weightwatchers®

FAMILY MEALS

250 Recipes for Bringing Family, Friends, and Food Together

HOUGHTON MIFFLIN HARCOURT

BOSTON NEW YORK 2016

For information about permission to reproduce selections
from this book, write to trade.permissions@hmhco.com or
to Permissions, Houghton Mifflin Harcourt Publishing Company,
3 Park Avenue, 19th Floor, New York, New York 10016.

www.hmhco.com

Library of Congress Cataloging-in-Publication Data is available

ISBN 978-0-544-71529-5 (hardcover);
ISBN 978-0-544-71532-5 (ebk)

Interior design by Empire Design Studio

Front cover photo: Turkey Tacos, 369
Back cover photos: Frozen Strawberry Yogurt, 38;
Teriyaki Turkey and Pineapple Kebabs, 253

Manufactured in China

C&C 10 9 8 7 6 5 4 3 2 1

About Weight Watchers International, Inc.

Weight Watchers International, Inc. is the world's leading commercial provider of weight management services, operating globally through a network of company-owned and franchise operations. Weight Watchers holds more than 36,000 meetings each week at which members receive group support and learn about healthy eating patterns, behavior modification, and physical activity. Weight Watchers provides innovative digital weight management products through its websites, mobile sites, and apps. Weight Watchers is the leading provider of online subscription weight management products in the world. In addition, Weight Watchers offers a wide range of products, publications, and programs for those interested in weight loss and weight control.

Weight Watchers Publishing Group

VP Content/Editor in Chief: Theresa DiMasi

Creative Director: Ed Melnitsky

Photo Director: Marybeth Dulany

Associate Editor: Katerina Gkionis

Food Editor: Eileen Runyan

Project Editor: Deborah Mintcheff

Contributing Writer: Alice K. Thompson

Contributing Editors: Lisa Chernick, Leslie Fink, MS, RD

Nutrition Consultant: Linda Wang

Contributing Recipe Developers: Sandra Gluck, Frank Melodia, Carol Prager

Photographer: John Kernick

Other Photographers: Antonis Achilleos, James Baigrie, Rita Maas, David Malosh, Johnny Miller, Con Poulos, Tina Rupp, Kate Sears, Dasha Wright, Romulo Yanes

Food Stylist: Simon Andrews

Other Food Sylists: Adrienne Anderson, Anne Disrude, Cyd McDowell, Michael Pederson, Lori Powell, Carrie Purcell, Maggie Ruggiero

Prop Stylist: Alistair Turnbull

Other Prop Stylists: Cathy Cook, Dani Fisher, Carla Gonzalez-Hart, Paige Hicks, Christina Lane, Karen Quatsoe, Theo Vamvounakis, Lynda White

Houghton Mifflin Harcourt

Publisher: Natalie Chapman

Editorial Director: Cindy Kitchel

Executive Editor: Anne Ficklen

Editorial Associate: Molly Aronica

Managing Editor: Marina Padakis Lowry

Art Director: Tai Blanche

Cover Design: Tai Blanche

Interior Design and Layout: Gary Tooth, Empire Design Studio

Production Director: Tom Hyland

BLUE CORN NACHOS, PAGE 212

CONTENTS

GATHER 'ROUND!

GREAT FOOD, AND THE JOY OF SHARING IT WITH FRIENDS AND family, is something we at Weight Watchers feel passionate about. Whether it's a special holiday that fills the house with laughter and joy or a simple weeknight dinner, we believe that enjoying food with the people we love enriches our lives. It's how some of our most important memories are made. *Family Meals* helps you build confidence in the kitchen and shows you simple ways to carve out time so that even busy families like yours can gather together for a well-balanced—and crazy-delicious—meal.

Discover recipes for weeknight entrees, including theme-night ideas for Italian, Mexican, Asian, and recipes for meat-and-potato lovers, gluten-free followers, or naturally adventurous eaters. Of course, life wouldn't be complete without special celebrations and holidays, so you'll also find crowd-pleasing meals that are healthy, casual, and tasty for everyone. Imagine a steaming bowl of chili, an incredibly flavored slow braise, or a hot, gooey mac and cheese. This book is full of delicious ideas! A bonus chapter offers ways to get everyone—including kids—involved in cooking, making mealtime even more fun.

Sharing food is a wonderful way to connect with friends and family each and every day. Our recipes emphasize nourishing foods like fresh fruits and vegetables, whole grains, lean proteins, and heart-friendly fats. With the food covered, it's easy for you to focus on each other.

Somewhere there's a table waiting. All we have to do is come together.

Cheers,

Theresa

ABOUT OUR RECIPES

While losing weight isn't only about what you eat, Weight Watchers realizes the critical role food plays in your success and overall good health. That's why our philosophy is to offer great-tasting, easy recipes that are nutritious as well as delicious. We create most of our recipes with the healthy and filling foods we love: lots of fresh fruits and vegetables, most of which have 0 SmartPoints value, and satisfying lean proteins, which are low in SmartPoints. We also try to ensure that our recipes fall within the recommendations of the U.S. Dietary Guidelines for Americans so that they support a diet that promotes health and reduces the risk of disease. If you have special dietary needs, consult with your health-care professional for advice on a diet that's best for you, then adapt these recipes to meet your specific nutritional needs.

GET STARTED, KEEP GOING, AND ENJOY GOOD NUTRITION

At Weight Watchers, we believe that eating well makes life better, no matter where you are on your weight-loss journey. These delicious recipes are ideal, whether you're just getting started or have already reached your goals on the SmartPoints plan. Unlike other weight-loss programs, which focus solely on calories, the SmartPoints plan guides you toward healthier foods that are lower in sugar and saturated fat, and higher in protein. But this isn't a diet—all food is "in." Eating well should be fun, energizing, and delicious so that healthy food choices become second nature.

To get maximum satisfaction from the foods you eat, we suggest that you keep the following information in mind while preparing our recipes.

● SmartPoints values are given for each recipe. The SmartPoints for each ingredient are assigned based on the number of calories, and amount of saturated fat, sugar, and protein per the ingredient quantity. The SmartPoints for each ingredient are then added together and divided by the number of servings, and the result is rounded.

● Recipes include approximate nutritional information: They are analyzed for Calories (Cal), Total Fat, Saturated Fat (Sat Fat), Sodium (Sod), Total Carbohydrates (Total Carb), Sugar, Dietary Fiber (Fib), and Protein (Prot). The nutritional values are obtained from the Weight Watchers database which is maintained by registered dietitians.

● Substitutions made to the ingredients could alter the per-serving nutritional information and may affect the SmartPoints.

● To boost flavor, we often include fresh herbs or a squeeze of citrus instead of some of the salt. If you don't have to restrict your sodium intake, feel free to add a touch more salt as desired.

● Recipes in this book that are designated gluten free do not contain any wheat (in all forms, including kamut, semolina, spelt, and triticale), barley, or rye, as well as any products that are made from these ingredients, such as breads, couscous, pastas, seitan, soy sauce, beer, malt vinegar, and malt beverages. Other foods such as salad dressings, Asian-style sauces, salsa and tomato sauce, shredded cheese, yogurt, and sour cream may be sources of gluten. Check ingredient labels carefully on packaged foods that we call for, as different brands of the same pre-made food product may or may not contain gluten. If you are following a gluten-free diet because you have celiac disease, please consult your health-care professional.

- Cook's Tip suggestions have a SmartPoints value of 0 unless otherwise stated.

- For information about the science behind lasting weight loss and more, please visit WeightWatchers.com/science.

- Calculations not what you expect? SmartPoints for the recipes in this book are calculated without counting any fruits and most vegetables, but the nutrition information does include the nutrient content from fruits and vegetables. This means you may get a different SmartPoints value if you calculate the SmartPoints based on the nutrition. To allow for your "free" fruits and veggies, use the SmartPoints assigned to the recipes. Also, please note, when fruits and veggies are liquefied or pureed (as in a smoothie), their nutrient content *is* incorporated into the recipe calculations, These nutrients can increase the SmartPoints.

- Alcohol is included in our SmartPoints calculations. Because alcohol information is generally not included on nutrition labels, it's not an option you can include when using the handheld or online calculator or in the Weight Watchers app. But since we include alcohol information that we get from our nutritionists, you might notice discrepancies between the SmartPoints you see here in our recipes, and the values you get using the calculator. The SmartPoints listed for our recipes are the most accurate values.

SIMPLY FILLING (THE NO-COUNT OPTION)

If counting SmartPoints isn't your thing, try Simply Filling, a no-count technique. To follow it, eat, just until satisfied, primarily from the list of Simply Filling foods found in your *Pocket Guide*. For more information, see your member guidebook.

CHOOSING INGREDIENTS

As you learn to eat more healthfully, consider the following to help you choose foods wisely:

Lean Meats and Poultry Purchase lean meats and poultry, and trim them of all visible fat before cooking. When poultry is cooked with the skin on, we recommend removing the skin before eating. Nutritional information for recipes that include meat, poultry, and fish is based on cooked, skinless boneless portions (unless otherwise stated), with the fat trimmed.

Seafood Whenever possible, our recipes call for seafood that's sustainable and deemed the most healthful for human consumption so that your choice of seafood is not only good for the oceans but also good for you. For more information about the best seafood choices and to download a pocket guide, go to the Environmental Defense Fund at **seafood.edf.org** or **seafoodwatch.org.**

Produce For best flavor, maximum nutrient content, and sometimes lower prices, buy fresh local produce, such as vegetables, leafy greens, and fruits, in season. Rinse them thoroughly before using, and keep a supply of cut-up vegetables and fruits in your refrigerator for convenient healthy snacks.

Whole Grains Explore your market for whole grain products such as whole wheat and whole grain breads and pastas, brown rice, bulgur, barley, cornmeal, whole wheat couscous, oats, and quinoa to enjoy with your meals.

READ THE RECIPE

Take a couple of minutes to read through the ingredients and directions before you start to prepare a recipe. This will prevent you from discovering midway through that you don't have an important ingredient or that a recipe requires several hours of marinating.

MAKING WISE CHOICES: HEALTHY STRATEGIES FOR EVERYDAY SITUATIONS

CONTROLLING PORTION SIZES

Knowing before a meal how much we should eat is a good start, but it's not the whole story. Many factors can influence how much we consume and whether we finish a meal feeling satisfied or hungry. The good news is that there are many ways we can give ourselves an advantage.

DRINK WATER BEFORE MEALS

Try drinking a full 12-ounce glass of water or seltzer a few minutes before you sit down at the table. It can give you a sense of fullness and help you avoid going back for seconds. Add a slice of orange, lemon, or cucumber to your glass for a hit of flavor and aroma.

SHRINK YOUR PLATES

Studies have shown that using large plates and bowls can encourage diners to take bigger portions. Serve food on smaller dinner plates (8 to 9 inches in diameter is great) and in bowls that hold no more than 16 ounces, and your brain will perceive the portions as more generous.

FILL HALF YOUR PLATE WITH VEGGIES

Most veggies are 0 SmartPoints, so enjoy! For instance, try a 0 SmartPoints option like steamed broccoli drizzled with lemon juice and a sprinkle of salt. Remember, even a single serving of prepared sides like grilled corn on the cob or green beans amandine can add more SmartPoints than you may want, so DIY and keep it simple.

FOCUS ON YOUR FOOD

Look at your food, concentrate on its flavors and textures, and discuss it with your fellow diners. Take small bites and put your fork down between each one to savor your meal. Being mindful of each mouthful will contribute to a sense of satiety and leave you happily aware of everything you ate.

LEAVE SERVING DISHES IN THE KITCHEN

A big bowl of pasta or a tray of lasagna on the table is an invitation for unplanned second helpings. Keep them in the kitchen to help you resist the temptation. If there are leftovers, store them out of sight in the refrigerator or freezer as soon as possible.

HAVE FRUIT OR DESSERT A LITTLE LATER

Finish your meal, then plan on a break of 20 minutes or so before having fruit or dessert. This will give your brain a chance to register that you've eaten, making a reasonably sized dessert more apt to satisfy. Or you might realize you're not hungry, and you won't need anything.

HOW TO STOP PICKING AND GRAZING WHILE YOU COOK

Ask any chef and they'll tell you a good cook always tastes food before serving it: It's the best way to ensure you've properly seasoned your dish or haven't left out a major ingredient. (No rosemary in that Rosemary Roasted Chicken? Good thing you caught it!) But for many of us, tasting our food can easily turn into nonstop picking and grazing that can really add up. Here are our favorite strategies for making sure you enjoy your meal at the table, not standing at the counter.

DON'T START HUNGRY

Preparing a delicious entrée while your stomach (and brain) are crying out for food is a recipe for disaster. Get in the habit of eating a reasonable snack that includes both protein and carbohydrates an hour or so before you start cooking. Good combos with staying power include plain low-fat Greek yogurt with chopped fruit, hummus and whole grain crackers, or a few almonds and a handful of plain air-popped popcorn.

DON'T TASTE WITH A DIRTY SPOON

When you're cooking, be sure to use your smallest spoon to taste the food (a demitasse one is perfect), and taste only once—"double dipping" is not only unsanitary but also doubles the amount you're actually eating. If you do need to taste twice (to adjust the amount of salt or pepper in a dish, for instance), first thoroughly wash your spoon or take out a clean one, then taste only half the amount you did the first time.

CHEW GUM OR MUNCH ON VEGGIES

Need a mouth fidget? Sugarless gum is a great one; when you do need to give food a taste test, you'll have to consciously remove the gum from your mouth, making mindless picking almost impossible. If you're not a gum fan, you can keep a cup of carrot or celery sticks in front of you to munch. Or brush your teeth with minty toothpaste; you won't want to nibble for a while.

DON'T LICK THE BOWL OR THE BEATERS

Many of us remember this treat from childhood, and some of us have continued the habit into adulthood. The truth is that eating a bunch of cookie dough or cake batter rarely satisfies as much as holding out for the real thing, although the SmartPoints you rack up doing it will definitely be real! So simply plop the bowl into the sink and give it a rinse.

REMEMBER THAT FOOD IS BEST ENJOYED WITH OTHERS

Remind yourself that great food tastes better when it's a shared experience, so save your appetite for the meal.

PLANNING FOR EATING AWAY FROM HOME

You've worked hard to make your own kitchen and work space weight-loss friendly. But what happens when you head out to a restaurant or to a celebration outside your home? What's the best way to make sure you have a great time *and* feel good about your food choices?

MARK MEALS OUT ON YOUR CALENDAR

Strategizing ahead a day or two can help you adjust your eating plan to accommodate celebrations and special dinners, either by budgeting extra from your Weekly Smart-Points Allowance or by thinking of ways to minimize overeating cues you might face when you get there. Remember, the point is to look forward to and enjoy eating out, so spend a little time coming up with a plan that you're comfortable with.

DECIDE WHAT SPLURGES ARE WORTH IT

If you really want to enjoy Uncle Lou's famous lasagna at a family reunion or have your heart set on a frozen margarita at your favorite Mexican spot, go for it! Think about strategies like skipping the pre-meal chips and dips and bypassing high-fat sides in favor of fresh fruits and vegetables so you'll finish the event content and energized, not overfull and lethargic.

DON'T SHOW UP HUNGRY

It's hard to make good choices when your stomach is growling. Plan to have a sensible snack before you head out, and remember to drink a glass or two of water when you arrive. You'll be more likely to stick to your plan if you start out feeling satisfied.

DON'T EAT MINDLESSLY

Before putting anything in your mouth, ask yourself "Is this worth the SmartPoints?" If the answer is yes, consume a reasonable portion. If the answer is no, don't eat it. If the food is already on your plate, remember that there's no harm in leaving it there. There's no such thing as the Clean Plate Club!

REMEMBER, IT'S NOT ONLY ABOUT THE FOOD

Sure, traditional celebrations and nights out in restaurants are enhanced by good food. But enjoying your surroundings and the company are also important. Focus more on connecting with friends and family, and you'll probably find it easier to make good choices and avoid unplanned overeating.

PACKING HEALTHY MEALS TO GO

There are a lot of reasons to take a meal with you when you're out for the day or for the evening. Eating at school or the office, or having a family meal at a park or event, is often healthier and more enjoyable when you bring the food you want rather than rely on restaurants or fast-food outlets. Plus it can save you a bundle, and tracking can be much simpler and more accurate. Here are some tried-and-true strategies that can easily become part of your daily and weekly routine.

START WITH A PLAN

A little organization can go a long way, whether you're packing your breakfast, your kid's lunch, or a meal for the whole family. Set aside time once a week or so to map out a strategy for packing up the meals you and your family prefer. Research what fruits and produce are in season, cull some recipes you'd like to try, and poll other members of your household about what healthy meals they might like. Once you've got all your ideas together, make a shopping list.

MAKE THE MOST OF LEFTOVERS

When you cook at home, think about doubling your recipe and refrigerating or freezing the extras to enjoy later. Dividing the food into individual portions and clearly labeling them with the dish's name, the date, and the SmartPoints before freezing is the most convenient approach. This game plan also works very well when you're cooking up staples like rice and other grains, or lentils.

GET THE RIGHT GEAR

A paper bag, a simple lunch box, or a reusable takeout container: These are all you really *need* to pack up a meal, but it's fun and practical to give yourself a few more options. And if you and your family like picnics, it can be a real time-saver to have a dedicated picnic basket that's already outfitted with cutlery, plates, containers, and more. The good news is that bringing your own food and drinks to work, school, or an event has become increasingly popular, and that has inspired manufacturers to create a whole new range of stylish and environmentally friendly packing options. See what design fits your needs and personality!

BEAT THE MORNING RUSH

Mornings can get hectic. Find a few moments in the evening to pack your meals for the next day. If you're taking something that's better assembled the same day, you can at least put out your lunch box or reusable bag so it's ready when you are.

ENLIST YOUR FAMILY

Do other members of your household eat meals at school or work? If they do, join forces to maximize the benefits you'll get from planning and cooking ahead. Even if everyone doesn't want the same lunch, you can save time by assembly-line packing items like snacks, fruit, and drinks the night before.

NEED SOME INSPIRATION?

The following recipes in this book are well suited to traveling:

CHAPTER 1

WEEKNIGHT DINNERS

When You Don't Have Much Time

We understand that with today's hectic lifestyles, cooking and sharing meals with family can be a challenge on weeknights. But help is here with recipes tailor-made for you, from cooking with pantry staples—check out our handy list on page 27—to make-ahead dishes. And they're all in our easy-to-follow sections—guaranteed to build your kitchen confidence and help get you organized. Short on time? Invite everyone to pitch in with the menu planning, shopping, and cooking to make mealtime at your house a happy occasion all week long. You can mix and match any of the recipes below to create tasty meals.

COOKING WITH STAPLES FROM YOUR PANTRY, REFRIGERATOR, AND FREEZER
Mains, Sides, and Desserts That Satisfy

SUPER-EASY NO-COOK RECIPES
From Starters to Mains and Desserts

MAKE IT AHEAD
Mains and Sides That Taste Even Better a Day or Two Later

SHORTCUT DISHES
Tasty Mains and Desserts That Use Convenience Foods

SLOW-COOKER CHILIES, STEWS, ROASTS, AND MORE
Simply Set It and Forget It!

HAVE BREAKFAST FOR DINNER
Mains That Are a Great Way to End the Day

BURRITOS WITH TURKEY AND PINTO BEANS

SERVES 4
20 Minutes or Less

2   teaspoons canola oil

¾   pound ground skinless turkey breast

1   (15½-ounce) can pinto beans, rinsed and drained

2   garlic cloves, minced

2   teaspoons chili powder

4   (8-inch) multigrain tortillas

8   tablespoons fat-free salsa

4   tablespoons shredded reduced-fat Cheddar cheese

2   scallions, thinly sliced

1. To make filling, heat oil in large skillet over medium-high heat. Add turkey and cook, breaking it up with wooden spoon, until browned, about 6 minutes. Add beans, garlic, and chili powder; cook, stirring occasionally, until heated through, about 2 minutes.

2. Meanwhile, warm tortillas according to package directions.

3. Place tortilla on work surface; spoon one-fourth of filling along center. Top with 2 tablespoons salsa and 1 tablespoon Cheddar; sprinkle with one-fourth of scallions. Fold sides of tortilla over to enclose filling. Place, seam side down, on platter. Repeat with remaining tortillas, filling, salsa, cheese, and scallions.

Per serving (1 burrito): 398 Cal, 11 g Total Fat, 3 g Sat Fat, 847 mg Sod, 43 g Total Carb, 4 g Sugar, 11 g Fib, 30 g Prot. SmartPoints value: 10

 Store It

Save money and keep Cheddar cheese fresher longer by buying it by the block at a big-box store. Tightly wrap it in plastic wrap and refrigerate up to 2 months. For longer storage, wrap the cheese in smaller portions in plastic wrap then in heavy foil and freeze up to 6 months. It will be a bit crumblier but will still be perfect for shredding.

BURRITOS WITH TURKEY
AND PINTO BEANS

GRILLED FLANK STEAK WITH ONIONS

SERVES 6
Gluten Free

3   tablespoons red wine vinegar

1   tablespoon olive oil

2   teaspoons dried oregano

1   large garlic clove, minced

¼   teaspoon black pepper

1   (1½-pound) lean flank steak, trimmed

¾   teaspoon salt

1   large red onion, cut into ¼-inch rounds

1. Combine vinegar, oil, oregano, garlic, and pepper in large zip-close plastic bag. Add steak; squeeze out air and seal bag. Turn bag until steak is evenly coated. Refrigerate, turning bag occasionally, at least 1 hour or up to 4 hours.

2. Meanwhile, preheat grill to medium-high or prepare medium-high fire.

3. Remove steak from marinade; discard marinade. Sprinkle steak with ½ teaspoon of salt. Spray onion with olive oil nonstick spray and sprinkle with remaining ¼ teaspoon salt.

4. Place steak on grill rack and grill, turning once, until instant-read thermometer inserted into side of steak registers 145°F, about 12 minutes. Transfer steak to cutting board and let rest 10 minutes.

5. Meanwhile, place onion rounds on grill rack and grill, turning occasionally, until lightly charred and tender, 7–9 minutes. Thinly slice steak against grain into 18 slices and place on platter; place onion on top.

Per serving (3 slices steak and ⅓ cup onion): 194 Cal, 9 g Total Fat, 3 g Sat Fat, 357 mg Sod, 3 g Total Carb, 1 g Sugar, 1 g Fib, 25 g Prot. SmartPoints value: 4

 Store It

Lean and flavorful flank steak is frequently on sale at the supermarket. Buy a few and freeze them, individually wrapped, up to 6 months.

APPLE AND CARROT SALAD

SERVES 8
20 Minutes or Less,
Gluten Free, Vegetarian

1   large red apple, unpeeled and cut into matchstick strips

1   large green apple, unpeeled and cut into matchstick strips

1½ tablespoons lemon juice

3   cups matchstick-cut carrots

¼   cup chopped fresh chives

1   tablespoon extra-virgin olive oil

1   teaspoon sugar

½   teaspoon salt

¼   teaspoon black pepper

½   cup crumbled feta cheese

Put apples in serving bowl and sprinkle with lemon juice; toss until coated evenly. Add carrots, chives, oil, sugar, salt, and pepper; toss until mixed well. Add feta and gently toss.

Per serving (¾ cup): 91 Cal, 4 g Total Fat, 2 g Sat Fat, 267 mg Sod, 13 g Total Carb, 9 g Sugar, 3 g Fib, 2 g Prot. SmartPoints value: 2

 Store It

To store carrots up to several weeks, place them in a zip-close plastic bag with a few holes poked in it (that will prevent too much moisture from accumulating) and store in the crisper drawer of your refrigerator.

SEAFOOD SALAD WITH
TOMATOES AND ORZO

SEAFOOD SALAD WITH TOMATOES AND ORZO

SERVES 4

½ cup regular or whole wheat orzo

3 teaspoons extra-virgin olive oil

1 (1-pound) bag frozen seafood medley (any combination of shrimp, calamari, scallops, mussels, clams, or crabmeat)

2 cups cherry tomatoes, preferably heirloom, halved or quartered

1 cup lightly packed micro greens or baby salad greens

½ cup diced red onion

1 tablespoon capers, drained and chopped

Grated zest and juice of ½ lemon

½ teaspoon salt

¼ teaspoon black pepper

1. Cook orzo according to package directions. Drain in colander and rinse under cold water to stop cooking. Drain again and transfer to serving bowl. Drizzle with 1 teaspoon of oil and toss until coated evenly. Set aside.

2. Bring large pot of water to boil. Add seafood and cook just until opaque in center, about 2 minutes. Drain in colander and rinse under cold water until cool. Drain again and add to orzo along with tomatoes, salad greens, onion, capers, lemon zest and juice, salt, pepper, and remaining 2 teaspoons oil; toss until mixed well.

Per serving (1¾ cups): 192 Cal, 5 g Total Fat, 1 g Sat Fat, 641 mg Sod, 19 g Total Carb, 3 g Sugar, 3 g Fib, 18 g Prot. SmartPoints value: 4

 Cook's Tip

Make this recipe gluten free by using brown rice orzo.

BROCCOLI WITH LEMON-GARLIC CRUMBS

SERVES 4
20 Minutes or Less,
Vegetarian

1   pound broccoli florets

1   tablespoon unsalted butter

1   garlic clove, minced

½   cup panko bread crumbs

1   teaspoon grated lemon zest

¼   teaspoon salt

1. Bring 1 inch of water to boil in large pot. Put broccoli in steamer basket and set in pot. Cook, covered, until broccoli is crisp-tender, about 5 minutes; drain.

2. Meanwhile, melt butter in medium nonstick skillet over medium-low heat. Add garlic and cook, stirring, until fragrant, about 30 seconds. Add panko; increase heat to medium and cook, stirring often, until lightly toasted, 2–3 minutes. Remove skillet from heat; stir in lemon zest and salt. Spoon broccoli into serving bowl and sprinkle with crumbs.

Per serving (about 1 cup): 116 Cal, 4 g Total Fat, 2 g Sat Fat, 268 mg Sod, 16 g Total Carb, 2 g Sugar, 3 g Fib, 5 g Prot. SmartPoints value: 3

 Store It

Garlic keeps longest when stored at a cool temperature in a moderate amount of humidity. So store it in the crisper drawer of your refrigerator, or at room temperature if you use often.

BROCCOLI WITH
LEMON-GARLIC CRUMBS

CURRIED CAULIFLOWER

SERVES 6
Gluten Free, Vegetarian

1   tablespoon olive oil

1   onion, chopped

3   large garlic cloves, minced

2   teaspoons ground cumin

2   teaspoons curry powder

1   teaspoon salt

⅛   teaspoon cayenne

1   head cauliflower, cut into
    small florets

1½ cups water

2   teaspoons sherry vinegar

1. Heat oil in Dutch oven over medium-high heat. Add onion and cook, stirring, until softened, about 5 minutes. Add garlic, cumin, curry powder, salt, and cayenne; cook, stirring, until fragrant, about 30 seconds.

2. Add cauliflower to Dutch oven and stir until coated with spice mixture. Stir in water and bring to boil. Reduce heat and simmer, covered, stirring occasionally, until cauliflower is tender, 8–10 minutes. With slotted spoon, transfer cauliflower to serving bowl. Keep warm.

3. Bring cooking liquid to boil; boil until reduced to ½ cup, about 4 minutes. Stir in vinegar. Spoon over cauliflower.

Per serving (1 cup): 58 Cal, 3 g Total Fat, 0 g Sat Fat, 421 mg Sod, 8 g Total Carb, 3 g Sugar, 3 g Fib, 2 g Prot. SmartPoints value: 1

 Store It

Over time spices lose their potency and therefore their flavor. As a basic rule, whole spices stay fresh for 3 to 4 years, while ground spices stay fresh for about 1 year.

MUST-HAVE PANTRY STAPLES

What can make getting family meals on the table easier—and keep you and yours healthier? The answer is a wisely stocked pantry: Your cupboard shelves, refrigerator, and freezer can be some of your best allies in weight loss, so commit to filling them with the kinds of healthful foods you and your family want.

To get started, take an inventory of what you already have on hand. Chances are you have a lot of the delicious, versatile ingredients used throughout this book. Take a look at our master checklist below and choose what you'd like to pick up. As you expand your pantry, planning and shopping will take less and less time each week.

ON YOUR SHELVES

Canned salmon and tuna (packed in water)

Canned beans

Whole grains, rice, and pasta

Plain dried, whole wheat dried, and panko bread crumbs

Canola, olive, and Asian (dark) sesame oil

Nonstick spray

Olives and capers

Roasted red peppers (not oil packed)

Salsa

Hot pepper sauce

Ketchup, Dijon mustard, and mayonnaise

Vinegars

Worcestershire, soy, and teriyaki sauces

Canned broth (chicken, beef, and vegetable)

Light (low-fat) coconut milk

Canned tomatoes (diced, whole, and crushed), tomato paste, and tomato sauce

All-purpose and whole wheat flours

Cornmeal

Old-fashioned (rolled) and quick-cooking oats

Granulated white, brown, and confectioners' sugars

Honey, maple syrup, and agave nectar

Baking powder and baking soda

Vanilla and almond extracts

Chocolate, chocolate chips, and unsweetened cocoa

Nuts and dried fruit

Peanut butter

Salt, black pepper, and dried herbs and spices

Garlic, onions, shallots, and potatoes

IN YOUR FREEZER

Chicken (assorted cuts, including ground skinless breast)

Beef (assorted cuts, including ground lean)

Lamb chops and ground lean lamb

Turkey (assorted cuts, including ground skinless breast)

Fish and shellfish

Vegetables (without sauce)

Unsweetened fruits and berries

Sandwich bread (reduced-calorie or regular, light English muffins)

Tortillas

Hot dog and hamburger rolls

IN YOUR FRIDGE

Fresh fruits and vegetables

Fresh herbs

Large eggs and fat-free egg substitute

Milk (fat-free)

Unsalted, salted, and light stick butter

Cheeses

Yogurt and (reduced-fat and fat-free) sour cream

CRISP DUTCH COCOA COOKIES

MAKES 42

Vegetarian

¼ cup old-fashioned (rolled) oats

1 cup white whole wheat flour

½ cup unsweetened Dutch process cocoa

¼ teaspoon baking soda

¼ teaspoon salt

½ cup (1 stick) unsalted butter, softened

1 cup sugar

1 large egg

2 teaspoons vanilla extract

1. Put oats in blender and process until finely ground.

2. Whisk together flour, cocoa, baking soda, and salt in small bowl; stir in ground oats.

3. With electric mixer on medium speed, beat butter and sugar in large bowl until creamy. Beat in egg and vanilla. Reduce mixer speed to low and stir in flour mixture just until blended. Refrigerate until dough is firm enough to shape, about 40 minutes.

4. Shape dough into 11-inch log and wrap tightly in plastic wrap. Refrigerate until very firm, at least 4 hours or up to overnight.

5. Preheat oven to 350°F. Spray two large baking sheets with nonstick spray.

6. Cut log into ¼-inch slices and place 2 inches apart on prepared baking sheets. Bake until cookies are slightly puffed, about 10 minutes. Transfer cookies to wire racks and let cool completely.

Per serving (1 cookie): 55 Cal, 3 g Total Fat, 1 g Sat Fat, 23 mg Sod, 8 g Total Carb, 5 g Sugar, 0 g Fib, 1 g Prot. SmartPoints value: 3

 Store It

Butter should be refrigerated in its original wrapper, which prevents it from spoiling or from picking up the flavors of other foods. Well wrapped, it will keep up to 3 weeks. For longer storage, overwrap the butter in heavy foil or place in a zip-close plastic bag and freeze up to 3 months.

CHOCOLATE FUDGE COOKIE BITES

MAKES 40
Vegetarian

1¾ cups all-purpose flour

1 teaspoon baking powder

¼ teaspoon salt

¾ cup granulated sugar

⅓ cup unsweetened cocoa

4 tablespoons butter, softened

½ cup unsweetened applesauce

1 teaspoon vanilla extract

2 tablespoons confectioners' sugar

1. Preheat oven to 375°F. Spray two nonstick baking sheets with nonstick spray or line regular baking sheets with parchment paper.

2. Whisk together flour, baking powder, and salt in small bowl.

3. With electric mixer on medium speed, beat granulated sugar, cocoa, and butter in large bowl until creamy. Beat in applesauce and vanilla. Reduce mixer speed to low and stir in flour mixture just until blended.

4. Roll dough into 40 marble-size balls and place 1 inch apart on prepared baking sheets. Bake until set, about 8 minutes. Let cookies cool on baking sheets about 1 minute. Transfer cookies to wire racks and let cool completely; dust with confectioners' sugar.

Per serving (1 cookie): 49 Cal, 1 g Total Fat, 1 g Sat Fat, 37 mg Sod, 9 g Total Carb, 4 g Sugar, 0 g Fib, 1 g Prot. SmartPoints value: 2

Cook's Tip

If the dough is too sticky to work with, refrigerate it for about 1 hour or until it is firmed up.

MIXED GREENS WITH VINAIGRETTE

SERVES 8
20 Minutes or Less,
Gluten Free, Vegetarian

- 1½ cups cherry tomatoes or grape tomatoes, halved
- ¼ cup lightly packed fresh flat-leaf parsley leaves
- 5 tablespoons water
- 2 tablespoons olive oil
- 2 tablespoons red wine vinegar
- 1 garlic clove, minced
- ¾ teaspoon sugar
- ¾ teaspoon salt
- ¼ teaspoon black pepper
- 12 cups lightly packed mixed baby salad greens

1. To make dressing, combine ½ cup of tomatoes, the parsley, water, oil, vinegar, garlic, sugar, salt, and pepper in blender or mini–food processor; pulse until smooth.

2. Put salad greens and remaining 1 cup tomatoes in salad bowl; drizzle dressing over and toss until coated evenly.

Per serving (1½ cups mixed greens with 2 tablespoons dressing): 70 Cal, 4 g Total Fat, 1 g Sat Fat, 295 mg Sod, 7 g Total Carb, 1 g Sugar, 4 g Fib, 4 g Prot. SmartPoints value: 1

 Cook's Tip

When purchasing cherry tomatoes, make sure they are firm without any signs of wilting or soft spots. Turn the container over to check the condition of the tomatoes in the bottom of the container.

MIXED GREENS
WITH VINAIGRETTE

COLD CUCUMBER SOUP

SERVES 4
20 Minutes or Less,
Gluten Free, Vegetarian

1½ cups plain low-fat yogurt

1 large cucumber, peeled, halved, seeded, and cut into chunks

4 scallions, coarsely chopped

3 tablespoons chopped fresh dill

1 cup fat-free milk

½ teaspoon salt

¼ teaspoon black pepper

4 tablespoons finely chopped orange or yellow bell pepper

1. Combine yogurt, cucumber, scallions, and 2 tablespoons of dill in blender; process until smooth. Pour into large bowl; stir in milk, salt, and black pepper.

2. Ladle soup evenly into 4 bowls. Top each serving with 1 tablespoon bell pepper and sprinkle with remaining 1 tablespoon dill.

Per serving (about 1¼ cups): 97 Cal, 2 g Total Fat, 1 g Sat Fat, 385 mg Sod, 13 g Total Carb, 11 g Sugar, 1 g Fib, 8 g Prot. SmartPoints value: 3

 Cook's Tip

No need to cook to enjoy a light and tasty soup. Be sure to use very cold yogurt and milk if planning to serve this summertime refresher right away. Keep the soup cold longer by serving it in chilled bowls.

TURKEY SALAD SOFT TACOS

SERVES 4
20 Minutes or Less

1 cup shredded skinless cooked turkey breast

3 tablespoons chopped fresh cilantro

2 tablespoons sliced pickled jalapeño, drained and finely chopped

2 tablespoons reduced-calorie mayonnaise

1 teaspoon grated lime zest

2 teaspoons lime juice

¼ teaspoon salt

4 (8-inch) fat-free flour tortillas, warmed

1 cup thinly sliced green leaf lettuce

1 large tomato, cut into ¼-inch dice

8 tablespoons shredded reduced-fat Cheddar cheese

1. Mix together turkey, cilantro, jalapeño, mayonnaise, lime zest and juice, and salt in medium bowl.

2. Lay tortillas on work surface. Put ¼ cup of turkey mixture on one half of each tortilla; top with ¼ cup of lettuce, one-fourth of tomato, and 2 tablespoons of Cheddar. Fold tortillas over to enclose filling.

Per serving (1 taco): 262 Cal, 4 g Total Fat, 1 g Sat Fat, 838 mg Sod, 26 g Total Carb, 4 g Sugar, 5 g Fib, 26 g Prot. SmartPoints value: 6

PORK, ORANGE, AND FENNEL SALAD

SERVES 4
20 Minutes or Less,
Gluten Free

2   tablespoons red wine vinegar

2   teaspoons olive oil

2   teaspoons water

¾   teaspoon kosher salt

½   teaspoon dried oregano

¼   teaspoon black pepper

4   cups lightly packed thickly
    sliced escarole

2   oranges, peeled and segmented

1   small fennel bulb, very thinly
    sliced

½   small red onion, thinly sliced

8   pitted Kalamata olives, halved

¾   pound roasted lean pork loin,
    trimmed and thinly sliced

1. To make dressing, whisk together vinegar, oil, water, salt, oregano, and pepper in small bowl; set aside.

2. Combine escarole, oranges, fennel, onion, and olives in large bowl. Drizzle dressing over and gently toss until coated evenly. Divide salad evenly among 4 plates and top evenly with pork.

Per serving (about 2 cups salad and ½ cup pork): 270 Cal, 12 g Total Fat, 3 g Sat Fat, 516 mg Sod, 14 g Total Carb, 7 g Sugar, 5 g Fib, 27 g Prot. SmartPoints value: 5

Cook's Tip

Make it faster: Instead of taking the time to peel and segment the oranges, use 2 cups drained refrigerated fresh citrus salad sections of red and white grapefruit and oranges. You'll find it packed in jars in the produce section of your supermarket.

WHITE BEAN, CITRUS, AND SALMON SALAD

SERVES 4
20 Minutes or Less,
Gluten Free

1   (15½-ounce) can small white beans, rinsed and drained

1   bunch arugula, stems trimmed and leaves chopped or torn

1   small red onion, diced

¼   cup lightly packed fresh flat-leaf parsley leaves, chopped

1   tablespoon extra-virgin olive oil

1   teaspoon grated lemon zest

3   tablespoons lemon juice

1   teaspoon chopped fresh thyme

½   teaspoon salt

½   teaspoon black pepper

1   (14¾-ounce) can pink or red salmon, large bones and skin removed, and flaked

Combine beans, arugula, onion, parsley, oil, lemon zest and juice, thyme, salt, and pepper in serving bowl; toss until mixed well. Add salmon and gently toss just until combined.

Per serving (1½ cups): 302 Cal, 9 g Total Fat, 1 g Sat Fat, 718 mg Sod, 27 g Total Carb, 2 g Sugar, 6 g Fib, 29 g Prot. SmartPoints value: 6

 Cook's Tip

To make this dish vegetarian, substitute diced firm tofu for the salmon. One 14-ounce package of firm tofu, diced, will reduce the per-serving SmartPoints value by 1.

TEX-MEX SHRIMP ROLLS

TEX-MEX SHRIMP ROLLS

SERVES 4
20 Minutes or Less

½ pound cooked medium shrimp, left whole or coarsely chopped

3 scallions, thinly sliced

¼ cup fat-free salsa

¼ cup fat-free mayonnaise

¼ cup lightly packed fresh cilantro leaves

¼ teaspoon salt

4 light whole wheat hotdog rolls, toasted

Toss together shrimp, scallions, salsa, mayonnaise, cilantro, and salt in medium bowl until mixed well. Fill rolls evenly with shrimp mixture.

Per serving (1 filled roll): 173 Cal, 2 g Total Fat, 1 g Sat Fat, 1,058 mg Sod, 23 g Total Carb, 4 g Sugar, 4 g Fib, 17 g Prot. SmartPoints value: 4

 Cook's Tip

For more luxurious rolls, substitute cooked lobster meat for the shrimp with no change in the SmartPoints value.

FROZEN STRAWBERRY YOGURT

SERVES 12
Gluten Free, Vegetarian

1   (1-pound) container strawberries, hulled and sliced

1   cup sugar

2   tablespoons lemon juice

    Pinch salt

1   cup vanilla low-fat yogurt

1   cup fat-free half-and-half

1. Combine strawberries, sugar, lemon juice, and salt in medium bowl; with potato masher, crush strawberries. Let stand, stirring occasionally, about 30 minutes.

2. Meanwhile, whisk together yogurt and half-and-half in large bowl until smooth. Stir into strawberry mixture. Cover and refrigerate until thoroughly chilled, about 2 hours (or place in freezer about 1 hour).

3. Pour strawberry mixture into ice-cream maker and freeze according to manufacturer's instructions. Transfer to freezer container and freeze until firm, at least 2 hours.

Per serving (⅓ cup): 106 Cal, 1 g Total Fat, 0 g Sat Fat, 67 mg Sod, 24 g Total Carb, 22 g Sugar, 1 g Fib, 2 g Prot. SmartPoints value: 5

FROZEN STRAWBERRY YOGURT

CHOCOLATE CHIP— PEANUT BUTTER PIE

SERVES 16
Vegetarian

½ cup reduced-fat creamy peanut butter

½ (8-ounce) package light cream cheese (Neufchâtel), softened

¼ cup fat-free cream cheese, softened

1 (12-ounce) can fat-free sweetened condensed milk

2 tablespoons lemon juice

1 cup thawed frozen light whipped topping

5 tablespoons mini semisweet chocolate chips

1 (6-ounce) prepared graham cracker piecrust

1. With electric mixer on medium speed, beat peanut butter, light cream cheese, and fat-free cream cheese in large bowl until smooth. Gradually beat in condensed milk and lemon juice until blended well.

2. With rubber spatula, fold in whipped topping and 4 tablespoons of chocolate chips just until whipped topping is no longer visible.

3. Spoon peanut-butter mixture into prepared piecrust and smooth top. Chop remaining 1 tablespoon chocolate chips and sprinkle over top. Cover pie loosely with plastic wrap and freeze until firm, at least 4 hours or up to overnight.

Per serving (¹⁄₁₆ of pie): 201 Cal, 8 g Total Fat, 3 g Sat Fat, 186 mg Sod, 27 g Total Carb, 21 g Sugar, 1 g Fib, 6 g Prot. SmartPoints value: 9

 Cook's Tip

This delectable peanut-buttery no-cook pie is a snap to put together. Pop it into the freezer to firm it up—no work there!

CHICKEN SAUSAGE, MUSHROOM, AND PASTA CASSEROLE

SERVES 8

12 ounces whole wheat rotini (about 3 cups)

1 teaspoon extra-virgin olive oil

½ cup panko bread crumbs

2 tablespoons grated Parmesan cheese

1 teaspoon dried oregano

½ pound fully cooked Italian-style chicken sausage, thinly sliced

1 yellow bell pepper, thinly sliced

1 onion, chopped

1 pound white or cremini mushrooms, sliced

2 tablespoons water

4 cups marinara sauce

1 cup shredded part-skim mozzarella cheese

1. Preheat oven to 350°F. Spray 9 x 13-inch baking dish with nonstick spray.

2. Cook rotini according to package directions. Drain in colander and return to pot.

3. Meanwhile, heat oil in large heavy nonstick skillet over medium heat. Add panko; reduce heat to medium-low and cook, stirring often, until golden, about 4 minutes. Transfer to small bowl; stir in Parmesan and oregano. Set aside. Wipe skillet clean.

4. Put sausage in skillet and cook over medium-high heat, stirring frequently, until browned, about 5 minutes. Transfer to plate and drain off any fat from skillet. Add bell pepper and onion to skillet; cook over medium-high heat, stirring frequently, until vegetables start to brown and soften, about 5 minutes. Add mushrooms and water; cook, stirring, until mushrooms are softened, about 8 minutes.

5. Add vegetables, sausage, and marinara to rotini; stir until mixed well. Spoon into prepared baking dish and sprinkle with mozzarella and reserved panko mixture. Bake until heated through and cheese is melted, about 25 minutes.

Per serving (about 1½ cups): 344 Cal, 9 g Total Fat, 2 g Sat Fat, 903 mg Sod, 50 g Total Carb, 10 g Sugar, 8 g Fib, 19 g Prot. SmartPoints value: 10

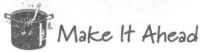 Make It Ahead

Prepare steps 2 through 5 of the recipe, setting aside the mozzarella, ½ cup of the sauce, and the panko mixture. Wrap the casserole tightly in plastic wrap and refrigerate up to 2 days. To reheat, let the casserole come to room temperature; drizzle with the reserved sauce, sprinkle with the cheese and panko mixture, and bake as directed.

STRACOTTO WITH
LEMON GREMOLATA

STRACOTTO WITH LEMON GREMOLATA

SERVES 6

1 (2-pound) lean beef chuck roast, trimmed

1½ teaspoons salt

½ teaspoon black pepper

2 tablespoons all-purpose flour

1 tablespoon olive oil

3 red onions, thinly sliced

2 large garlic cloves, minced

1 (8-ounce) package sliced white mushrooms

1 (14½-ounce) can petite diced tomatoes

1 cup dry red wine

½ cup chopped fresh flat-leaf parsley

Grated zest of 1 lemon

1. Sprinkle beef with salt and pepper; coat evenly with flour, pressing lightly so it adheres.

2. Heat oil in medium Dutch oven over medium heat. Add beef and cook until browned on all sides, about 10 minutes; transfer to plate. Add onions to pot and cook, stirring, until softened, about 5 minutes. Add half of garlic and cook, stirring, until fragrant, about 30 seconds.

3. Add mushrooms, tomatoes, and wine to Dutch oven; cook, scraping up browned bits from bottom of pot, about 3 minutes. Increase heat and bring to boil; reduce heat and simmer until mushrooms are softened, about 5 minutes. Return beef and any accumulated juices to pot; reduce heat and simmer, covered, stirring occasionally and turning beef every 30 minutes, until beef is fork-tender, about 2 hours. Transfer beef to board.

4. Bring vegetable mixture to boil over medium-high heat; boil, stirring frequently, until reduced to 4 cups, about 12 minutes.

5. Meanwhile, to make gremolata, stir together parsley, lemon zest, and remaining garlic in small bowl. Cut beef on diagonal into 12 slices. Serve sprinkled with gremolata and accompanied by vegetables with sauce.

Per serving (2 slices beef, generous ⅔ cup vegetables with sauce, and 1½ tablespoons gremolata): 320 Cal, 12 g Total Fat, 4 g Sat Fat, 810 mg Sod, 13 g Total Carb, 5 g Total Sugar, 3 g Fib, 35 g Prot. SmartPoints value: 7

 Make It Ahead

Prepare the pot roast through step 5, but do not make the gremolata. Transfer the beef and sauce to one or two airtight containers and refrigerate up to 4 days or freeze up to 3 months. To reheat, if frozen, thaw the meat and sauce in the refrigerator overnight. Transfer to a large skillet. Cook, covered, over medium-low heat until heated through, about 10 minutes. Prepare the gremolata.

WINTER BEEF STEW

SERVES 4

1   tablespoon canola oil

1   pound lean boneless beef top
    sirloin, trimmed and cut into
    1½-inch chunks

1   large red onion, cut into
    ½-inch slices

2   garlic cloves, crushed with side
    of large knife

5   teaspoons red wine vinegar

1   bay leaf

3   fresh thyme sprigs

½   teaspoon salt

¼   teaspoon black pepper

1   cup apple juice or cider

1   cup beef broth

2   carrots, thinly sliced

2   cups hot cooked egg noodles

2   tablespoons finely chopped
    fresh flat-leaf parsley

1. Heat oil in Dutch oven over medium-high heat. Add beef and cook until browned on all sides, about 6 minutes, transferring beef to plate as it is browned; set aside.

2. Add onion and garlic to Dutch oven. Reduce heat to medium and cook, stirring occasionally, until onion is golden, about 10 minutes. Stir in vinegar, bay leaf, thyme, salt, and pepper. Add apple juice, scraping to loosen any browned bits on bottom of pot. Add broth and bring to simmer. Return beef with any accumulated juices and the carrots to pot. Reduce heat and simmer, covered, until beef is fork-tender and carrots are softened, about 1½ hours. Remove and discard bay leaf and thyme sprigs.

3. Divide noodles evenly among 4 plates or large shallow bowls; top evenly with stew and sprinkle with parsley.

Per serving (about 1 cup stew and ½ cup noodles): 352 Cal, 9 g Total Fat, 2 g Sat Fat, 603 mg Sod, 35 g Total Carb, 10 g Sugar, 3 g Fib, 31 g Prot. SmartPoints value: 8

 Make It Ahead

Prepare the stew through step 2. Transfer to an airtight container and let cool. Cover and refrigerate up to 4 days or freeze up to 3 months. To reheat, if frozen, thaw the stew in the refrigerator overnight. Transfer to a medium saucepan. Cook, covered, over medium heat, stirring occasionally until heated through, about 10 minutes. Meanwhile, cook the noodles.

LENTIL AND BLACK BEAN CHILI

SERVES 8
Gluten Free, Vegetarian

1½ cups French green lentils, picked over

1 tablespoon olive oil

1 large onion, chopped

1 large red bell pepper, diced

4 large garlic cloves, minced (about 2 tablespoons)

3 tablespoons chili powder

2 teaspoons dried oregano

1½ teaspoons ground cumin

1 teaspoon kosher salt

½ teaspoon cayenne

1 (29-ounce) can diced fire-roasted tomatoes with chiles

2 (15½-ounce) cans black beans, rinsed and drained

½ cup chopped fresh cilantro

1. Combine lentils with enough water to cover by several inches in large saucepan; bring to boil. Reduce heat to low and simmer, partially covered, until lentils are tender but retain a little bite, 10–15 minutes; drain well and set aside.

2. Meanwhile, heat oil in Dutch oven over medium heat. Add onion, bell pepper, and garlic; cook, stirring, until bell pepper is softened, about 8 minutes.

3. Stir together chili powder, oregano, cumin, salt, and cayenne in cup; add to onion mixture, stirring to combine. Cook, stirring often, until chili is fragrant, about 1 minute. Stir tomatoes and beans into chili. Simmer, covered, until flavors are blended, about 10 minutes longer. Stir in lentils and cilantro.

Per serving (about 1 cup): 277 Cal, 3 g Total Fat, 0 g Sat Fat, 1,101 mg Sod, 48 g Total Carb, 2 g Sugar, 20 g Fib, 18 g Prot. SmartPoints value: 6

 Make It Ahead

Prepare the chili through step 3, but do not stir in the cilantro. Transfer to an airtight container and let cool. Cover and refrigerate up to 4 days or freeze up to 3 months. To reheat, if frozen, thaw the chili in the refrigerator overnight. Transfer to a medium saucepan. Cook, covered, over medium heat, stirring occasionally until heated through, about 10 minutes. Stir in the cilantro.

INDIAN-STYLE QUINOA WITH CRANBERRIES, PISTACHIOS, AND MINT

SERVES 6
Gluten Free, Vegetarian

1   cup quinoa, rinsed

1¾ cups reduced-sodium
     vegetable broth

1   tablespoon curry powder

1   teaspoon salt

½   teaspoon cinnamon

½   pound green beans, trimmed
     and halved crosswise

2   teaspoons olive oil

2   large celery stalks, sliced

1   red onion, chopped

½   cup dried cranberries

¼   cup unsalted pistachios, chopped

¼   cup lightly packed fresh mint
     leaves, torn

2   tablespoons chopped fresh chives

     Grated zest and juice of 1 large
     lemon

1. Combine quinoa, broth, curry powder, salt, and cinnamon in medium saucepan; bring to boil. Reduce heat and simmer, covered, until liquid is absorbed and quinoa is tender, about 15 minutes; transfer to serving bowl and let cool.

2. Meanwhile, bring 1 inch of water to boil in medium nonstick skillet. Add green beans and cook, covered, until crisp-tender, about 5 minutes. Drain in colander; rinse under cold water to stop cooking. Drain again. Add beans to quinoa. Wipe skillet dry.

3. Heat oil in skillet over medium heat. Add celery and onion; cook, stirring occasionally, until onion is softened, about 5 minutes. Add to quinoa along with all remaining ingredients; toss until mixed well. Serve at room temperature.

Per serving (scant 1 cup): 209 Cal, 6 g Total Fat, 1 g Sat Fat, 470 mg Sod, 35 g Total Carb, 9 g Sugar, 6 g Fib, 6 g Prot. SmartPoints value: 6

 Make It Ahead

Prepare the recipe through step 3, but do not stir in the mint and chives. Cover and refrigerate up to 3 days. Let stand at room temperature about 1 hour. Stir in the mint and chives.

INDIAN-STYLE QUINOA
WITH CRANBERRIES,
PISTACHIOS, AND MINT

FARMERS' MARKET TOMATO,
EGGPLANT, AND ZUCCHINI CASSEROLE

FARMERS' MARKET TOMATO, EGGPLANT, AND ZUCCHINI CASSEROLE

SERVES 4
Gluten Free, Vegetarian

- 2 teaspoons olive oil
- 1 small eggplant (about ¾ pound), unpeeled and cut into 1-inch chunks
- 1 onion, chopped
- 3 large garlic cloves, minced
- 1 teaspoon kosher salt
- ½ teaspoon black pepper
- ¼ cup chopped fresh flat-leaf parsley
- ¼ cup chopped fresh basil
- 2 tablespoons chopped fresh oregano
- ¾ pound small tomatoes, preferably heirloom, cut into ¼-inch slices
- 1 large zucchini (about ¾ pound), cut into ¼-inch slices
- ¼ cup grated Asiago or Parmesan cheese

1. Preheat oven to 400°F. Spray shallow 8-cup casserole dish or 9-inch deep-dish pie plate with olive oil nonstick spray.

2. Heat oil in large cast-iron or heavy nonstick skillet over medium-high heat. Add eggplant, onion, garlic, ½ teaspoon of salt, and ¼ teaspoon of pepper; cook, stirring, until eggplant is very tender and browned in spots, about 10 minutes, reducing heat if eggplant browns too quickly. Transfer to prepared casserole dish.

3. Mix together parsley, basil, oregano, and remaining ½ teaspoon salt and ¼ teaspoon pepper in small bowl; sprinkle evenly over eggplant. Arrange tomato and zucchini slices on top of eggplant in alternating rows, overlapping slices.

4. Bake until vegetables are tender and browned along edge, 25–30 minutes. Sprinkle evenly with Asiago and bake until softened, about 2 minutes longer. Serve hot, warm, or at room temperature.

Per serving (1 cup): 116 Cal, 5 g Total Fat, 2 g Sat Fat, 594 mg Sod, 15 g Total Carb, 8 g Sugar, 5 g Fib, 4 g Prot. SmartPoints value: 2

 Make It Ahead

Prepare the casserole as directed through step 4 (in a microwavable casserole or pie plate if planning to serve hot). Let come to room temperature, then cover and refrigerate up to 2 days. To serve hot, cover the dish with a sheet of wax paper and microwave on High until heated through, about 5 minutes. To serve at room temperature, let the dish stand at room temperature up to 2 hours.

ROASTED TRI-COLOR PEPPERS AND RED ONION

SERVES 4
Gluten Free, Vegetarian

1   red bell pepper, cut into 1½-inch pieces

1   yellow bell pepper, cut into 1½-inch pieces

1   orange bell pepper, cut into 1½-inch pieces

1   large red onion, cut into ½-inch wedges

1   tablespoon olive oil

2   teaspoons chopped fresh rosemary, thyme, or a combination

½   teaspoon salt

¼   teaspoon black pepper

1. Preheat oven to 425°F. Spray large baking sheet with olive oil nonstick spray.

2. Combine bell peppers and onion in large bowl; spray with nonstick spray and toss until coated. Add oil, rosemary, salt, and black pepper; toss until coated evenly.

3. Spoon vegetable mixture onto prepared baking sheet and spread to form single layer. Roast 10 minutes; turn vegetables. Roast until browned in spots and tender, 10–15 minutes longer.

Per serving (¾ cup): 69 Cal, 4 g Total Fat, 1 g Sat Fat, 295 mg Sod, 9 g Total Carb, 4 g Sugar, 2 g Fib, 1 g Prot. SmartPoints value: 1

 Make It Ahead

Prepare this dish as directed. Transfer to an airtight container and let cool. Cover and refrigerate up to 3 days. To serve warm, transfer the vegetable mixture to a microwavable dish. Cover with a sheet of wax paper and microwave on High, stirring several times, just until warmed through, about 3 minutes. To serve at room temperature, let the dish stand out up to 2 hours.

GREEN BEANS OREGANATA

SERVES 4
20 Minutes or Less,
Gluten Free, Vegetarian

1   pound green beans, trimmed
    and cut into 1½-inch pieces

4   teaspoons olive oil

3   large shallots, chopped
    (about ½ cup)

2   garlic cloves, minced

1   large tomato, cut into ½-inch dice

½   teaspoon dried oregano

½   teaspoon salt

¼   teaspoon black pepper

¼   cup lightly packed fresh flat-leaf
    parsley leaves

1. Bring ½ inch of water to boil in large skillet over medium-high heat. Add green beans and cook, covered, until crisp-tender, about 5 minutes; drain in colander. Rinse under cold water to stop cooking; set aside.

2. Wipe skillet dry. Heat oil in skillet over medium heat. Add shallots and garlic; cook, stirring, until shallots are softened, about 4 minutes. Add tomato and oregano; cook until tomato begins to release its juice, about 2 minutes.

3. Add green beans, salt, and pepper to skillet; cook, stirring, until heated through, about 2 minutes. Spoon into serving bowl and sprinkle with parsley.

Per serving (1½ cups): 101 Cal, 5 g Fat, 1 g Sat Fat, 305 mg Sod, 14 g Total Carb, 3 g Sugar, 5 g Fib, 3 g Prot. SmartPoints value: 1

 Make It Ahead

You can cook the green beans as directed in step 1 up to a day ahead. Refresh them under cold water, then drain, transfer to a zip-close plastic bag, and refrigerate. When ready to serve, continue with steps 2 and 3.

GRILLED STEAK WITH ROASTED PEPPER SALSA

SERVES 4
Gluten Free

¾ teaspoon kosher salt

½ teaspoon smoked paprika

½ teaspoon black pepper

1 (1-pound) lean sirloin steak, ¾ inch thick, trimmed

½ cup salsa verde

⅓ cup frozen corn kernels, thawed

⅓ cup roasted red pepper (not oil packed), drained and finely diced

2 tablespoons chopped fresh basil

1. To make rub, stir together salt, paprika, and black pepper in cup. Rub spice mixture on both sides of steak; lightly spray with olive oil nonstick spray.

2. Heat grill pan over medium-high heat until hot. Put steak in pan and grill until instant-read thermometer inserted into side of steak registers 145°F, about 5 minutes per side. Transfer to cutting board and let stand 5 minutes.

3. Meanwhile, to make salsa, stir together salsa verde, corn, roasted pepper, and basil in serving bowl. Cut steak on diagonal into 12 very thin slices. Serve with salsa.

Per serving (3 slices steak and ¼ cup salsa): 182 Cal, 4 g Total Fat, 2 g Sat Fat, 665 mg Sod, 8 g Total Carb, 3 g Sugar, 1 g Fib, 27 g Prot. SmartPoints value: 3

 Cook's Tip

Accompany this steak dinner with a side of warm corn tortillas. One corn tortilla for each serving will up the SmartPoints value by 2.

GREEK SALAD WITH GRILLED CHICKEN TENDERS

SERVES 4
20 Minutes or Less,
Gluten Free

1   pound chicken tenders

1   teaspoon dried Greek seasoning

½   teaspoon kosher salt

½   teaspoon black pepper

1   tablespoon extra-virgin olive oil

1   tablespoon red wine vinegar

1   (10-ounce) package cut-up romaine lettuce

6   pitted Kalamata olives, chopped or sliced

1   (8- to 9-ounce) package cooked beets, cut into wedges

¼   cup crumbled reduced-fat feta cheese

1. Heat grill pan over medium-high heat until hot. Sprinkle chicken with Greek seasoning, ¼ teaspoon of salt, and ¼ teaspoon of pepper; lightly spray with olive oil nonstick spray. Place chicken in pan and grill until cooked through, 5–6 minutes per side. Transfer to cutting board and let cool slightly.

2. Meanwhile, to make dressing, whisk together oil, vinegar, and remaining ¼ teaspoon salt and ¼ teaspoon pepper in large serving bowl. Add romaine and olives; toss until coated evenly.

3. Cut chicken into 1½-inch pieces. Place on top of salad along with beets and feta.

Per serving (2 cups salad, about ⅔ cup chicken, ⅓ cup beets, and 1 tablespoon feta): 231 Cal, 10 g Total Fat, 2 g Sat Fat, 785 mg Sod, 9 g Total Carb, 6 g Sugar, 3 g Fib, 28 g Prot. SmartPoints value: 4

 Cook's Tip

Using already-cooked beets really cuts down on kitchen time. Look for them in the refrigerated section of the produce area in your supermarket. If you can find organic beets, they will be even more flavorful.

MEXICAN-STYLE SLOPPY JOES

SERVES 4

20 Minutes or Less

1 teaspoon canola oil

½ pound ground lean beef (7% fat or less)

1 cup packaged cut-up butternut squash, cut into ½-inch dice

1 teaspoon chili powder

½ teaspoon ground cumin

1¼ cups mild or medium fat-free salsa

1 (7-ounce) can Mexican-style corn, drained, or 1 cup frozen corn kernels, thawed

2 multigrain English muffins, split and toasted

8 tablespoons shredded reduced-fat Mexican cheese blend

1. Preheat broiler or toaster oven.

2. Heat oil in large nonstick skillet over medium heat. Add beef and cook, breaking it up with wooden spoon, until lightly browned, about 4 minutes. Stir in squash, chili powder, and cumin; cook, covered, stirring occasionally, until squash is tender, about 8 minutes. Stir in salsa and corn; simmer, stirring occasionally, until flavors are blended, about 2 minutes longer.

3. Place English muffins, cut side up, on broiler rack. Top each with 2 tablespoons Mexican cheese blend and broil until cheese is melted, about 1 minute. Spoon scant ¾ cup beef mixture on each muffin half.

Per serving (½ English muffin, ¾ cup beef mixture, and 2 tablespoons cheese): 281 Cal, 8 g Total Fat, 3 g Sat Fat, 723 mg Sod, 33 g Total Carb, 5 g Sugar, 5 g Fib, 22 g Prot. SmartPoints value: 6

THAI-FLAVORED
SALMON CAKES

THAI-FLAVORED SALMON CAKES

SERVES 4
20 Minutes or Less

½ cup fat-free egg substitute

2 tablespoons chopped
fresh cilantro

1½ teaspoons Thai red or
green curry paste

½ teaspoon kosher salt

2 (6-ounce) cans skinless boneless
pink salmon, drained

½ red bell pepper, finely diced

⅓ cup instant potato flakes

1 scallion, thinly sliced

¼ cup plain dried bread crumbs

2 teaspoons canola oil

4 lime wedges

Sriracha for serving

1. Whisk together egg substitute, cilantro, curry paste, and salt in large bowl. Add salmon, bell pepper, potato flakes, scallion, and bread crumbs; stir with fork until mixture begins to hold together. Shape mixture into 4 (¾-inch-thick) patties.

2. Heat 1 teaspoon of oil in large nonstick skillet over medium heat. Add patties and cook until browned, about 4 minutes. Gently turn patties over; add remaining 1 teaspoon oil to pan. Cook until patties are browned and cooked through, about 4 minutes longer. Serve with lime wedges and Sriracha.

Per serving (1 salmon cake): 198 Cal, 7 g Total Fat, 1 g Sat Fat, 724 mg Sod, 11 g Total Carb, 2 g Sugar, 1 g Fib, 21 g Prot. SmartPoints value: 4

PENNE WITH ROASTED CAULIFLOWER

SERVES 6

2 ounces diced pancetta (about ⅓ cup)

1 (12-ounce) bag fresh cauliflower florets, cut into 1½-inch chunks

1 (14½-ounce) can diced tomatoes with basil and oregano, drained, juice reserved

8 ounces whole wheat penne

2 tablespoons chopped fresh flat-leaf parsley

1 tablespoon capers, drained and coarsely chopped

½ teaspoon kosher salt

¼ teaspoon black pepper

1. Preheat oven to 450°F.

2. Sprinkle pancetta on heavy rimmed baking sheet; spread cauliflower on top to form single layer. Roast until pancetta is crisp and cauliflower is browned, about 15 minutes. Remove baking sheet from oven; add drained tomatoes and toss gently to combine.

3. Meanwhile, cook penne according to package directions. Drain and return to pot. Add cauliflower-tomato mixture, reserved tomato juice, parsley, capers, salt, and pepper to penne; gently toss until mixed well. Divide cauliflower-pasta mixture evenly among 6 plates or large shallow bowls.

Per serving (1⅓ cups): 242 Cal, 6 g Total Fat, 2 g Sat Fat, 442 mg Sod, 33 g Total Carb, 4 g Sugar, 5 g Fib, 9 g Prot. SmartPoints value: 7

STRAWBERRY MERINGUE MOUSSE

SERVES 12
20 Minutes or Less,
Gluten Free, Vegetarian

1 (1-pound) container fresh strawberries, hulled and sliced

⅔ cup light sour cream

1 (12-ounce) container thawed frozen reduced-fat whipped topping

8 (2-inch) vanilla meringue cookies, coarsely crushed (generous 2 cups)

1. Stir together strawberries and sour cream in large bowl; gently fold in whipped topping just until blended.

2. Spoon ½ cup of strawberry mixture into each of 12 wine-glasses or dessert dishes. Top each with 2 tablespoons cookies. Top evenly with remaining strawberry mixture and sprinkle with remaining cookies.

Per serving (about 1 cup): 106 Cal, 3 g Total Fat, 2 g Sat Fat, 39 mg Sod, 17 g Total Carb, 13 g Sugar, 1 g Fib, 1 g Prot. SmartPoints value: 5

 Cook's Tip

When purchasing fresh strawberries, look for firm, shiny, bright red berries with no white area at the top, which would indicate berries that were picked under ripe.

PEAR AND CRANBERRY CLAFOUTIS

SERVES 6
Vegetarian

⅓ cup dried cranberries

1 cup low-fat (1%) milk

¼ cup + 1 tablespoon granulated sugar

¼ cup all-purpose flour

½ teaspoon cinnamon

¼ teaspoon salt

¾ cup fat-free egg substitute

½ teaspoon vanilla extract

1 (15-ounce) can pear halves in juice, drained

1 tablespoon confectioners' sugar

1. Preheat oven to 375°F. Spray 8-inch square baking dish or casserole dish with nonstick spray.

2. Combine cranberries with enough hot water to cover in small bowl; let stand until softened, about 10 minutes.

3. Meanwhile, to make batter, pour milk into medium microwavable bowl. Microwave on High until hot, about 2 minutes. Whisk together granulated sugar, flour, cinnamon, and salt in large bowl. Gradually whisk in egg substitute and vanilla until smooth; whisk in hot milk until blended.

4. Cut each pear half into 4 wedges. Arrange in prepared baking dish. Drain cranberries and sprinkle over pears; pour batter over. Bake until clafoutis is puffed, golden along edges, and knife inserted into center comes out clean, about 30 minutes. Let cool in baking dish on wire rack until warm, about 5 minutes. Dust with confectioners' sugar just before serving.

Per serving (⅙ of clafoutis): 141 Cal, 1 g Total Fat, 0 g Sat Fat, 174 mg Sod, 29 g Total Carb, 23 g Sugar, 2 g Fib, 5 g Prot. SmartPoints value: 5

 Cook's Tip

Clafoutis is a French dessert that originated in the Limousin region. Simple and homey, it is made by spreading a layer of fruit—traditionally black cherries—in a shallow baking dish, covering it with a sweetened egg batter, and baking it.

PEAR AND CRANBERRY
CLAFOUTIS

PINEAPPLE SHORTCAKES

SERVES 8

Vegetarian

2½ tablespoons sugar

¼ + ⅛ teaspoon cinnamon

1   (16.3-ounce) tube refrigerated reduced-fat buttermilk biscuits

2   tablespoons fat-free egg substitute

5   cups (½-inch) diced fresh pineapple (about 1 pineapple)

1   cup thawed frozen fat-free whipped topping

1. Preheat oven to 350°F.

2. Mix together ½ tablespoon of sugar and ¼ teaspoon of cinnamon in cup.

3. Place biscuits about 2 inches apart on ungreased large baking sheet. Brush tops with egg substitute and sprinkle evenly with cinnamon-sugar mixture. Bake until golden, 14–18 minutes.

4. Meanwhile, to make filling, combine pineapple, remaining 2 tablespoons sugar, and ⅛ teaspoon cinnamon in large skillet; cook over high heat, stirring frequently, until pineapple is tender, about 5 minutes.

5. Split biscuits; let cool slightly, about 3 minutes. Place bottoms of biscuits on 8 plates. Top each with about ⅓ cup pineapple filling and 2 tablespoons whipped topping. Cover with tops of biscuits and serve warm.

Per serving (1 filled shortcake): 149 Cal, 2 g Total Fat, 1 g Sat Fat, 321 mg Sod, 32 g Total Carb, 18 g Sugar, 2 g Fib, 3 g Prot. SmartPoints value: 4

TURKEY-AND-VEGETABLE STEW

SERVES 6

2 teaspoons canola oil

3 scallions, thinly sliced

2 tablespoons minced peeled fresh ginger

1½ cups chicken broth

3 tablespoons all-purpose flour

2 tablespoons lime juice

1¼ teaspoons garam masala

½ teaspoon salt

¼ teaspoon black pepper

1 pound small red potatoes, scrubbed and quartered

2 carrots, halved lengthwise and cut into 2-inch lengths

1 (2¾-pound) bone-in turkey thigh, skin removed and trimmed

Chopped fresh mint

1. Heat oil in medium skillet over medium heat. Add scallions and ginger; cook, stirring occasionally, until scallions begin to soften, about 3 minutes.

2. Whisk together broth and flour in small bowl until smooth. Add broth mixture to skillet and cook, whisking constantly, 2 minutes. Whisk in lime juice, garam masala, salt, and pepper. Increase heat to medium-high and bring to boil. Reduce heat and simmer, whisking often, 2 minutes.

3. Put potatoes and carrots in 5- or 6-quart slow cooker. Place turkey on top of vegetables; add broth mixture. Cover and cook until turkey and vegetables are fork-tender, 3–4 hours on High or 5–6 hours on Low.

4. Transfer turkey thigh to cutting board. Remove and discard bone. Cut turkey into 1-inch chunks and return to slow cooker; stir to combine. Ladle stew evenly into 6 bowls and sprinkle with mint.

Per serving (generous 1 cup): 339 Cal, 11 g Total Fat, 3 g Sat Fat, 757 mg Sod, 19 g Carb, 3 g Sugar, 2 g Fib, 43 g Prot. SmartPoints value: 7

 Cook's Tip

Turkey thighs are budget friendly and cook up moist and flavorful in a slow cooker. They are readily available especially around the holidays. Pick up a package or two and freeze for recipes like this one. Just be sure to thaw the thighs in the refrigerator—not on the counter.

CHICKEN AND
BLACK BEAN CHILI

CHICKEN AND BLACK BEAN CHILI

SERVES 6
Gluten Free

1   teaspoon canola oil

1   pound skinless boneless chicken thighs, trimmed and cut into ½-inch pieces

2   tablespoons chili powder

2   large red bell peppers, chopped

1   large onion, chopped

1   (15½-ounce) can black beans, rinsed and drained

1   (14½-ounce) can diced tomatoes

½   cup chicken broth

2   garlic cloves, minced

2   teaspoons cumin

1   teaspoon dried oregano

½   teaspoon salt

¼   teaspoon black pepper

2   tablespoons cornmeal

1. Heat oil in large heavy skillet over medium-high heat. Add chicken and sprinkle with 1 tablespoon of chili powder; cook, stirring occasionally, until browned, about 5 minutes. Transfer chicken to 5- or 6-quart slow cooker.

2. Add remaining 1 tablespoon chili powder, the bell peppers, onion, beans, tomatoes, broth, garlic, cumin, oregano, salt, and black pepper to slow cooker; stir to combine. Cover and cook until chicken and vegetables are fork-tender, 4–5 hours on High or 8–9 hours on Low.

3. About 20 minutes before cooking time is up, gradually stir cornmeal into chili until blended. Cover and cook on High until mixture bubbles and thickens, about 15 minutes. Ladle chili evenly into 6 bowls.

Per serving (about ¾ cup): 223 Cal, 5 g Total Fat, 1 g Sat Fat, 734 mg Sod, 24 g Total Carb, 4 g Sugar, 8 g Fib, 22 g Prot. SmartPoints value: 4

 Cook's Tip

Top each serving with 2 tablespoons of reduced-fat sour cream, 1 tablespoon of shredded reduced-fat Cheddar cheese, and a sprinkling of scallion for an additional 2 SmartPoints.

POT ROAST WITH POTATOES AND GREEN OLIVES

SERVES 6

2   teaspoons olive oil

1   small red onion, chopped

½   cup dry red wine

2   tablespoons all-purpose flour

1   cup chicken broth

½   cup orange juice

¾   teaspoon salt

½   teaspoon paprika

½   teaspoon ground cumin

1   pound small yellow potatoes, scrubbed and halved or quartered

1   (1½-pound) lean boneless bottom round roast, trimmed

⅓   cup pimiento-stuffed olives, halved

     Chopped fresh cilantro

1. Heat oil in medium skillet over medium heat. Add onion and cook, stirring, until softened, about 5 minutes.

2. Whisk together wine and flour in small bowl until smooth. Add to onion and cook, whisking constantly, 1 minute. Whisk in broth, orange juice, salt, paprika, and cumin. Increase heat to medium-high and bring to boil. Reduce heat and simmer, whisking often, 2 minutes.

3. Put potatoes in 5- or 6-quart slow cooker. Place beef on top of potatoes; add broth mixture. Cover and cook until beef is fork-tender, 4–5 hours on High or 8–9 hours on Low.

4. Transfer beef to cutting board. Cut into 6 pieces.

5. Stir olives into slow cooker. Divide beef, potatoes, and sauce evenly among 6 plates; sprinkle with cilantro.

Per serving (1 piece beef with about 1 cup potatoes and sauce): 350 Cal, 17 g Total Fat, 5 g Sat Fat, 688 mg Sod, 18 g Carb, 3 g Sugar, 2 g Fib, 26 g Prot. SmartPoints value: 10

 Cook's Tip

Slow cooking meat in a sauce that is prepared on the stovetop is an easy way to ensure that the finished dish will be infused with lots of flavor and has just the right consistency.

SLOW-COOKER LASAGNA

SERVES 6

2 teaspoons olive oil

1 pound ground lean beef (7% fat or less)

1 small onion, chopped

1 garlic clove, minced

1 (28-ounce) can crushed tomatoes

1 (15½-ounce) can tomato sauce

1 teaspoon dried oregano

1 teaspoon salt

½ teaspoon dried basil

¼ teaspoon red pepper flakes

1½ cups shredded part-skim mozzarella cheese

1 cup part-skim ricotta cheese

6 lasagna noodles

½ cup grated Parmesan cheese

1. Heat oil in large heavy nonstick skillet over medium-high heat. Add beef, onion, and garlic; cook, breaking up beef with wooden spoon, until no longer pink, about 5 minutes. Stir in crushed tomatoes, tomato sauce, oregano, salt, basil, and pepper flakes; reduce heat and simmer 5 minutes to allow flavors to blend.

2. Meanwhile, stir together 1 cup of mozzarella and the ricotta in medium bowl.

3. Spoon one-third of beef mixture into 5-quart slow cooker. Break 3 lasagna noodles in half and arrange over beef mixture; top with half of mozzarella mixture. Repeat layers once; top with remaining beef mixture. Cover and cook on Low 4–6 hours. Remove cover and turn off heat.

4. Sprinkle remaining ½ cup mozzarella and the Parmesan over beef mixture. Cover and set aside until mozzarella is melted and lasagna sets up, about 10 minutes.

Per serving (⅙ of lasagna): 402 Cal, 16 g Total Fat, 8 g Sat Fat, 1346 mg Sod, 31 g Total Carb, 8 g Sugar, 4 g Fib, 36 g Prot. SmartPoints value: 10

 Cook's Tip

An arugula, Belgian endive, and radicchio salad dressed with balsamic vinegar would be a refreshing way to begin the meal.

RED CURRY BEEF WITH PINEAPPLE AND SNOW PEAS

SERVES 6

- 2 teaspoons canola oil
- 1 onion, chopped
- 1 (13½-ounce) can light (low-fat) coconut milk
- 2 tablespoons all-purpose flour
- 2 tablespoons Thai red curry paste
- ⅛ teaspoon cayenne or to taste
- ½ cup chicken broth
- 2 tablespoons lime juice
- 1 tablespoon honey
- 1 pound small red potatoes, scrubbed and halved or quartered
- 1 (1½-pound) lean bottom round steak, trimmed and cut into 1-inch chunks
- 2 cups fresh pineapple chunks
- ¾ pound snow peas, trimmed
- 1 teaspoon salt
  Chopped fresh cilantro
  Lime wedges

1. Heat oil in medium skillet over medium heat. Add onion and cook, stirring, until softened, about 5 minutes.

2. Whisk together coconut milk, flour, 1 tablespoon of curry paste, and the cayenne in medium bowl until smooth. Add coconut-milk mixture to skillet and cook, whisking constantly, about 2 minutes. Whisk in broth, lime juice, and honey. Increase heat to medium-high and bring to boil. Reduce heat and simmer, whisking often, 2 minutes.

3. Place potatoes and beef in 5- or 6-quart slow cooker; add coconut-milk mixture. Cover and cook until beef is fork-tender, 4–5 hours on High or 8–9 hours on Low. Stir in pineapple, snow peas, remaining 1 tablespoon curry paste, and the salt. Cover and cook on High until snow peas are crisp-tender, about 5 minutes. Ladle stew evenly into 6 bowls and sprinkle with cilantro. Serve with lime wedges.

Per serving (about 1½ cups): 415 Cal, 19 g Total Fat, 8 g Sat Fat, 546 mg Sod, 33 g Carb, 13 g Sugar, 4 g Fib, 28 g Prot. SmartPoints value: 11

 Cook's Tip

Instead of the pineapple, you can use chopped fresh mango or papaya for a flavor change.

RED CURRY BEEF WITH
PINEAPPLE AND SNOW PEAS

BOLOGNESE SAUCE WITH SPAGHETTI

SERVES 8

2   teaspoons olive oil

1   small fennel bulb, chopped

1   small onion, chopped

1   carrot, cut into ¼-inch dice

1   celery stalk, cut into ¼-inch dice

4   garlic cloves, minced

½   pound ground lean beef (7% fat or less)

½   pound ground lean pork

1   teaspoon salt

¼   teaspoon red pepper flakes

¼   teaspoon black pepper

1   (28-ounce) can crushed tomatoes

½   cup grated Parmesan cheese

⅓   cup reduced-fat (2%) milk

1   (16-ounce) package whole wheat spaghetti

½   cup chopped fresh basil

1. Heat oil in large pot over medium-high heat. Add fennel, onion, carrot, and celery; cook, stirring, until onion is softened, about 5 minutes. Add garlic and cook, stirring, until fragrant, about 30 seconds. Add beef, pork, salt, pepper flakes, and black pepper; cook, breaking up meat with wooden spoon, until browned, 6–8 minutes. Transfer to 5- or 6-quart slow cooker.

2. Stir tomatoes into beef mixture. Cover and cook until sauce is slightly thickened, 3½ hours on Low. Stir in ¼ cup of Parmesan and the milk. Cover and cook on Low 30 minutes longer.

3. Meanwhile, cook spaghetti in same large pot according to package directions. Drain.

4. Divide spaghetti evenly among 8 bowls; top evenly with meat sauce. Sprinkle with remaining ¼ cup Parmesan and the basil.

Per serving (scant 1 cup pasta, ¾ cup sauce, and 1 tablespoon Parmesan): 346 Cal, 7 g Total Fat, 3 g Sat Fat, 594 mg Sod, 51 g Total Carb, 4 g Sugar, 8 g Fib, 25 g Prot. SmartPoints value: 8

 Cook's Tip

Slow cookers are perfect for making big-batch meals such as this one. Make this Italian classic when you are feeding a crowd or when you want to have leftovers for another meal. Store the sauce in the refrigerator in an airtight container up to 4 days or frozen up to 4 months. Thaw in the refrigerator and gently reheat.

PORK AND WHITE BEAN STEW

SERVES 6

2   teaspoons canola oil

3   scallions, thinly sliced

1   jalapeño pepper, seeded
     and minced

1½ cups chicken broth

3   tablespoons all-purpose flour

½   teaspoon ground cumin

½   teaspoon ground coriander

½   teaspoon salt

1   (1½-pound) lean boneless pork
     loin roast, trimmed and cut into
     1-inch chunks

1   (15½-ounce) can cannellini (white
     kidney) beans, rinsed and drained

     Chopped fresh cilantro

1. Heat oil in medium skillet over medium heat. Add scallions and jalapeño; cook, stirring occasionally, until beginning to soften, about 3 minutes.

2. Whisk together broth and flour in small bowl until smooth. Add to skillet and cook, whisking constantly, about 2 minutes. Whisk in cumin, coriander, and salt. Increase heat to medium-high and bring to boil. Reduce heat and simmer, whisking often, about 2 minutes.

3. Combine pork and beans in 5- or 6-quart slow cooker; add broth mixture. Cover and cook until pork is fork-tender, 3–4 hours on High or 5–6 hours on Low. Ladle stew evenly into 6 bowls. Sprinkle with cilantro.

Per serving (about 1 cup): 299 Cal, 10 g Total Fat, 3 g Sat Fat, 443 mg Sod, 20 g Total Carb, 1 g Sugar, 4 g Fib, 32 g Prot. SmartPoints value: 7

LAMB AND FENNEL MEATBALLS
IN TOMATO SAUCE

LAMB AND FENNEL MEATBALLS IN TOMATO SAUCE

SERVES 8

1   pound ground lean lamb

2   large eggs, lightly beaten

1   small onion, finely chopped

1   garlic clove, minced

¾   teaspoon fennel seeds

½   teaspoon salt

⅛   teaspoon black pepper

1   (26.46-ounce) carton tomato sauce with basil

1   (14½-ounce) can diced tomatoes with garlic and onion

⅓   cup all-purpose flour

1   tablespoon olive oil

½   cup thinly sliced fresh basil

1. Stir together lamb, eggs, onion, garlic, fennel seeds, salt, and pepper in medium bowl until mixed well. With damp hands, form into 24 meatballs.

2. Combine tomato sauce and diced tomatoes in 3- or 4-quart slow cooker.

3. Spread flour on sheet of wax paper; coat meatballs with flour, shaking off excess.

4. Heat oil in large nonstick skillet over medium heat. Cook meatballs in two batches, turning often, until browned on all sides, about 5 minutes, transferring meatballs to paper towel–lined plate to drain. Add meatballs to slow cooker, spooning sauce over.

5. Cover and cook until meatballs are cooked through and sauce is slightly thickened, about 3 hours on Low. Divide meatballs and sauce evenly among 8 bowls. Sprinkle with basil.

Per serving (¾ cup meatballs with sauce): 253 Cal, 16 g Total Fat, 6 g Sat Fat, 881 mg Sod, 13 g Total Carb, 6 g Sugar, 2 g Fib, 13 g Prot. SmartPoints value: 7

Cook's Tip

Serve our tasty meatballs and sauce over whole wheat pappardelle noodles. One cup of cooked whole wheat pappardelle per serving will up the SmartPoints value by 5.

SPICY SLOW-COOKER VEGETARIAN CHILI

SERVES 6
Gluten Free, Vegetarian

1   (29-ounce) can diced fire-roasted
    tomatoes with garlic

3   tablespoons tomato paste

1   tablespoon olive oil

1   tablespoon chili powder

1   teaspoon ground cumin

¾   teaspoon salt

½   teaspoon chipotle chile powder

2   large zucchini, cut into ¾-inch
    dice (about 4 cups)

2   cups frozen corn kernels

1   (15½-ounce) can black beans,
    rinsed and drained

1   (15½-ounce) can pinto beans,
    rinsed and drained

2   poblano peppers, seeded and
    diced (about 1¾ cups)

¾   cup chopped fresh cilantro

1. Stir together tomatoes, tomato paste, oil, chili powder, cumin, salt, and chipotle chile powder in 4- or 5-quart slow cooker. Stir in zucchini, corn, black beans, pinto beans, and poblanos. Cover and cook on Low until vegetables are tender, about 6 hours.

2. Stir in cilantro and enough water to create saucy consistency, if needed.

Per serving (about 1½ cups): 258 Cal, 4 g Total Fat, 1 g Sat Fat, 1049 mg Sod, 48 g Total Carb, 11 g Sugar, 13 g Fib, 13 g Prot. SmartPoints value: 6

 Cook's Tip

For a touch of richness, serve the chili topped with light sour cream. Two tablespoons of light sour cream for each serving will up the SmartPoints value by 2.

EGG, CANADIAN BACON, AVOCADO, AND TOMATO SANDWICHES

SERVES 4
30 Minutes or Less

1½   teaspoons canola oil

4   (½-ounce) slices Canadian bacon

4   light English muffins, split and toasted

3   large eggs

4   large egg whites

1   scallion, thinly sliced

½   teaspoon salt

¼   teaspoon black pepper

½   Hass avocado, halved, pitted, peeled, and cut into 8 slices

1   large plum tomato, cut into 8 slices

1. Heat 1 teaspoon of oil in large heavy nonstick skillet over medium-high heat. Add bacon and cook, turning, until lightly browned, 1½–2 minutes. Place 1 slice of bacon on bottom of each English muffin. Keep warm.

2. Remove skillet from heat; add remaining ½ teaspoon oil. Beat eggs, egg whites, scallion, salt, and pepper in medium bowl until blended; pour into skillet. Cook over medium heat until eggs begin to set, about 1½ minutes, pushing egg mixture toward center of skillet to form large, soft curds; continue cooking until eggs are just set, about 3 minutes longer.

3. Place one-fourth of eggs on top of each slice of bacon. Top with 2 avocado slices and 2 tomato slices; cover with tops of English muffins.

Per serving (1 sandwich): 224 Cal, 8 g Total Fat, 2 g Sat Fat, 727 mg Sod, 26 g Total Carb, 2 g Sugar, 7 g Fib, 16 g Prot. SmartPoints value: 6

 Cook's Tip

To make this dish vegetarian, omit the Canadian bacon. The SmartPoints value will be reduced by 1.

EGG WHITE FRITTATA WITH CHEDDAR AND VEGGIES

SERVES 4
Gluten Free, Vegetarian

1½ cups egg whites
    (about 8 large eggs)

½   teaspoon salt

¼   teaspoon black pepper

2   teaspoons olive oil

2   any-color bell peppers, diced

1   red onion, thinly sliced

1   cup shredded reduced-fat
    Cheddar cheese

2   scallions, sliced on diagonal

1. Whisk together egg whites, salt, and black pepper in large bowl until frothy.

2. Heat oil in 10-inch heavy ovenproof nonstick skillet over medium-high heat. Add bell peppers and onion; cook, stirring occasionally, until softened, about 5 minutes. Add egg whites and cook, stirring occasionally, until beginning to set, about 2 minutes. Reduce heat and cook, without stirring, until eggs are almost set, about 6 minutes longer.

3. Meanwhile, preheat broiler.

4. Sprinkle Cheddar over frittata. Broil 5 inches from heat until cheese is melted and eggs are set, 1–2 minutes. Sprinkle with scallions. Cut into 4 wedges.

Per serving (1 wedge): 142 Cal, 5 g Total Fat, 2 g Sat Fat, 619 mg Sod, 7 g Total Carb, 4 g Sugar, 2 g Fib, 18 g Prot. SmartPoints value: 3

 Cook's Tip

If you have leftovers, wrap them in plastic wrap and refrigerate up to 3 days. A wedge of this tasty frittata makes an excellent sandwich filling.

EGG WHITE FRITTATA WITH
CHEDDAR AND VEGGIES

ITALIAN PEPPER AND EGG SANDWICHES

SERVES 4
20 Minutes or Less,
Vegetarian

2   teaspoons olive oil

1   small onion, thinly sliced

1   large green pepper, such as cubanelle or Italian frying, thinly sliced

1   garlic clove, minced

4   large eggs

3   large egg whites

½   teaspoon salt

¼   teaspoon black pepper

4   reduced-calorie hamburger rolls, toasted if desired

1. Heat oil in large nonstick skillet over medium heat. Add onion and green pepper; cook, stirring, until softened, about 8 minutes. Add garlic and cook, stirring, until fragrant, about 30 seconds longer. Transfer vegetables to plate.

2. Whisk together eggs, egg whites, salt, and black pepper in medium bowl. Pour into skillet and cook over medium heat until eggs begin to set, about 1½ minutes, pushing eggs toward center of skillet to form large, soft curds. Return vegetables to skillet and continue cooking, stirring occasionally, until eggs are just set, about 2 minutes longer.

3. Place about ¾ cup egg-vegetable mixture on bottom of each roll; cover with tops of rolls.

Per serving (1 sandwich): 205 Cal, 8 g Total Fat, 2 g Sat Fat, 595 mg Sod, 22 g Total Carb, 4 g Sugar, 4 g Fib, 13 g Prot. SmartPoints value: 6

 Cook's Tip

Enjoy a cappuccino with these Italian-style breakfast sandwiches. An 8-ounce cappuccino made with low-fat (1%) milk will up the SmartPoints value by 3, while an 8-ounce cappuccino made with reduced-fat (2%) milk will up the SmartPoints value by 2.

MEXICAN BREAKFAST BURRITOS

SERVES 6

Vegetarian

6 tablespoons light sour cream

6 tablespoons fat-free salsa

1 teaspoon canola oil

½ onion, chopped

1 poblano pepper, chopped

1 (16-ounce) carton fat-free egg substitute

1 teaspoon ground cumin

¾ teaspoon kosher salt

   Pinch cayenne

6 (8-inch) whole wheat tortillas

12 tablespoons reduced-fat shredded Cheddar cheese or Mexican cheese blend

1. Preheat oven to 350°F.

2. Stir together sour cream and salsa in small bowl; set aside.

3. Heat oil in large heavy nonstick skillet over medium-high heat. Add onion and poblano; cook, stirring, until softened, about 5 minutes.

4. Meanwhile, beat egg substitute, cumin, salt, and cayenne in medium bowl. Pour over vegetable mixture and cook until eggs begin to set, about 1½ minutes, pushing egg mixture toward center of skillet to form large, soft curds; continue cooking eggs just until set, about 4 minutes longer.

5. Place 1 tortilla on square of foil big enough to wrap it in. Spoon about ½ cup egg mixture down center of tortilla. Top with 2 tablespoons each salsa mixture and Cheddar; fold two opposite sides of tortilla and roll up burrito-style to enclose filling. Wrap tightly in foil. Place wrapped burrito on baking sheet and repeat with remaining ingredients, making total of 6 burritos. Bake until heated through, 10–15 minutes.

Per serving (1 burrito): 224 Cal, 4 g Total Fat, 2 g Sat Fat, 825 mg Sod, 38 g Total Carb, 3 g Sugar, 4 g Fib, 17 g Prot. SmartPoints value: 5

 Cook's Tip

To make this dish gluten free, substitute corn tortillas for the whole wheat tortillas with no change in the SmartPoints value.

PERUVIAN POTATO CAKES
WITH POACHED EGGS

PERUVIAN POTATO CAKES WITH POACHED EGGS

SERVES 4

Gluten Free, Vegetarian

1   pound baking potatoes, peeled and sliced

2   large garlic cloves, coarsely chopped

¾   cup shredded part-skim mozzarella cheese

½   cup frozen corn kernels, thawed and patted dry

4   scallions, thinly sliced

¼   cup chopped fresh cilantro + additional for sprinkling

3   tablespoons grated Parmesan cheese

½   teaspoon salt

2   teaspoons canola oil

1   tablespoon distilled white vinegar

4   large eggs

    Hot pepper sauce for serving

1. Preheat oven to 250°F. Line baking sheet with parchment paper; spray with nonstick spray.

2. Put potatoes and garlic in medium saucepan and add enough cold water to cover by 1 inch; bring to boil over high heat. Reduce heat and cook until potatoes are fork-tender, 10–12 minutes; drain. Transfer to large bowl. With potato masher, mash potatoes and garlic until smooth. Add mozzarella, corn, scallions, ¼ cup of cilantro, the Parmesan, and salt, stirring until mixed well. Shape potato mixture into 8 (¾-inch-thick) patties using about ⅓ cup potato mixture for each patty.

3. Heat oil in large deep nonstick skillet over medium heat. Add 4 patties and cook until golden brown, about 3 minutes per side. Transfer to prepared baking sheet and place in oven to keep warm. Repeat with remaining 4 patties. Wipe skillet clean.

4. To poach eggs, half-fill skillet with water and bring to boil; add vinegar. Reduce heat to bare simmer. Break 1 egg into cup. Holding cup close to water, slip egg into water. Repeat with remaining eggs. Cook until whites of eggs are firm but yolks are still soft, about 5 minutes. With slotted spoon, transfer one egg at a time to paper towel–lined plate to drain.

5. To serve, place 2 potato patties on each of 4 plates; top with 1 egg and sprinkle with cilantro. Serve with hot sauce.

Per serving (2 potato patties and 1 egg): 279 Cal, 12 g Total Fat, 5 g Sat Fat, 568 mg Sod, 27 g Total Carb, 3 g Sugar, 3 g Fib, 17 g Prot. SmartPoints value: 8

 Make It Ahead

The potato patties can be prepared up to 1 day ahead and refrigerated, but let them come to room temperature before browning in the skillet.

YOGURT PANCAKES WITH FRESH RASPBERRY SAUCE

SERVES 4
Vegetarian

1   cup fresh or thawed frozen unsweetened raspberries

¼   cup + 2 tablespoons sugar

1   tablespoon lemon juice

1⅓   cups all-purpose flour

1   teaspoon baking powder

¼   teaspoon baking soda

½   teaspoon salt

1   cup plain fat-free yogurt

¾   cup fat-free milk

1   large egg

1   tablespoon + ½ teaspoon canola oil

1. To make raspberry sauce, combine raspberries, ¼ cup of sugar, and the lemon juice in small saucepan and set over medium heat. Cook, stirring, until chunky sauce is formed, about 5 minutes. Transfer to serving bowl; set aside.

2. To make pancakes, whisk together flour, remaining 2 tablespoons sugar, the baking powder, baking soda, and salt in large bowl. Whisk together yogurt, milk, egg, and 1 tablespoon oil in small bowl until blended well. Add yogurt mixture to flour mixture, stirring just until combined.

3. Coat large nonstick griddle or skillet with remaining ½ teaspoon oil. Set over medium heat. Pour ¼ cupfuls of batter onto griddle. Cook until bubbles appear and edges of pancakes look dry, 2–3 minutes. Turn and cook until golden brown, about 2 minutes longer. Transfer pancakes to plate and keep warm. Repeat with remaining batter, spraying griddle between batches, making total of 12 pancakes. Serve with sauce.

Per serving (3 pancakes and about 3 tablespoons sauce): 336 Cal, 5 g Total Fat, 1 g Sat Fat, 572 mg Sod, 62 g Total Carb, 27 g Sugar, 3 g Fib, 11 g Prot. SmartPoints value: 12

 Cook's Tip

Begin with glasses of freshly squeezed orange juice for a good dose of vitamin C. A 4-ounce glass of orange juice per serving will up the SmartPoints value by 3.

QUINOA AND APPLE BREAKFAST CEREAL

SERVES 6

Gluten Free, Vegetarian

1 cup quinoa, rinsed

1 teaspoon canola oil

1 tablespoon butter

2 apples, peeled, cored, and cut into ¾-inch chunks

2 cups water

¼ cup fat-free milk

3 tablespoons brown sugar

½ teaspoon cinnamon + additional for sprinkling

1. Put quinoa in medium bowl with enough water to cover and soak 5 minutes; drain in fine-mesh sieve. Rinse under cold water and drain again.

2. Heat oil in large skillet over medium heat. Add ½ tablespoon of butter and cook until melted and sizzling. Add apples and cook, turning occasionally, until softened and beginning to caramelize, 5–10 minutes; remove skillet from heat and keep warm.

3. Meanwhile, combine quinoa and 2 cups water in medium saucepan and bring to boil over medium-high heat; boil 1 minute. Reduce heat to low and simmer, covered, until quinoa is tender and liquid is absorbed, about 10 minutes. Remove saucepan from heat and fluff quinoa with fork. Stir in remaining ½ tablespoon butter, the milk, brown sugar, and ½ teaspoon of cinnamon until butter is melted; stir in apples. Spoon evenly into 6 bowls and sprinkle with cinnamon.

Per serving (⅔ cup): 189 Cal, 4 g Total Fat, 1 g Sat Fat, 27 mg Sod, 34 g Total Carb, 14 g Sugar, 4 g Fib, 5 g Prot. SmartPoints value: 6

FRESH CORN AND BLUEBERRY PANCAKES

SERVES 6
Vegetarian

2   cups all-purpose flour

½   cup yellow cornmeal

2   tablespoons sugar

1   tablespoon + 1 teaspoon baking powder

1   teaspoon salt

1¾ cups reduced-fat (2%) milk

½   cup fat-free egg substitute

2   tablespoons canola oil

¾   cup fresh or frozen blueberries

¾   cup fresh corn kernels (about 2 ears of corn) or frozen corn kernels

¼   cup pure maple syrup, warmed

1. Whisk together flour, cornmeal, sugar, baking powder, and salt in medium bowl. Make a well in middle of flour mixture (see Cook's Tip). Combine milk, egg substitute, and oil in well; with fork, stir until mixed well. With rubber spatula, stir flour mixture into milk mixture just until flour mixture is moistened (batter will be lumpy). Gently stir in blueberries and corn.

2. Spray griddle with nonstick spray and set over medium heat. Pour scant ¼ cupfuls of batter onto griddle. Cook until bubbles appear and edges of pancakes look dry, about 3 minutes. Turn and cook until golden brown, about 3 minutes longer. Transfer pancakes to platter and keep warm. Repeat with remaining batter, spraying griddle between batches, making total of 24 pancakes. Serve with maple syrup.

Per serving (4 pancakes and 2 teaspoons maple syrup): 363 Cal, 7 g Total Fat, 1 g Sat Fat, 789 mg Sod, 65 g Total Carb, 19 g Sugar, 3 g Fib, 10 g Prot. SmartPoints value: 12

Cook's Tip

Making a "well" is a classic cooking technique that is used when combining wet and dry ingredients for pasta dough, gnocchi, pancakes, and quick breads. Here's how: Whisk together the dry ingredients in a large bowl, then push it towards the side of the bowl to create an empty space in the middle—the well. Pour the wet ingredients into the well, beat them with a fork, then gradually stir in the dry ingredients until thoroughly mixed.

FRESH CORN AND
BLUEBERRY PANCAKES

CHAPTER 2
ANYTIME ENTERTAINING

Company Is Always Welcome

Gathering family and friends together is about celebrating the bonds that connect us and sharing food with the people who matter the most to us. Whether the occasion is a relaxing Sunday-afternoon brunch in the kitchen or a pull-out-all-the-stops fancy affair in the dining room, spending time with those closest to us enriches our lives and brings us joy. In this chapter, look for a tempting array of recipes organized by occasion so you can easily create your own delicious, healthful menus for small or large gatherings that will create wonderful memories.

IT'S THE WEEKEND—TIME FOR BRUNCH
Drinks, Mains, Sides, and Desserts That Set the Mood

LIGHT UP THE GRILL
Starters, Mains, Sides, and Desserts for on and off the Grill

SPRING BOUNTY
Mains, Sides, and Desserts That Show Off the Best of the Season

COCONUT-CUCUMBER SPLASH

SERVES 4
Gluten Free, Vegetarian

1   (33½-ounce) container coconut water
2   mini (Persian) cucumbers, thinly sliced
4   fresh mint sprigs
    Juice of 1 lime
1   tablespoon light agave nectar
1   tablespoon grated peeled fresh ginger

Pour coconut water into large pitcher. Add cucumbers, mint, lime juice, agave, and ginger; stir until mixed well. Refrigerate until well chilled, at least 1 hour or up to 2 days. Pour into 4 ice cube–filled glasses.

Per serving (1 cup): 74 Cal, 1 g Total Fat, 0 g Sat Fat, 249 mg Sod, 16 g Total Carb, 11 g Sugar, 4 g Fib, 2 g Prot. SmartPoints value: 3

 Cook's Tip

Refreshing and elegant, this nonalcoholic drink is the perfect accompaniment to just about any brunch dish.

APRICOT BELLINIS

SERVES 6
20 Minutes or Less, Gluten Free, Vegetarian

¾   cup chilled apricot nectar
3   cups well-chilled champagne, sparkling wine, or prosecco
¼   cup fresh raspberries
6   fresh mint sprigs

Spoon 2 tablespoons nectar into each of 6 champagne flutes or wineglasses; top with champagne. Garnish each drink with a few raspberries and mint sprig.

Per serving (1 drink): 103 Cal, 0 g Total Fat, 0 g Sat Fat, 10 mg Sod, 7 g Total Carb, 6 g Sugar, 1 g Fib, 0 g Prot. SmartPoints value: 4

 Cook's Tip

Prosecco is similar to champagne and other sparkling wines but is a bit fruitier and usually less expensive, making it a great choice for gatherings. We've mixed it with apricot nectar, but it is also great with passion fruit or mango nectar.

WARM SPINACH SALAD
WITH BACON, CHICKEN,
AND BLUE CHEESE

WARM SPINACH SALAD WITH BACON, CHICKEN, AND BLUE CHEESE

SERVES 6
Gluten Free

2   tablespoons cider vinegar

1   teaspoon Dijon mustard

¾   teaspoon salt

¼   teaspoon black pepper

1   (5-ounce) bag baby spinach

2   cups lightly packed coarsely chopped radicchio

6   slices reduced-fat bacon, cut crosswise into ½-inch pieces

½   pound cremini mushrooms, sliced (about 3½ cups)

1   large red onion, thinly sliced

1   pound cooked skinless boneless chicken breasts, cut into bite-size pieces

1   large Granny Smith apple, unpeeled, halved, cored, and thinly sliced

¼   cup crumbled blue cheese

1. Whisk together vinegar, mustard, salt, and pepper in small bowl; set aside.

2. Toss together spinach and radicchio in salad bowl; set aside.

3. Cook bacon in large heavy skillet until crisp and browned, about 8 minutes. With slotted spoon, transfer bacon to paper towel–lined plate to drain.

4. Set skillet over medium-high heat. Add mushrooms and onion; cook, stirring, until onion begins to brown, about 6 minutes. Add vinegar mixture and chicken; cook, stirring, until chicken is warmed through, about 1 minute. Add to spinach mixture and toss until spinach is slightly wilted. Transfer to serving bowl. Top with bacon, apple, and blue cheese; toss until combined. Serve warm.

Per serving (1½ cups): 219 Cal, 7 g Total Fat, 3 g Sat Fat, 585 mg Sod, 10 g Total Carb, 6 g Sugar, 3 g Fib, 29 g Prot. SmartPoints value: 3

 **Cook's Tip**

Enjoy gluten-free multigrain bread alongside this classic salad. Half a slice of gluten-free multigrain bread per serving will up the SmartPoints value by 2.

POACHED EGGS WITH ASPARAGUS AND DILL

SERVES 2
20 Minutes or Less,
Gluten Free, Vegetarian

2   teaspoons distilled white vinegar

2   large eggs

½   bunch pencil (thin) asparagus, trimmed

1   tablespoon lemon juice

1   teaspoon extra-virgin olive oil

1   tablespoon chopped fresh dill

¼   teaspoon salt

⅛   teaspoon black pepper

1. Bring 4 cups water to boil in medium deep skillet. Reduce heat to bare simmer; add vinegar. Break 1 egg into cup. Holding cup close to water, slip egg into water. Repeat with remaining egg. Cook until whites are firm but yolks are still soft, about 5 minutes. With slotted spoon, transfer eggs, one at a time, to paper towel–lined plate to drain. Keep warm.

2. Meanwhile, combine asparagus and 1 tablespoon water in glass pie plate. Cover loosely with sheet of wax paper; microwave on High until asparagus are crisp-tender, 2–3 minutes. Drain. Drizzle lemon juice and oil over asparagus; toss until coated evenly.

3. To serve, divide asparagus evenly between 2 plates. Top each with 1 egg and sprinkle with dill, salt, and pepper.

Per serving (about 12 asparagus and 1 egg): 124 Cal, 7 g Total Fat, 2 g Sat Fat, 364 mg Sod, 7 g Total Carb, 3 g Sugar, 3 g Fib, 10 g Prot. SmartPoints value: 3

Cook's Tip

Crisp slices of bacon served alongside this dish will put it over the top. Three slices of crisp-cooked turkey bacon or reduced-fat bacon per serving will up the SmartPoints value by 3.

BACON AND CHEDDAR STRATA

SERVES 6

2 teaspoons canola oil

4 slices turkey bacon, cut into ¼-inch pieces

2 cups (1-inch) pieces asparagus or diced green bell pepper

1 small onion, chopped

6 slices reduced-calorie whole wheat bread

4 large eggs

5 large egg whites

¾ cup fat-free milk

2 teaspoons Dijon mustard

½ teaspoon salt

¼ teaspoon black pepper

2 tablespoons grated Parmesan cheese

1 cup shredded reduced-fat Cheddar cheese

1. Heat oil in large ovenproof skillet over medium heat. Add bacon and cook, stirring, until browned, about 4 minutes. Add asparagus and onion; cook, stirring, until softened, about 5 minutes. Transfer to plate and keep warm.

2. Preheat broiler.

3. Spray same skillet with nonstick spray. Arrange slices of bread in bottom of skillet, fitting them snugly and overlapping as needed.

4. Whisk together eggs, egg whites, milk, mustard, salt, and pepper in medium bowl; pour over bread, allowing milk mixture to soak in. Sprinkle bread with 1 tablespoon of Parmesan. Set skillet over medium heat and cook, shaking pan frequently, until egg mixture is almost cooked through, about 5 minutes.

5. Place skillet under broiler 5 inches from heat and broil until egg mixture is set, about 2 minutes. Remove skillet from broiler (leave broiler on); top bread with bacon-vegetable mixture, Cheddar, and remaining 1 tablespoon Parmesan. Return to broiler until Cheddar is melted, about 2 minutes longer.

Per serving (1½ cups): 208 Cal, 9 g Total Fat, 3 g Sat Fat, 651 mg Sod, 15 g Total Carb, 4 g Sugar, 3 g Fib, 19 g Prot. SmartPoints value: 6

CINNAMON-RAISIN BAKED FRENCH TOAST

SERVES 8
Vegetarian

8   slices cinnamon-swirl raisin
    bread, halved on diagonal

6   large eggs

1   cup fat-free half-and-half

3   tablespoons turbinado sugar

1   teaspoon vanilla extract

¾   teaspoon cinnamon

    Pinch nutmeg

    Pinch salt

1   tablespoon confectioners' sugar

1. Spray 8 x 11-inch baking dish or casserole dish with nonstick spray.

2. Arrange bread in prepared baking dish, overlapping slices, if needed.

3. Whisk together eggs, half-and-half, 2 tablespoons of sugar, the vanilla, cinnamon, nutmeg, and salt in medium bowl. Pour egg mixture evenly over bread, lightly pressing bread to help it absorb egg mixture. Cover and refrigerate at least 1 hour or up to overnight.

4. Preheat oven to 350°F.

5. Uncover dish and sprinkle French toast with remaining 1 tablespoon sugar. Bake until puffed and browned, about 35 minutes. Let cool about 10 minutes. Dust with confectioners' sugar and serve.

Per serving (2 half slices): 164 Cal, 5 g Total Fat, 2 g Sat Fat, 214 mg Sod, 22 g Total Carb, 8 g Sugar, 1 g Fib, 8 g Prot. SmartPoints value: 6

Cook's Tip

Try our French toast topped with your favorite fruit: cherries, sliced strawberries, plump blueberries, or sliced bananas are all good choices.

CINNAMON-RAISIN
BAKED FRENCH TOAST

GRILLED ASPARAGUS, ORANGE, RED ONION, AND FETA SALAD

SERVES 6
Gluten Free, Vegetarian

1   pound asparagus, trimmed

¼   teaspoon salt

⅛   teaspoon black pepper

1   head red leaf lettuce, torn (about 6 cups)

2   large navel oranges, segmented, membranes reserved

¾   cup fresh or frozen green peas

1   small red onion, thinly sliced

⅓   cup crumbled feta or Gorgonzola cheese

2   tablespoons reduced-fat vinaigrette

1. Preheat grill to high or prepare hot fire.

2. Put asparagus on small rimmed baking sheet. Spray with olive oil nonstick spray and sprinkle with salt and pepper; toss until coated evenly. Spread asparagus on grill rack and grill until lightly charred and tender, about 2 minutes per side.

3. Transfer asparagus to plate and let cool; cut into 1-inch pieces.

4. Combine asparagus, lettuce, orange segments, peas, onion, feta, and vinaigrette in salad bowl; toss until coated evenly.

Per serving (generous 1 cup): 104 Cal, 3 g Total Fat, 1 g Sat Fat, 281 mg Sod, 17 g Total Carb, 11 g Sugar, 5 g Fib, 5 g Prot. SmartPoints value: 2

 Cook's Tip

Instead of using store-bought dressing, whip up this flavorful vinaigrette in minutes: In a small jar with a tight-fitting lid, combine 3 tablespoons water, 2 tablespoons balsamic vinegar, 2 tablespoons red wine vinegar, 4 teaspoons extra-virgin olive oil, 1 heaping teaspoon Dijon mustard, 1 minced shallot, 1 minced small garlic clove, ½ teaspoon salt, and ¼ teaspoon black pepper; shake until blended well. The SmartPoints value will remain the same.

BLUE CHEESE—PEAR SALAD

SERVES 6
20 Minutes or Less,
Gluten Free, Vegetarian

½ cup low-fat buttermilk

½ cup crumbled blue cheese

1 garlic clove, minced

¼ teaspoon black pepper

1 bunch arugula, trimmed

1 small head romaine lettuce, torn

3 pears, unpeeled, halved, cored, and thinly sliced

¼ cup chopped walnuts, toasted

1. To make dressing, stir together buttermilk, blue cheese, garlic, and pepper in small bowl.

2. Gently toss together arugula, romaine, and pears in salad bowl; drizzle with dressing and toss until coated evenly. Sprinkle with walnuts.

Per serving (about 2 cups): 150 Cal, 7 g Total Fat, 3 g Sat Fat, 192 mg Sod, 19 g Total Carb, 11 g Sugar, 5 g Fib, 6 g Prot. SmartPoints value: 3

 Cook's Tip

You can substitute pecans for the walnuts and apples for the pears if they look better at the market. Or use a variety of pears—brown skinned, red skinned, and yellow skinned—to really impress.

DEEP CHOCOLATE
CHIFFON CAKE

DEEP CHOCOLATE CHIFFON CAKE

SERVES 16

Vegetarian

3 ounces bittersweet chocolate, chopped

½ cup unsweetened Dutch process cocoa

1 cup boiling water

2 cups all-purpose flour

1½ cups granulated sugar

2 teaspoons baking powder

¾ teaspoon salt

4 large eggs, separated and at room temperature

⅓ cup canola oil

1½ teaspoons vanilla extract

3 large egg whites, at room temperature

½ teaspoon cream of tartar

1 tablespoon confectioners' sugar

1. Preheat oven to 325°F.

2. Stir together chocolate and cocoa in medium bowl; add boiling water and let stand 5 minutes. Whisk until chocolate is melted and mixture is smooth. Let cool.

3. Whisk together flour, 1 cup of granulated sugar, the baking powder, and salt in large bowl. To cooled cocoa mixture, add egg yolks, oil, and vanilla, and whisk until blended. Stir cocoa mixture into flour mixture until blended (mixture will be stiff).

4. With electric mixer on medium speed, beat the 7 egg whites and cream of tartar in large bowl until soft peaks form when beaters are lifted. Add remaining ½ cup granulated sugar, 2 tablespoons at a time, beating until stiff peaks form and sugar is dissolved.

5. With rubber spatula, stir one-fourth of beaten whites into chocolate mixture to lighten it. Fold remaining whites, one-third at a time, into chocolate mixture, just until no longer visible.

6. Scrape batter into ungreased 10-inch tube pan with removable bottom; smooth top. Bake until cake springs back when lightly pressed, about 1 hour 5 minutes. Invert cake onto its legs or neck of wine bottle and let cool completely. Run thin knife around cake to loosen from side and center tube of pan. Remove cake from pan and place on serving plate. Dust with confectioners' sugar.

Per serving (¹⁄₁₆ of cake): 227 Cal, 9 g Total Fat, 3 g Sat Fat, 198 mg Sod, 35 g Total Carb, 20 g Sugar, 2 g Fib, 5 g Prot. SmartPoints value: 10

CINNAMON-SUGAR PINEAPPLE WITH COCONUT SORBET

SERVES 4
20 Minutes or Less,
Gluten Free, Vegetarian

3   tablespoons sugar

½   teaspoon cinnamon

     Pinch black pepper

4   (¾-inch) slices fresh pineapple, cored

2   tablespoons chopped fresh cilantro

1⅓ cups coconut sorbet

4   tablespoons sliced almonds, toasted

1. Stir together sugar, cinnamon, and pepper in cup.

2. Place 1 slice of pineapple on each of 4 dessert plates. Sprinkle evenly with cinnamon-sugar mixture and cilantro. Top each slice of pineapple with ⅓-cup scoop of sorbet. Sprinkle evenly with almonds.

Per serving (1 slice pineapple, ⅓ cup sorbet, and 1 tablespoon almonds): 154 Cal, 3 g Total Fat, 0 g Sat Fat, 4 mg Sod, 32 g Total Carb, 29 g Sugar, 2 g Fib, 2 g Prot. SmartPoints value: 7

 Cook's Tip

The combination of sugar, cinnamon, black pepper, and pineapple is unexpectedly delicious.

BEEF NACHOS

SERVES 8
20 Minutes or Less,
Gluten Free

32 baked low-fat corn tortilla chips

2 teaspoons canola oil

6 ounces ground lean beef
   (7% fat or less)

¾ cup diced tomatoes with chiles

⅔ cup canned fat-free refried beans

½ teaspoon dried oregano

½ teaspoon salt

½ cup shredded reduced-fat
   Cheddar cheese or Mexican
   cheese blend

3 scallions, sliced (about ½ cup)

2 jalapeño peppers, seeded and
   minced

1. Preheat broiler.

2. Arrange tortilla chips very close together on baking sheet in single layer; set aside.

3. Heat oil in large nonstick skillet over medium heat. Add beef and cook, breaking it up with wooden spoon, until browned, about 4 minutes. Stir in tomatoes, beans, oregano, and salt; cook, stirring occasionally, until heated through, about 5 minutes.

4. Spoon beef mixture evenly over chips; sprinkle evenly with Cheddar. Broil about 5 inches from heat until cheese is melted, about 30 seconds. Sprinkle with scallions and jalapeños.

Per serving (4 garnished chips): 113 Cal, 3 g Total Fat, 1 g Sat Fat, 432 mg Sod, 12 g Total Carb, 1 g Sugar, 2 g Fib, 9 g Prot. SmartPoints value: 3

 Cook's Tip

This is the perfect finger food to share while getting the grill going for a barbecue get-together. If you like things really spicy, add additional jalapeños or use pickled jalapeños instead of the fresh ones.

CREAMY SPINACH-PARMESAN DIP

SERVES 8
20 Minutes or Less,
Gluten Free, Vegetarian

1   pound baby spinach

¾   cup light sour cream

¼   cup grated Parmesan cheese

1   garlic clove, minced

⅛   teaspoon nutmeg

⅛   teaspoon salt

1. Bring 1 inch of water to boil in large pot. Add spinach and cook, covered, until wilted, about 5 minutes. Drain in colander, then rinse under cool water to stop cooking. Squeeze out excess liquid.

2. Combine spinach, sour cream, Parmesan, garlic, nutmeg, and salt in food processor; process until smooth.

Per serving (about ¼ cup dip): 57 Cal, 3 g Total Fat, 2 g Sat Fat, 144 mg Sod, 4 g Total Carb, 0 g Sugar, 1 g Fib, 4 g Prot. SmartPoints value: 2

 Cook's Tip

Serve the dip with lightly grilled bell pepper wedges of assorted colors for a touch of smoky flavor.

GRILLED CHICKEN WITH SUMMER CORN–TOMATO SALAD

SERVES 4
Gluten Free

1½ cups corn kernels
    (about 3 ears of corn)

1   large tomato, diced

4   scallions, sliced

¼   cup chopped fresh cilantro

4   tablespoons lime juice

2   teaspoons extra-virgin olive oil

1   teaspoon ground cumin

1   teaspoon salt

¾   teaspoon smoked paprika

4   (5-ounce) skinless boneless
    chicken breasts

1. **Bring 1 inch of water to boil in medium saucepan. Put corn in steamer basket and lower into saucepan. Cook, covered, until corn is tender, about 4 minutes. Lift steamer basket out of pan and let corn cool.**

2. **Spray grill rack with nonstick spray. Preheat grill to medium-high or prepare medium-high fire.**

3. **Meanwhile, mix together corn, tomato, scallions, cilantro, 2 tablespoons of lime juice, the oil, ¼ teaspoon of cumin, ¼ teaspoon of salt, and ¼ teaspoon of paprika in medium bowl; set aside to allow flavors to blend.**

4. **Combine remaining 2 tablespoons lime juice, ¾ teaspoon cumin, ¾ teaspoon salt, and ½ teaspoon paprika in cup; rub all over chicken. Spray chicken with nonstick spray. Place chicken on grill rack and grill until cooked through, about 5 minutes per side. Place chicken on 4 plates. Spoon corn salad on top or alongside.**

Per serving (1 chicken breast and ⅔ cup salad): 260 Cal, 7 g Total Fat, 1 g Sat Fat, 754 mg Sod, 19 g Total Carb, 4 g Sugar, 3 g Fib, 33 g Prot. SmartPoints value: 5

 Cook's Tip

Take advantage of summer's bounty of corn for this dish. Choose Butter and Sugar, which has yellow and white kernels, Silver Queen, which is made up of tender white kernels, or always-reliable yellow corn.

GRILLED T-BONE WITH BARBECUE SAUCE

SERVES 4
Gluten Free

2 tablespoons chili sauce
   or ketchup

1 tablespoon packed dark
   brown sugar

1 tablespoon Worcestershire sauce

1 garlic clove, minced

2 teaspoons coarse-grained
   mustard

1 teaspoon grated peeled
   fresh ginger

1 (1-pound) lean T-bone steak
   (about 1½ inches thick), trimmed

1. Spray grill rack with nonstick spray. Preheat grill to high or prepare hot fire.

2. To make barbecue sauce, stir together chili sauce, brown sugar, Worcestershire sauce, garlic, mustard, and ginger in small bowl.

3. Brush some of sauce on both sides of steak. Place steak on grill rack and grill, brushing with remaining sauce, until instant-read thermometer inserted into side of steak registers 145°F, about 6 minutes per side. Transfer steak to cutting board and let stand 10 minutes before slicing against grain.

Per serving (3 ounces steak): 276 Cal, 18 g Total Fat, 7 g Sat Fat, 233 mg Sod, 7 g Total Carb, 5 g Sugar, 1 g Fib, 22 g Prot. SmartPoints value: 9

ROSEMARY-GRILLED SALMON

SERVES 6
Gluten Free

2 teaspoons grated lemon zest

¼ cup lemon juice

1 tablespoon olive oil

2 teaspoons chopped fresh rosemary + 6 sprigs

¾ teaspoon salt

¼ teaspoon black pepper

6 (6-ounce) salmon steaks

6 (¼-inch) slices lemon

1. Stir together lemon zest and juice, oil, chopped rosemary, salt, and pepper in small bowl. Arrange salmon in shallow baking dish; drizzle with lemon-juice mixture. Refrigerate 15 minutes.

2. Meanwhile, spray grill rack with nonstick spray. Preheat grill to medium-high or prepare medium-high fire.

3. With tongs, push 3 rosemary sprigs through grill rack onto lit burners. Place salmon and slices of lemon on grill rack and grill until fish is just opaque throughout and lemon is lightly charred along edges, about 5 minutes per side. Discard marinade. Transfer salmon to platter; top with grilled lemon slices and remaining 3 rosemary sprigs.

Per serving (1 salmon steak): 337 Cal, 21 g Total Fat, 4 g Sat Fat, 391 mg Sod, 2 g Total Carb, 0 g Sugar, 0 g Fib, 34 g Prot. SmartPoints value: 8

 Cook's Tip

Firm-fleshed fish is always the best choice for grilling. Halibut, catfish, arctic char, and brook trout are also good choices. Keep in mind that thinner fish takes less time to cook.

GRILLED CORN WITH SMOKED PAPRIKA—LIME BUTTER

SERVES 6
Gluten Free, Vegetarian,
20 Minutes or Less

6   ears of corn, husks and
    silk removed

3   tablespoons light stick butter

4   teaspoons lime juice

1   teaspoon smoked paprika

⅛   teaspoon salt

3   tablespoons chopped
    fresh cilantro

1. **Spray grill rack with nonstick spray. Preheat grill to medium-high or prepare medium-high fire.**

2. **Place corn on grill rack and grill, turning occasionally, until lightly charred in spots and tender, about 10 minutes.**

3. **Meanwhile, combine butter, lime juice, paprika, and salt in microwaveable cup; microwave on High until butter is melted, about 20 seconds.**

4. **Place corn on platter; drizzle with butter mixture and sprinkle with cilantro, turning until coated evenly.**

Per serving (1 ear of corn and about 1½ teaspoons butter mixture): 121 Cal, 5 g Total Fat, 3 g Sat Fat, 81 mg Sod, 20 g Total Carb, 3 g Sugar, 2 g Fib, 3 g Prot. SmartPoints value: 5

Cook's Tip

For an additional layer of flavor, sprinkle the corn with crumbled cotija cheese just before serving. One tablespoon of cotija cheese per serving will up the SmartsPoints value by 2.

GRILLED VEGETABLE KEBABS

SERVES 4
Gluten Free, Vegetarian

¼ cup chopped fresh flat-leaf parsley

1 garlic clove, minced

1 teaspoon olive oil

½ teaspoon salt

⅛ teaspoon black pepper

2 green bell peppers, each cut into 8 pieces

12 grape tomatoes

12 cremini mushrooms

1. Preheat grill to high or prepare hot fire.

2. Mix together parsley, garlic, oil, salt, and black pepper in medium bowl. Add bell peppers, tomatoes, and mushrooms and toss until coated evenly. Thread vegetables onto 4 long metal skewers, dividing evenly.

3. Place skewers on grill rack and grill, turning, until vegetables are tender and lightly charred, about 10 minutes.

Per serving (1 kebab): 45 Cal, 2 g Total Fat, 0 g Sat Fat, 299 mg Sod, 7 g Total Carb, 4 g Sugar, 2 g Fib, 3 g Prot. SmartPoints value: 0

 Cook's Tip

Turn any leftovers into a tasty salad by tossing the vegetables with a handful of mixed fresh herbs. Or turn it into a rice and vegetable medley by tossing the vegetables with a mix of fresh herbs and 2 cups of warm cooked brown rice for an extra 3 SmartPoints value for 4 servings.

RASPBERRY-YOGURT POPS

RASPBERRY-YOGURT POPS

MAKES 8

Gluten Free, Vegetarian

3   cups fresh or thawed frozen unsweetened raspberries

1   ripe banana

1   (6-ounce) container raspberry fat-free Greek yogurt

½   cup light (reduced-fat) coconut milk

3   tablespoons honey

½   teaspoon grated lemon zest

1   tablespoon lemon juice

1. Put raspberries in food processor and process until smooth. Pour puree through fine-mesh sieve set over medium bowl, pressing hard to extract as much puree as possible. Discard seeds.

2. Combine raspberry puree, banana, yogurt, coconut milk, honey, and lemon zest and juice in food processor; process until smooth.

3. Divide raspberry mixture evenly among 8 ice-pop molds. Insert wooden craft stick into each mold. Cover and freeze until firm, at least 4 hours or up to 1 day.

4. To serve, dip bottom of each mold into hot water about 10 seconds to loosen. Remove pops from molds.

Per serving (1 ice pop): 82 Cal, 1 g Total Fat, 1 g Sat Fat, 10 mg Sod, 17 g Total Carb, 11 g Sugar, 4 g Fib, 3 g Prot. SmartPoints value: 2

 Cook's Tip

Don't have ice-pop molds? Use 8 wax-coated paper cups and wooden craft sticks. Fill the cups with the berry mixture and cover tightly with foil; poke the sticks through the foil (this will keep the sticks upright while the mixture freezes).

PLUM-APRICOT BUCKLE

SERVES 10
Vegetarian

1   cup cake flour

1   teaspoon baking powder

½   teaspoon salt

½   cup low-fat buttermilk

½   cup sugar

1   large egg

¼   cup canola oil

1   teaspoon vanilla extract

6   Italian (prune) plums, pitted and cut into ½-inch wedges

6   small apricots, pitted and cut into ½-inch wedges

Topping

3   tablespoons cake flour

2   tablespoons sugar

1   tablespoon unsalted butter, softened

½   teaspoon cinnamon

1. Preheat oven to 375°F. Spray 9-inch springform pan with nonstick spray.

2. Whisk together flour, baking powder, and salt in large bowl. Whisk together buttermilk, sugar, egg, oil, and vanilla in medium bowl. Add buttermilk mixture to flour mixture, stirring just until blended. Pour batter into prepared pan. Arrange plums and apricots on top, spacing evenly.

3. To make topping, with your fingers, mix together flour, sugar, butter, and cinnamon in small bowl until crumbly; sprinkle evenly over fruit.

4. Bake until buckle is browned and bubbly, about 35 minutes. Let cool in pan on wire rack about 20 minutes. Release side of pan. Serve warm or at room temperature.

Per serving (¹⁄₁₀ of buckle): 205 Cal, 7 g Total Fat, 1 g Sat Fat, 186 mg Sod, 32 g Total Carb, 19 g Sugar, 1 g Fib, 3 g Prot. SmartPoints value: 7

 Cook's Tip

A buckle is a cakelike dessert that got its name because of the way the cake bakes up around the fruit and then "buckles." If you can't find Italian plums, use red or black plums instead.

LAMB AND VEGETABLE KEBABS

SERVES 6
Gluten Free

¾ cup beef broth

2 tablespoons Dijon mustard

½ lemon, cut into 3 thick slices

1 garlic clove, crushed with side of large knife

1¼ pounds lean leg of lamb, trimmed and cut into 18 chunks

2 red bell peppers, each cut into 6 pieces

6 cremini mushrooms, halved

¼ teaspoon salt

⅛ teaspoon black pepper

2 teaspoons olive oil

1 teaspoon chopped fresh thyme

1. To make marinade, mix together ½ cup of broth, 1 tablespoon of mustard, the lemon, and garlic in large bowl; add lamb and stir until coated evenly. Cover and refrigerate at least 4 hours or up to 6 hours.

2. Preheat grill pan over medium heat.

3. Thread 3 pieces of lamb, 2 pieces of bell pepper, and 2 pieces of mushroom onto each of 6 (12-inch) metal skewers. Sprinkle with salt and black pepper; discard marinade.

4. To make basting mixture, stir together remaining ¼ cup broth, 1 tablespoon mustard, the oil, and thyme in small bowl; brush all over kebabs. Place kebabs in grill pan and grill 5 minutes; turn and brush with basting mixture. Continue to grill until lamb is browned and vegetables are tender, about 5 minutes longer.

Per serving (1 kebab): 147 Cal, 5 g Total Fat, 1 g Sat Fat, 342 mg Sod, 4 g Total Carb, 1 g Sugar, 1 g Fib, 21 g Prot. SmartPoints value: 3

Cook's Tip

You can also cook the kebabs on an outdoor grill over medium heat; keep in mind that the cooking time may be different.

GRILLED CHICKEN BREASTS WITH RHUBARB-MANGO SALSA

SERVES 4

Gluten Free

Grated zest and juice of 1 lemon

4　tablespoons coarsely chopped fresh basil

2　garlic cloves, minced

3　teaspoons olive oil

1　teaspoon salt

¼　teaspoon black pepper

4　(5-ounce) skinless boneless chicken breasts

1　small mango, pitted, peeled, and cut into ¼-inch dice

1　rhubarb stalk, trimmed and cut into ¼-inch dice (1 cup)

¾　cup (¼-inch) diced English (seedless) cucumber

1　jalapeño pepper, seeded and chopped

1　tablespoon honey

2　teaspoons white balsamic vinegar

1　small shallot, minced

1. To make marinade, combine lemon zest and juice, 2 tablespoons of basil, the garlic, 2 teaspoons of oil, ¾ teaspoon of salt, and the pepper in large zip-close plastic bag; add chicken. Squeeze out air and seal bag. Turn to coat chicken. Refrigerate at least 1 hour or up to 3 hours.

2. To make salsa, stir together mango, rhubarb, cucumber, remaining 2 tablespoons basil, the jalapeño, honey, vinegar, shallot, and remaining 1 teaspoon oil and ¼ teaspoon salt in small bowl until mixed well. Cover and refrigerate at least 30 minutes or up to 1 hour to allow flavors to blend.

3. Spray grill pan with nonstick spray and preheat over medium heat. Remove chicken from marinade; discard marinade. Place chicken in grill pan and grill until cooked through, about 5 minutes per side. Place chicken on platter and top evenly with salsa.

Per serving (1 chicken breast and ½ cup salsa): 266 Cal, 7 g Total Fat, 1 g Sat Fat, 748 mg Sod, 19 g Total Carb, 14 g Sugar, 2 g Fib, 31 g Prot. SmartPoints value: 5

 Cook's Tip

Rhubarb stalks are perfectly safe to eat raw. It is the leaves that are poisonous. The subtle, tart flavor of uncooked rhubarb is a perfect match for the deeply sweet mango and crisp and crunchy cucumber, while a touch of honey rounds it out.

GRILLED CHICKEN BREASTS
WITH RHUBARB-MANGO SALSA

ASIAN-SPICED SALMON WITH BABY BOK CHOY AND SHIITAKES

SERVES 4

⅓ cup reduced-sodium soy sauce

1 tablespoon rice vinegar

1 tablespoon honey

1 tablespoon Asian (dark) sesame oil

3 large garlic cloves, minced (1 tablespoon)

1 tablespoon minced peeled fresh ginger

½ teaspoon sambal oelek (hot chili sauce) or chili garlic sauce

4 (6-ounce) skinless salmon fillets

4 baby bok choy, halved lengthwise

½ pound shiitake mushrooms, stemmed and caps halved

3 cups lightly packed shredded red cabbage

2 scallions, chopped

2 tablespoons sesame seeds, toasted

1. Stir together soy sauce, vinegar, honey, sesame oil, garlic, ginger, and sambal oelek in large bowl; add salmon and turn to coat. Marinate in refrigerator about 15 minutes.

2. Meanwhile, set racks in upper and lower thirds of oven and preheat oven to 450°F. Line two rimmed baking sheets with foil; spray with nonstick spray.

3. Place salmon in center of one prepared baking sheet; reserve marinade. Add bok choy to marinade; toss until coated. Arrange bok choy around salmon in single layer. Add mushrooms and cabbage to marinade; toss until coated. Spread on second prepared baking sheet to form even layer.

4. Place salmon on top rack and cabbage-mushroom mixture on bottom rack; roast until salmon is just opaque in center and vegetables are tender, about 15 minutes. Sprinkle salmon with scallions and sesame seeds; serve cabbage-mushroom mixture and bok choy alongside.

Per serving (1 salmon fillet and about 1 cup vegetables): 433 Cal, 24 g Total Fat, 4 g Sat Fat, 834 mg Sod, 16 g Total Carb, 7 g Sugar, 4 g Fib, 38 g Prot. SmartPoints value: 10

 Cook's Tip

To make this dish gluten free, use gluten-free soy sauce, which is readily available in supermarkets.

STIR-FRIED ASPARAGUS AND SUGAR SNAP PEAS

SERVES 4
20 Minutes or Less,
Vegetarian

5   tablespoons vegetable broth

2   cups sugar snap peas, trimmed

2   cups asparagus, cut into
     1½-inch pieces

2   garlic cloves, minced

1   teaspoon minced peeled
     fresh ginger

2   teaspoons grated lemon zest

2   teaspoons teriyaki sauce

⅛   teaspoon salt

1. Heat 3 tablespoons of broth in large deep skillet or wok over high heat. Add sugar snap peas and asparagus; stir-fry until crisp-tender, about 3 minutes, adding 1 tablespoon broth if mixture seems dry.

2. Add remaining 2 tablespoons broth, the garlic, and ginger to skillet; stir-fry until fragrant, about 1 minute. Add lemon zest, teriyaki sauce, and salt; stir-fry 1 minute longer.

Per serving (about 1 cup): 41 Cal, 0 g Total Fat, 0 g Sat Fat, 263 mg Sod, 9 g Total Carb, 2 g Sugar, 4 g Fib, 3 g Prot. SmartPoints value: 0

 Cook's Tip

Asparagus is available pencil (thin), regular, and jumbo. To store it for several days, trim the ends and stand the stalks in about 1 inch of water in a large measuring cup or jar, then loosely cover with a plastic bag and refrigerate.

FAVA BEANS WITH
BABY PEAS AND TOMATOES

FAVA BEANS WITH BABY PEAS AND TOMATOES

SERVES 4

Gluten Free, Vegetarian

1½ cups shelled fava beans
(about 1½ pounds pods)

3 teaspoons extra-virgin olive oil

1 small onion, chopped (½ cup)

½ pound plum tomatoes, seeded
and diced

2 garlic cloves, minced

1 cup fresh or thawed frozen
baby peas

½ cup vegetable broth

1 teaspoon chopped fresh thyme

2 teaspoons lemon juice

½ teaspoon salt

¼ teaspoon black pepper

1. Bring small saucepan of water to boil; add fava beans and cook 1 minute. Drain in colander; rinse under cold water to stop cooking. Remove tough outer skins by splitting beans open and squeezing out beans; discard skins.

2. Heat 2 teaspoons of oil in large nonstick skillet over medium heat. Add onion and cook until softened, about 5 minutes. Add tomatoes and garlic; cook until tomatoes start to soften, about 2 minutes. Stir in fava beans, peas, broth, and thyme. Cook, stirring occasionally, until beans and peas are just tender, 2–3 minutes longer.

3. Remove skillet from heat; stir in lemon juice, salt, and pepper. Transfer to serving bowl. Drizzle with remaining 1 teaspoon oil.

Per serving (generous ½ cup): 120 Cal, 4 g Total Fat, 1 g Sat Fat, 465 mg Sod, 18 g Total Carb, 9 g Sugar, 6 g Fib, 6 g Prot. SmartPoints value: 4

 Cook's Tip

Serve this tasty dish on a bed of spring greens, such as dandelions, which you can forage for right in your own backyard. They are at their most tender and mild when they've just emerged from the ground and before they've flowered. *Note:* Do not pick dandelions that have been sprayed with chemicals.

FRISÉE SALAD WITH GRILLED APRICOTS, SPRING RADISHES, AND SNOW PEAS

SERVES 4
20 Minutes or Less,
Gluten Free, Vegetarian

6   small apricots (about ½ pound), pitted and halved, or 3 peaches (about 10 ounces), pitted and quartered

½   teaspoon salt

2   tablespoons orange juice

1   tablespoon rice vinegar

2   teaspoons extra-virgin olive oil

1½ teaspoons honey

¼   teaspoon Dijon mustard

¼   teaspoon black pepper

¼   pound snow peas, trimmed

6   cups lightly packed torn frisée or inner escarole leaves

5   radishes, preferably Easter egg or French breakfast, trimmed and thinly sliced

1   ounce reduced-fat feta cheese, crumbled

1. Spray grill pan with nonstick spray and set over medium heat. Spray cut sides of apricots with nonstick spray and sprinkle with ¼ teaspoon of salt. Place apricots, cut side down, in grill pan and grill until lightly charred, 2–3 minutes; turn and grill just until tender, about 2 minutes longer. Transfer to plate and let cool.

2. To make dressing, put 4 apricot halves in blender along with orange juice, vinegar, oil, honey, mustard, remaining ¼ teaspoon salt, and the pepper. Process until smooth. Set aside.

3. Bring small saucepan of water to boil; add snow peas and cook 1 minute. Drain in colander; rinse under cold water to stop cooking, then pat dry with paper towel. Cut snow peas on diagonal into ½-inch-wide pieces.

4. To serve, gently toss together frisée, snow peas, radishes, and feta with half of dressing in salad bowl. Top with remaining grilled apricots. Drizzle remaining dressing over apricots.

Per serving (about 2 cups): 103 Cal, 4 g Total Fat, 1 g Sat Fat, 403 mg Sod, 14 g Total Carb, 11 g Sugar, 3 g Fib, 4 g Prot. SmartPoints value: 2

Cook's Tip

Easter egg radishes range from white to pink to crimson to purple, all in one colorful bunch. Their flesh is bright white and crisp with a mild flavor. French breakfast radishes are about 3 inches long. They are bright red at the top and white at the root end. They have a crisp texture and sweet flavor.

FRISÉE SALAD WITH GRILLED
APRICOTS, SPRING RADISHES,
AND SNOW PEAS

BUTTERMILK PANNA COTTA WITH STRAWBERRIES

SERVES 4
Gluten Free

1   teaspoon unflavored gelatin

1½ tablespoons water

1   vanilla bean, split

1   cup low-fat buttermilk

¾   cup fat-free half-and-half

⅓   cup + 1 tablespoon sugar

2   cups strawberries, hulled and thinly sliced

1   teaspoon grated orange zest

1. Spray 4 (6-ounce) ramekins or custard cups with nonstick spray.

2. Sprinkle gelatin over the water in cup. Let stand until gelatin is softened, about 5 minutes.

3. Meanwhile, with edge of small knife, scrape seeds from vanilla bean; reserve pod and seeds.

4. Combine buttermilk, half-and-half, ⅓ cup of sugar, and the vanilla bean pod and seeds in medium saucepan. Cook over medium heat, stirring occasionally, until sugar is dissolved, about 2 minutes. Remove saucepan from heat; stir in gelatin mixture until completely dissolved. Pour buttermilk mixture through sieve set over medium bowl; discard vanilla bean pod. Divide buttermilk mixture evenly among prepared ramekins. Cover and refrigerate until chilled and set, at least 4 hours or up to 1 day (the longer it sets, the firmer it will be).

5. Toss together strawberries and orange zest with remaining 1 tablespoon sugar in small bowl. Cover and refrigerate at least 20 minutes or up to 1 hour.

6. To serve, run tip of thin knife around edge of each ramekin to loosen panna cotta. Dip bottoms of ramekins, one at a time, into bowl of hot water about 5 seconds. Unmold by inverting each panna cotta onto dessert plate. Surround with strawberries.

Per serving (1 panna cotta and ½ cup berries): 156 Cal, 2 g Total Fat, 1 g Sat Fat, 131 mg Sod, 33 g Total Carb, 29 g Sugar, 2 g Fib, 4 g Prot. SmartPoints value: 7

Cook's Tip

Spring is the time to begin savoring local strawberries. Bright red, juicy, and bursting with flavor, they are the perfect complement to this vanilla-scented eggless custard.

BUTTERMILK PANNA COTTA
WITH STRAWBERRIES

RHUBARB-CHERRY CRUMBLE

SERVES 9
Vegetarian

2 cups (¾- to 1-inch) pieces rhubarb

2 cups pitted fresh or thawed frozen sweet cherries

½ cup cherry preserves

½ cup + 2 tablespoons all-purpose flour

½ cup old-fashioned (rolled) oats

⅓ cup packed dark brown sugar

½ teaspoon cinnamon

¼ teaspoon nutmeg

¼ teaspoon salt

4 tablespoons cold unsalted butter, cut into pieces

1. Preheat oven to 375°F. Spray 2-quart baking dish with nonstick spray.

2. Stir together rhubarb, cherries, and preserves in large bowl. Add 2 tablespoons of flour and stir until fruit is coated. Spoon into prepared baking dish; set aside.

3. Stir together remaining ½ cup flour, the oats, brown sugar, cinnamon, nutmeg, and salt in medium bowl. With pastry blender or two knives used scissors fashion, cut in butter until mixture resembles coarse crumbs.

4. Spoon crumb topping over fruit. Bake until fruit is bubbly, 25–30 minutes. Let cool 10–15 minutes before serving.

Per serving (about ¾ cup): 197 Cal, 6 g Total Fat, 3 g Sat Fat, 74 mg Sod, 35 g Total Carb, 20 g Sugar, 2 g Fib, 2 g Prot. SmartPoints value: 8

Cook's Tip

Fresh rhubarb and sweet cherries are harbingers of spring. Tart and crunchy when raw, rhubarb turns soft and flavorful when baked. Substitute raspberry or apricot preserves for the cherry preserves to bring in a different flavor element, if you like.

CHERRY CLAFOUTIS

SERVES 6
Vegetarian

½ pound sweet cherries, pitted and halved, or frozen unsweetened pitted cherries

3 large eggs

1 cup low-fat (1%) milk

2 tablespoons brandy

1½ teaspoons vanilla extract

⅛ teaspoon salt

⅔ cup all-purpose flour

⅓ cup + 1 tablespoon confectioners' sugar

1. Preheat oven to 375°F. Spray 10-inch pie plate or quiche pan with nonstick spray.

2. Spread cherries in prepared pie plate forming even layer; set aside.

3. Whisk eggs in large bowl until frothy; whisk in milk, brandy, vanilla, and salt. Whisk together flour and ⅓ cup of confectioners' sugar in small bowl. Gradually whisk flour mixture into egg mixture until smooth batter is formed; pour over cherries.

4. Bake 10 minutes. Reduce oven temperature to 300°F. Bake until clafoutis is puffed and toothpick inserted into center comes out clean, about 35 minutes. Allow clafoutis to cool (it will sink in center). Just before serving, dust with remaining 1 tablespoon confectioners' sugar.

Per serving (⅙ of clafoutis): 173 Cal, 3 g Total Fat, 1 g Sat Fat, 102 mg Sod, 27 g Total Carb, 15 g Sugar, 1 g Fib, 6 g Prot. SmartPoints value: 6

 Cook's Tip

Originally from the Limousin region of France, a clafoutis is a homey, easy-to-make baked fruit-and-custard dessert. Although cherries are traditional, try apples, pears, peaches, or nectarines cut into cubes, or whole raspberries, blackberries, or blueberries.

CRUNCHY OVEN-FRIED DRUMSTICKS WITH THYME AND PARMESAN

SERVES 6

1   cup fat-free buttermilk

2   garlic cloves, crushed through a press

1   teaspoon salt

6   (¼-pound) skinless chicken drumsticks

½   cup whole wheat panko bread crumbs

2   tablespoons grated Parmesan cheese

2   teaspoons chopped fresh thyme or ¾ teaspoon dried

     Pinch cayenne

1. Combine buttermilk, garlic, and salt in large zip-close plastic bag; add chicken. Squeeze out air and seal bag; turn to coat chicken. Refrigerate, turning bag occasionally, at least 20 minutes or up to 1 day.

2. Place rack in lower third of oven and preheat oven to 400°F. Line baking sheet with foil; spray with nonstick spray.

3. Mix together panko, Parmesan, thyme, and cayenne on sheet of wax paper. Remove chicken from marinade; discard marinade. Coat drumsticks, one at a time, in panko mixture, pressing gently so it adheres. Lightly spray drumsticks with nonstick spray and place on prepared baking sheet.

4. Bake until browned and instant-read thermometer inserted into drumstick (not touching bone) registers 165°F, about 35 minutes.

Per serving (1 drumstick): 243 Cal, 12 g Total Fat, 3 g Sat Fat, 599 mg Sod, 9 g Total Carb, 2 g Sugar, 1 g Fib, 23 g Prot. SmartPoints value: 6

Cook's Tip

Buttermilk is great at tenderizing chicken and adding flavor. To take this oven-fried chicken on the road, let it cool, then layer between sheets of wax paper in an airtight container. It is safe to keep at cool room temperature up to 2 hours. For longer storage, pack it in a cooler surrounded by ice packs.

CRUNCHY OVEN-FRIED
DRUMSTICKS WITH THYME
AND PARMESAN

LEBANESE CHICKEN-PITA SALAD

SERVES 4

1   pound thin-sliced chicken breasts, cut into thin strips

¾   teaspoon salt

¼   teaspoon black pepper

3   teaspoons olive oil

3   (6-inch) whole wheat pita breads, split, toasted, and cooled

12   cherry tomatoes, halved

1   cucumber, peeled, seeded, and cut into ½-inch pieces

2   scallions, sliced

¼   cup lightly packed chopped fresh mint

¼   cup lightly packed chopped fresh cilantro

3   tablespoons lemon juice

½–1 teaspoon ground cumin

1. Sprinkle chicken with ½ teaspoon of salt and ⅛ teaspoon of pepper. Heat 1 teaspoon of oil in large heavy nonstick skillet over medium-high heat. Add chicken and cook, stirring, until cooked through, about 5 minutes; transfer to serving bowl.

2. Break cooled pitas into 1-inch pieces and add to chicken along with tomatoes, cucumber, scallions, mint, cilantro, lemon juice, remaining 2 teaspoons oil, the cumin, and remaining ¼ teaspoon salt and ⅛ teaspoon pepper. Toss until mixed well.

Per serving (about 2 cups): 296 Cal, 8 g Total Fat, 1 g Sat Fat, 798 mg Sod, 29 g Total Carb, 3 g Sugar, 5 g Fib, 29 g Prot. SmartPoints value: 6

Cook's Tip

When shopping, choose scallions that are bright green with no sign of browning or wilting.

ROAST BEEF SANDWICHES WITH HORSERADISH MAYONNAISE

SERVES 4

20 Minutes or Less

¼ cup reduced-calorie mayonnaise

2½ teaspoons prepared horseradish

¼ teaspoon black pepper

8   slices reduced-calorie rye bread, toasted

8   (1-ounce) slices lean roast beef, trimmed

2   large plum tomatoes, each cut into 8 crosswise slices

2   cups lightly packed baby arugula

1. Stir together mayonnaise, horseradish, and pepper in small bowl. Spread about 1½ teaspoons mayonnaise mixture on each slice of toast.

2. Top each of 4 slices of toast with 2 slices roast beef, 4 slices tomato, and ½ cup arugula. Cover with remaining slices toast.

Per serving (1 sandwich): 260 Cal, 10 g Total Fat, 2 g Sat Fat, 841 mg Sod, 24 g Total Carb, 5 g Sugar, 7 g Fib, 19 g Prot. SmartPoints value: 7

Cook's Tip

To make these sandwiches gluten free, use 4 slices of gluten-free bread and make the sandwiches open face. Using 1 slice of gluten-free bread per serving will up the per-serving SmartsPoints value by 1.

RUSTIC TUNA PANZANELLA

SERVES 6
20 Minutes or Less

2   tablespoons extra-virgin olive oil

2   tablespoons red wine vinegar

1   large garlic clove, minced

½   teaspoon salt

¼   teaspoon black pepper

1   (8-ounce) piece day-old country-style whole wheat bread, thickly sliced, toasted, and cut into 1-inch cubes

1½   pounds tomatoes, coarsely chopped

½   English (seedless) cucumber, quartered lengthwise and sliced

1   yellow bell pepper, cut into ¾-inch pieces

½   red onion, thinly sliced

10   fresh basil leaves, torn

2   tablespoons nonpareil (tiny) capers, drained

2   (5-ounce) cans chunk light tuna in water, drained

1. To make dressing, whisk together oil, vinegar, garlic, salt, and black pepper in large salad bowl.

2. Add bread cubes, tomatoes, cucumber, bell pepper, onion, basil, and capers to dressing; toss until mixed well. Coarsely flake tuna into salad; gently toss just until combined.

Per serving (about 2 cups): 219 Cal, 6 g Total Fat, 1 g Sat Fat, 636 mg Sod, 26 g Total Carb, 5 g Sugar, 3 g Fib, 16 g Prot. SmartPoints value: 5

 Cook's Tip

The panzanella will be at its best if allowed to stand for about 1 hour before being served, giving the flavors a chance to meld.

POTATO SALAD

SERVES 4
Gluten Free

1½ pounds red potatoes, scrubbed

3 slices turkey bacon

¼ cup reduced-calorie mayonnaise

2 tablespoons red wine vinegar

2 tablespoons chopped fresh flat-leaf parsley

½ teaspoon salt

¼ teaspoon black pepper

½ cup chopped scallions

1. Combine potatoes with enough water to cover in large saucepan; bring to boil. Reduce heat and simmer until potatoes are fork-tender, about 20 minutes; drain. When potatoes are cool enough to handle, cut into bite-size chunks.

2. Meanwhile, cook bacon in medium skillet over medium heat until crisp; transfer to paper towel–lined plate to drain. Break bacon into pieces.

3. Stir together mayonnaise, vinegar, parsley, salt, and pepper in large bowl. Add potatoes, bacon, and scallions; gently toss until coated with dressing.

Per serving (about ¾ cup): 197 Cal, 7 g Total Fat, 2 g Sat Fat, 544 mg Sod, 30 g Total Carb, 3 g Sugar, 3 g Fib, 5 g Prot. SmartPoints value: 6

Cook's Tip

Potato salad is quintessential picnic food. Pack it into an airtight container surrounded by ice packs in a cooler and it will stay fresh for hours.

HOMEMADE VEGETABLE PICKLES

SERVES 12
Gluten Free, Vegetarian

½ pound green beans, trimmed

5 carrots, cut into sticks

12 radishes, halved

2½ cups distilled white vinegar

1½ cups water

½ cup sugar

¼ cup pickling spices

2 tablespoons kosher salt

2–3 large garlic cloves, peeled and halved (optional)

1. Bring large pot of water to boil. Add green beans, carrots, and radishes; cook just until tender, 2–3 minutes. Drain in colander; rinse under cold water to stop cooking. Drain again. Pack vegetables into 2 (1-quart) or 4 (1-pint) sterilized mason jars, dividing evenly.

2. Combine vinegar, water, sugar, pickling spices, salt, and garlic (if using) in medium saucepan. Cook over medium heat, stirring occasionally, until sugar and salt are dissolved. Ladle mixture evenly into jars. Let cool; seal jars and refrigerate at least 1 day or up to 1 month.

Per serving (½ cup drained pickles): 57 Cal, 0 g Total Fat, 0 g Sat Fat, 960 mg Sod, 13 g Total Carb, 10 g Sugar, 1 g Fib, 1 g Prot. SmartPoints value: 2

 Cook's Tip

When you have a bounty of home-grown vegetables or feel like taking advantage of locally grown veggies at a farmers' market, make it a fun family project and pickle them together. For more information and tips on safe canning and pickling, visit the National Center for Home Food Preservation's website: nchfp.uga.edu.

ROASTED BEET AND WHEAT BERRY SALAD

SERVES 6
Vegetarian

2   pounds red and/or golden beets, scrubbed and trimmed

2½ teaspoons kosher salt

1   cup wheat berries

2   tablespoons orange juice

1   tablespoon orange preserves

1   tablespoon extra-virgin olive oil

1   tablespoon cider vinegar

4   scallions, chopped

⅓   cup chopped fresh flat-leaf parsley

¼   teaspoon table salt

¼   teaspoon black pepper

⅓   cup crumbled soft goat cheese

1. Preheat oven to 400°F. Spray small rimmed baking sheet with nonstick spray.

2. Put beets on prepared baking sheet; lightly spray with nonstick spray and sprinkle with ½ teaspoon of kosher salt. Tightly cover pan with foil; roast until beets are tender when pierced with small knife, 45–60 minutes. Remove beets from oven and let cool.

3. Meanwhile, cover wheat berries with 2 inches of water in small saucepan. Add 1 teaspoon kosher salt and bring to boil; reduce heat to low and simmer, covered, until wheat berries are tender, 50–60 minutes. Drain and set aside.

4. When beets are cool enough to handle, use paper towel to help slip off skins. Dice beets or cut into thick matchstick strips; set aside.

5. To make vinaigrette, whisk together orange juice, preserves, oil, vinegar, and remaining 1 teaspoon kosher salt.

6. Transfer wheat berries to serving bowl. Add beets, scallions, parsley, fine salt, pepper, and vinaigrette; toss until mixed well and coated evenly with dressing. Sprinkle with goat cheese.

Per serving (about ¾ cup): 225 Cal, 5 g Total Fat, 1 g Sat Fat, 1047 mg Sod, 41 g Total Carb, 13 g Sugar, 9 g Fib, 8 g Prot. SmartPoints value: 5

 Cook's Tip

To make this dish gluten free, substitute 1 cup uncooked quinoa for the wheat berries. The SmartPoints value will remain the same.

RED AND WHITE QUINOA SALAD WITH CORN AND PEPPERS

SERVES 6
Gluten Free, Vegetarian

2	cups water
½	cup white quinoa, rinsed
½	cup red quinoa, rinsed
1	ear of corn, husk and silk removed and kernels cut off
½	red bell pepper, diced
½	yellow bell pepper, diced
2	tablespoons lemon juice
1½	tablespoons grated orange zest (about 1 large orange)
⅓	cup orange juice
1	teaspoon olive oil
¼	teaspoon salt
⅛	teaspoon black pepper
2	tablespoons chopped almonds, toasted

1. Bring 2 cups water to boil in medium saucepan; add quinoa. Reduce heat and simmer, covered, until quinoa is tender and water is absorbed, about 15 minutes. Transfer quinoa to serving bowl and let cool.

2. Add corn, bell peppers, lemon juice, orange zest and juice, oil, salt, and black pepper to cooled quinoa. Toss until mixed well; sprinkle with almonds.

Per serving (about ¾ cup): 155 Cal, 4 g Total Fat, 0 g Sat Fat, 99 mg Sod, 25 g Total Carb, 3 g Sugar, 3 g Fib, 5 g Prot. SmartPoints value: 4

 Cook's Tip

We used ½ cup of red quinoa and ½ cup of white quinoa in this recipe, but you can use just one type, if you prefer.

MINI BLUEBERRY COBBLERS

SERVES 4
Vegetarian

3 cups fresh blueberries

3 tablespoons + 1 teaspoon turbinado sugar

Grated zest and juice of 1 small lemon

¼ teaspoon almond extract

Pinch ground ginger

1 cup reduced-fat baking mix

¼ cup + 2 tablespoons low-fat buttermilk

1. Preheat oven to 400°F. Spray 4 (6-ounce) ramekins or baking dishes with nonstick spray.

2. Toss together blueberries, 3 tablespoons of sugar, the lemon zest and juice, almond extract, and ginger in large bowl; divide evenly among prepared ramekins.

3. To make biscuits, combine baking mix and buttermilk in small bowl, stirring just until blended. Spoon dough evenly over filling; sprinkle with remaining 1 teaspoon sugar.

4. Place ramekins on small rimmed baking sheet. Bake until crust is golden and filling is bubbly, about 20 minutes. Serve warm or at room temperature.

Per serving (1 cobbler): 259 Cal, 3 g Total Fat, 0 g Sat Fat, 460 mg Sod, 57 g Total Carb, 27 g Sugar, 4 g Fib, 5 g Prot. SmartPoints value: 7

 Cook's Tip

Pack the cooled cobblers in a large covered plastic container, cushioned with paper towels to keep them stable, for a special picnic dessert.

GOOEY ROCKY ROAD BARS

SERVES 16

4 ounces chocolate wafer cookies

3 tablespoons unsalted butter, melted

¾ teaspoon salt

½ cup mini semisweet chocolate chips

¼ cup walnuts, chopped

½ cup fat-free sweetened condensed milk

½ cup mini marshmallows, coarsely chopped

1. Preheat oven to 350°F. Line 8-inch square baking pan with parchment paper or nonstick foil.

2. Put wafer cookies in food processor and pulse until fine crumbs form. (Or place cookies in large zip-close plastic bag and crush with rolling pin.) Transfer crumbs to small bowl; stir in butter and salt until crumbs are evenly moistened. Transfer to prepared pan, pressing to form even layer.

3. Sprinkle chocolate chips and walnuts over crust. Pour condensed milk over and sprinkle with marshmallows. Bake until chocolate is melted and marshmallows begin to brown, about 15 minutes.

4. Let cool in pan on a wire rack. Refrigerate until firm. Cut bars into 4 strips, then cut each strip crosswise into 4 pieces, making total of 16 bars.

Per serving (1 bar): 119 Cal, 6 g Total Fat, 3 g Sat Fat, 170 mg Sod, 16 g Total Carb, 12 g Sugar, 1 g Fib, 2 g Prot. SmartPoints value: 6

 Cook's Tip

Keep these bars in the refrigerator until ready to leave for your picnic. Cover the baking pan with a sheet of foil and you're good to go.

GOOEY ROCKY ROAD BARS

PROVENÇAL BEEF STEW

SERVES 6
Gluten Free

1   pound lean round steak, trimmed and cut into 1-inch chunks

1   teaspoon canola oil

2   cups white or cremini mushrooms, sliced

1   small onion, chopped

2   garlic cloves, minced

2   large carrots, sliced

1   (15½-ounce) can pinto beans, rinsed and drained

1½ cups beef broth

1   (14½-ounce) can crushed tomatoes

½   teaspoon dried oregano, crumbled

½   teaspoon salt

¼   teaspoon dried thyme

¼   teaspoon black pepper

1. Put beef in 5-quart slow cooker.

2. Heat oil in large nonstick skillet over medium heat. Add mushrooms, onion, and garlic; cook, stirring, until onion is softened, about 5 minutes. Add to slow cooker along with carrots and half of beans.

3. Put remaining beans and ½ cup of broth in blender and process until smooth; stir into mushroom mixture. Add remaining 1 cup broth, the tomatoes, oregano, salt, thyme, and pepper. Cover and cook on High until beef is fork-tender and carrots are softened, 6–7 hours.

Per serving (1¼ cups): 208 Cal, 5 g Total Fat, 2 g Sat Fat, 771 mg Sod, 18 g Total Carb, 5 g Sugar, 5 g Fib, 22 g Prot. SmartPoints value: 4

Cook's Tip

Accompany this hearty stew with a side of oven-roasted Brussels sprouts. Trim and halve Brussels sprouts and transfer to a large rimmed baking sheet. Spray them with olive oil nonstick spray and season with salt and pepper; toss until coated evenly. Spread the sprouts to form an even layer; roast in a 425°F oven, turning once or twice, until tender, about 25 minutes.

BROCCOLI AND SAUSAGE CASSEROLE

SERVES 8

1 large garlic clove, halved

1 (12-ounce) piece Italian bread, split

1 large red onion, cut into thin wedges

4 cups broccoli florets

1 teaspoon olive oil

¾ pound sweet or hot Italian-style turkey sausages, casings removed

1 cup chicken broth

½ teaspoon salt

¼ teaspoon black pepper

¼ teaspoon red pepper flakes

¾ cup shredded reduced-fat sharp Cheddar cheese

1. Set racks in lower third and middle of oven and preheat oven to 400°F. Spray two large baking sheets with olive oil nonstick spray.

2. Rub garlic over cut sides of bread. Place bread, cut side up, on one side of prepared baking sheet; spread onion alongside. Spread broccoli on second prepared baking sheet. Spray vegetables and bread with nonstick spray, tossing vegetables until coated evenly. Roast, stirring vegetables after 10 minutes and turning bread over, until broccoli is tender and bread is crisp, about 20 minutes. Cut bread into ½-inch cubes.

3. Reduce oven temperature to 350°F. Spray 9-inch square baking dish or casserole dish with nonstick spray.

4. Heat oil in large heavy nonstick skillet over medium heat. Cook sausage, breaking it up with wooden spoon, until no longer pink, about 10 minutes. Add broccoli, onion, bread cubes, broth, salt, black pepper, and pepper flakes, stirring until mixed well.

5. Spoon 3 cups of broccoli mixture into prepared baking dish; sprinkle with ¼ cup of Cheddar. Top with remaining broccoli mixture and sprinkle with remaining ½ cup cheese. Bake until cheese is melted and casserole is heated through, about 30 minutes.

Per serving (⅛ of casserole): 225 Cal, 7 g Total Fat, 2 g Sat Fat, 823 mg Sod, 27 g Total Carb, 2 g Sugar, 3 g Fib, 15 g Prot. SmartPoints value: 5

LINGUINE WITH BRUSSELS SPROUTS, WALNUTS, AND PARMESAN

SERVES 4

8   ounces linguine

2   tablespoons diced pancetta or prosciutto

1   teaspoon olive oil

3   large garlic cloves, minced

3   cups Brussels sprouts, trimmed and thinly sliced

1   mini sweet red pepper, sliced into thin rings, or ¼ cup diced red bell pepper

¾   teaspoon salt

¼   teaspoon black pepper

¼   teaspoon red pepper flakes

⅓   cup chicken broth

4   tablespoons grated Parmesan cheese

1   teaspoon grated lemon zest

1   tablespoon lemon juice

¼   cup walnuts, chopped and toasted

1. Cook linguine according to package directions. Drain and keep warm, reserving ½ cup of pasta cooking water.

2. Meanwhile, cook pancetta in large heavy nonstick skillet over medium heat until crisp, about 5 minutes. With slotted spoon, transfer pancetta to plate.

3. Add oil and garlic to skillet; cook, stirring, until fragrant, about 30 seconds. Add Brussels sprouts, sweet pepper, salt, black pepper, and pepper flakes; cook, stirring, until sprouts are crisp-tender, about 3 minutes. Add broth and cook, tossing mixture, until broth is almost evaporated, about 1 minute longer.

4. Add linguine to skillet along with reserved ¼ cup cooking water. Cook, stirring, adding more water if needed, until sprouts are just tender, 1–2 minutes. Remove skillet from heat; stir in 2 tablespoons of Parmesan and the lemon zest and juice. Transfer to serving bowl; top with walnuts, pancetta, and remaining 2 tablespoons cheese.

Per serving (1½ cups): 400 Cal, 12 g Total Fat, 3 g Sat Fat, 708 mg Sod, 52 g Total Carb, 4 g Sugar, 5 g Fib, 16 g Prot. SmartPoints value: 11

 Cook's Tip

To make this dish gluten free, substitute brown rice linguine for the whole wheat linguine with no change in the SmartPoints value.

LINGUINE WITH BRUSSELS
SPROUTS, WALNUTS, AND
PARMESAN

ROASTED DUMPLING SQUASH
AND ROMANESCO WITH SAGE

ROASTED DUMPLING SQUASH AND ROMANESCO WITH SAGE

SERVES 6

Gluten Free, Vegetarian

2   (10-ounce) dumpling or delicata squash

½   small head (about 1 pound) Romanesco broccoli, broccoflower, or cauliflower

12   large fresh sage leaves, torn

1½   tablespoons white balsamic vinegar

1   tablespoon olive oil

1   teaspoon kosher salt

¼   teaspoon black pepper

1. Place rack in middle of oven and preheat oven to 425°F. Line large rimmed baking sheet with nonstick foil.

2. Cut squash in half through stem end and scrape out seeds. Cut crosswise (lengthwise if using sweet dumpling squash) into ½-inch crescents and put in large bowl. Cut Romanesco into 1-inch florets and add to squash along with sage, vinegar, oil, salt, and pepper; toss until vegetables are coated evenly.

3. Spread vegetables on prepared baking sheet forming single layer. Roast, stirring once or twice, until lightly browned and tender, about 30 minutes.

Per serving (⅔ cup): 76 Cal, 3 g Total Fat, 0 g Sat Fat, 342 mg Sod, 13 g Total Carb, 4 g Sugar, 3 g Fib, 2 g Prot. SmartPoints value: 1

 Cook's Tip

Fall is the perfect time to try the different varieties of broccoli that are available in farmers' markets and specialty food stores. Romanesco broccoli, an Italian heirloom variety with a beautiful apple-green whorled head, may appear to be a new variety of psychedelic broccoli or cauliflower, but it has actually been enjoyed in Italy since the 16th century.

ROASTED CARROTS AND PARSNIPS

SERVES 8
Gluten Free, Vegetarian

8   carrots, cut into thick
     matchstick strips

6   parsnips, cut into thick
     matchstick strips

1   tablespoon chopped fresh thyme
     or 1 teaspoon dried

1   teaspoon salt

½   teaspoon black pepper

1   tablespoon olive oil

1. Preheat oven to 400°F. Spray rimmed baking sheet with olive oil nonstick spray.

2. Combine carrots and parsnips on prepared baking sheet. Sprinkle with thyme, salt, and pepper; drizzle with oil, tossing until coated evenly. Spread vegetables to form single layer. Roast 20 minutes; toss vegetables and roast until tender and beginning to caramelize, about 15 minutes longer.

Per serving (about ⅔ cup): 131 Cal, 2 g Total Fat, 0 g Sat Fat, 344 mg Sod, 28 g Total Carb, 9 g Sugar, 8 g Fib, 2 g Prot. SmartPoints value: 4

 Cook's Tip

In the fall, you will find the sweetest, freshest carrots and parsnips at local farmers' markets.

KALE AND ESCAROLE CAESAR SALAD

SERVES 4
20 Minutes or Less,
Gluten Free

⅓ cup plain low-fat Greek yogurt

4 tablespoons grated Parmesan cheese

2 tablespoons lemon juice

1 tablespoon extra-virgin olive oil

2 teaspoons Worcestershire sauce

1 anchovy packed in oil, drained and minced

1 garlic clove, minced

½ teaspoon Dijon mustard

¼ teaspoon kosher salt

Pinch black pepper

4 cups lightly packed baby kale

4 cups lightly packed coarsely chopped escarole

1. To make dressing, whisk together yogurt, 2 tablespoons of Parmesan, the lemon juice, oil, Worcestershire sauce, anchovy, garlic, mustard, salt, and pepper in small bowl.

2. Combine kale and escarole in salad bowl; add dressing and toss until slightly wilted. Sprinkle with remaining 2 tablespoons cheese.

Per serving (2 cups): 114 Cal, 6 g Total Fat, 2 g Sat Fat, 326 mg Sod, 11 g Total Carb, 1 g Sugar, 3 g Fib, 7 g Prot. SmartPoints value: 2

Cook's Tip

To make this dish vegetarian, omit the Worcestershire sauce and anchovy and season with salt with no change in the SmartPoints value.

ARUGULA SALAD WITH QUINCE, POMEGRANATE, AND PECANS

SERVES 6

Gluten Free, Vegetarian

- 1 cup unsweetened pomegranate or cranberry juice
- 2 tablespoons honey
- 1½ tablespoons cider vinegar
- ¼ teaspoon ground cardamom or cinnamon
- 1 (½-pound) ripe quince or Golden Delicious apple
- 2 teaspoons olive oil
- 1 garlic clove, lightly crushed with side of large knife
- ½ teaspoon salt
- ¼ teaspoon black pepper
- 1 (5-ounce) container baby arugula
- ¼ cup pecans, toasted and broken into pieces
- ¼ cup pomegranate seeds
- 3 tablespoons pecorino-Romano cheese shavings

1. Whisk together pomegranate juice, honey, vinegar, and cardamom in medium saucepan.

2. Peel and quarter quince; cut out fuzzy core and seeds. Cut each quarter into 4 or 5 wedges and add to pomegranate-juice mixture; bring to boil. Reduce heat to low and cook, covered, until quince is tender, about 12 minutes. (If using apple, cook until softened, about 5 minutes.) Remove pan from heat; with slotted spoon, transfer quince to small bowl. Reserve poaching liquid.

3. To make vinaigrette, add oil, garlic, salt, and pepper to poaching liquid; bring to boil and cook until reduced to about ⅓ cup, about 8 minutes. Discard garlic. Let cool to room temperature.

4. Toss together arugula, quince, pecans, pomegranate seeds, and vinaigrette in large salad bowl until coated evenly. Divide salad evenly among 6 plates and top with Romano shavings.

Per serving (about 1½ cups): 196 Cal, 9 g Total Fat, 2 g Sat Fat, 379 mg Sod, 30 g Total Carb, 19 g Sugar, 3 g Fib, 3 g Prot. SmartPoints value: 7

 Cook's Tip

Quinces are greenish-yellow and resemble lumpy pears. Though available year-round, California-grown quinces are in stores in autumn. Choose quinces that are free of blemishes and discolorations. When ripe, they turn pale yellow and remain quite hard but exude a delicate, sweet floral aroma.

CHOCOLATE-MARSHMALLOW BARK

SERVES 16
Gluten Free

8   ounces best-quality bittersweet chocolate

2   teaspoons butter

3   cups mini marshmallows

1. Line 9-inch square baking pan with heavy foil.

2. Place chocolate and butter in medium bowl and set over saucepan of simmering water. Cook, stirring, until melted and smooth; remove saucepan from heat and stir in marshmallows.

3. Scrape chocolate mixture into prepared pan; spread to form even layer. Refrigerate until chocolate is set, at least 1 hour or up to overnight. Cut bark into 4 strips, then cut each strip crosswise into 4 pieces, making total of 16 pieces.

Per serving (1 piece): 105 Cal, 8 g Total Fat, 5 g Sat Fat, 14 mg Sod, 12 g Total Carb, 6 g Sugar, 2 g Fib, 2 g Prot. SmartPoints value: 5

Cook's Tip

We like the contrast of bittersweet chocolate against the sweetness of the marshmallows, but you can use semisweet chocolate instead, if you like.

APPLE-WALNUT PHYLLO PURSES

SERVES 4
Vegetarian

2   large Granny Smith apples, peeled, cored, and diced

2   tablespoons + 2 teaspoons brown sugar

2   teaspoons all-purpose flour

1¼ teaspoons apple pie spice

4   (12 x 17-inch) sheets phyllo dough, thawed if frozen

2   tablespoons chopped walnuts

1. Preheat oven to 375°F. Spray 4 (8-ounce) ramekins or custard cups with nonstick spray.

2. Mix together apples, 2 tablespoons of brown sugar, the flour, and apple pie spice in medium bowl.

3. Lay 1 phyllo sheet on cutting board. (Keep remaining phyllo covered with damp kitchen towel and plastic wrap to prevent it from drying out.) Lightly spray phyllo with nonstick spray and cut into quarters. Stack phyllo. Repeat with remaining phyllo sheets, making total of 4 stacks.

4. Gently ease each phyllo stack into a prepared ramekin, pressing it against bottom and side. Divide filling evenly among ramekins and sprinkle with walnuts. Gather edges of phyllo together to partially cover filling. Lightly spray filling with nonstick spray and sprinkle with remaining 2 teaspoons brown sugar.

5. Place ramekins on small rimmed baking sheet. Bake until phyllo is golden and filling is bubbly, about 25 minutes. Serve warm.

Per serving (1 purse): 183 Cal, 4 g Total Fat, 1 g Sat Fat, 96 mg Sod, 36 g Total Carb, 20 g Sugar, 4 g Fib, 2 g Prot. SmartPoints value: 5

APPLE-WALNUT PHYLLO PURSES

OLD-FASHIONED CHICKEN POTPIE

SERVES 6

1 teaspoon butter

2 cups sliced white or cremini mushrooms

1 small onion, chopped

3 cups coarsely chopped cooked skinless boneless chicken breast

2 cups frozen mixed vegetables

1 cup chicken broth

½ teaspoon salt

¼ teaspoon paprika

¼ teaspoon dried thyme

¼ teaspoon black pepper

½ cup fat-free evaporated milk

2 tablespoons all-purpose flour

4 pieces reduced-fat crescent roll dough

1. Preheat oven to 375°F. Spray 10-inch shallow round baking dish or casserole dish with nonstick spray.

2. Spray large pot with nonstick spray. Add butter and melt over medium heat. Add mushrooms and onion; cook, stirring, until softened, about 5 minutes. Stir in chicken, mixed vegetables, broth, salt, paprika, thyme, and pepper. Reduce heat and simmer, covered, until vegetables are tender, about 15 minutes.

3. Meanwhile, whisk together ¼ cup of evaporated milk and the flour in small bowl until smooth; stir into chicken mixture. Cook over medium heat, stirring constantly, until sauce bubbles and thickens, about 2 minutes. Stir in remaining ¼ cup evaporated milk and cook 3 minutes longer.

4. Spoon chicken mixture into prepared baking dish. Unroll crescent rolls and arrange around inside edge of baking dish to form border (the middle will not be covered). Bake until crust is golden brown and filling is bubbly, about 15 minutes.

Per serving (⅙ of potpie): 259 Cal, 7 g Total Fat, 2 g Sat Fat, 561 mg Sod, 21 g Total Carb, 5 g Sugar, 3 g Fib, 28 g Prot. SmartPoints value: 6

 Cook's Tip

No dish warms the body and soul as deliciously as a homemade chicken potpie. Start your meal with a wintery salad of escarole, pomegranate seeds, and radicchio dressed with balsamic vinegar and sprinkled with salt and pepper.

RIGATONI WITH CREAMY SAUSAGE SAUCE

SERVES 4

8 ounces whole wheat rigatoni

½ pound sweet Italian-style turkey sausages, casings removed

½ pound cremini mushrooms, quartered

2 large garlic cloves, minced

1½ cups fat-free milk

2 tablespoons all-purpose flour

1 cup frozen baby peas

½ teaspoon salt

¼ teaspoon black pepper

½ cup roasted red peppers (not oil packed), sliced

½ cup sliced scallions

3 tablespoons grated Parmesan cheese

1. Cook rigatoni according to package directions. Drain in colander and return to pot; keep warm.

2. Meanwhile, cook sausages in large nonstick skillet over medium heat, breaking meat up with wooden spoon, until no longer pink, about 5 minutes; with slotted spoon, transfer to medium bowl. Add mushrooms to skillet and cook, stirring, until browned and tender, about 4 minutes. Stir in garlic and cook, stirring, until fragrant, about 30 seconds longer.

3. Whisk together milk and flour in glass measuring cup until smooth; stir into skillet along with peas, salt, and black pepper; bring to boil. Reduce heat and simmer until sauce is thickened and peas are tender, about 3 minutes. Return sausages to skillet along with roasted peppers and scallions; remove skillet from heat. Add sausage mixture and Parmesan to rigatoni; stir until mixed well.

Per serving (about 2 cups): 401 Cal, 7 g Total Fat, 2 g Sat Fat, 880 mg Sod, 63 g Total Carb, 9 g Sugar, 8 g Fib, 26 g Prot. SmartPoints value: 11

Cook's Tip

This hearty dish is easily doubled for larger gatherings. It can be prepared up to 2 hours ahead and left out at room temperature. For longer storage, spoon it into one or two baking dishes and refrigerate, covered, up to 2 days. To serve, reheat, covered, in a 300°F oven for about 30 minutes.

PEPPERED BEEF TENDERLOIN WITH PORT WINE SAUCE

SERVES 4

1 teaspoon whole black peppercorns

1 teaspoon fennel seeds

¾ teaspoon salt

2 teaspoons olive oil

1 (1-pound) lean beef tenderloin, trimmed

1 small onion, finely chopped

⅔ cup ruby port wine

2 teaspoons all-purpose flour

½ cup beef broth

1 teaspoon Dijon mustard

2 teaspoons unsalted butter

1. Preheat oven to 400°F.

2. Combine peppercorns, fennel seeds, and ½ teaspoon of salt in small zip-close plastic bag; press out air and seal bag. With meat mallet or rolling pin, pound until crushed. Spread spice mixture on sheet of wax paper. Roll tenderloin in spice mixture until coated, pressing so it adheres.

3. Heat oil in small heavy flameproof roasting pan over medium-high heat. Add beef and cook until browned on all sides, about 8 minutes.

4. Transfer pan to oven and roast until instant-read thermometer inserted into center of beef registers 145°F, about 30 minutes. Transfer to cutting board and let stand 10 minutes.

5. Meanwhile, to make sauce, spray roasting pan with nonstick spray and set over medium heat. Add onion and cook, stirring, until softened, about 5 minutes. Add wine and cook, stirring, 2 minutes. Whisk in flour and cook, stirring, about 1 minute. Whisk in broth, mustard, and remaining ¼ teaspoon salt; bring to boil. Cook, stirring, until sauce bubbles and thickens, about 4 minutes longer. Remove pan from heat; swirl in butter until melted. Cut beef against grain into 12 slices and serve with sauce.

Per serving (3 slices beef and 2 tablespoons sauce): 272 Cal, 11 g Fat, 4 g Sat Fat, 644 mg Sod, 5 g Total Carb, 1g Sugar, 1 g Fib, 26 g Prot. SmartPoints value: 7

 Cook's Tip

A spice grinder or mini food processor is the fastest way to grind spices, although a coffee grinder also works well. Just be sure to wipe the inside of the grinder clean when you are finished so the taste of your coffee isn't affected by the spices.

CURRY-SPICED SWEET POTATO– QUINOA CAKES

SERVES 4
Gluten Free, Vegetarian

2   cups water

1   cup quinoa, rinsed

1   pound sweet potatoes, peeled and cut into 1-inch chunks

1   tablespoon grated peeled fresh ginger

1   tablespoon finely chopped shallot

1   tablespoon curry powder

1¼ teaspoons ground cumin

¾   teaspoon salt

2   teaspoons olive oil

1. Combine 2 cups water and quinoa in medium saucepan; bring to boil. Reduce heat and cook, covered, until liquid is absorbed and quinoa is tender, about 15 minutes. Transfer to large bowl.

2. Meanwhile, combine potatoes with enough salted water to cover in small saucepan; bring to boil. Reduce heat and simmer, covered, until fork-tender, about 12 minutes; drain. Return potatoes to saucepan and coarsely mash with fork.

3. Add potatoes, ginger, shallot, curry powder, cumin, and salt to quinoa; stir until mixed well. Shape mixture into 4 (¾-inch-thick) patties.

4. Heat oil in large nonstick skillet over medium heat. Add patties and cook until browned and heated through, about 5 minutes per side.

Per serving (1 cake): 284 Cal, 5 g Total Fat, 1 g Sat Fat, 506 mg Sod, 52 g Total Carb, 5 g Sugar, 7 g Fib, 8 g Prot. SmartPoints value: 9

Cook's Tip

Make these unusual cakes even tastier by serving them topped with plain fat-free Greek yogurt or hummus (any variety you like). Three tablespoons of plain fat-free Greek yogurt will up the SmartPoints value by 1, while 2 tablespoons of hummus will up the per-serving SmartPoints value by 2.

SAGE-AND-GARLIC-INFUSED PARSNIP PUREE

SERVES 6
Gluten Free, Vegetarian

2½ pounds parsnips, cubed (about 7 cups)

¾ cup low-fat (1%) milk, warmed

1 tablespoon unsalted butter

1½–2 teaspoons finely chopped fresh sage

1 small garlic clove, minced

1 teaspoon kosher salt

¼ teaspoon black pepper

1. Combine parsnips with enough salted water to cover in large saucepan; bring to boil. Reduce heat and simmer, covered, until fork-tender, about 15 minutes.

2. Drain parsnips and let cool slightly. Transfer to blender or food processor; add milk, butter, sage, garlic, salt, and pepper. Pulse until smooth.

Per serving (⅔ cup): 171 Cal, 3 g Total Fat, 1 g Sat Fat, 353 mg Sod, 35 g Total Carb, 11 g Sugar, 9 g Fib, 3 g Prot. SmartPoints value: 7

BROCCOLI RABE WITH CANNELLINI BEANS

SERVES 4
Gluten Free, Vegetarian

1 pound broccoli rabe, coarsely chopped

1½ tablespoons extra-virgin olive oil

3 large garlic cloves, minced

1 (15½-ounce) can cannellini (white kidney) beans, rinsed and drained

2 tablespoons lemon juice

¼ teaspoon salt

⅛ teaspoon black pepper

1. Bring large pot of salted water to boil over high heat. Add broccoli rabe and cook just until tender, 3–4 minutes; drain in colander and set aside.

2. Combine oil and garlic in middle of large nonstick skillet and set over low heat. Cook, stirring, until garlic is very tender but not colored, about 10 minutes, keeping garlic in center of pan to avoid browning.

3. Add beans, broccoli rabe, lemon juice, salt, and pepper to skillet; toss until combined well. Increase heat to medium and cook, stirring, until heated through, about 5 minutes.

Per serving (generous 1 cup): 199 Cal, 6 g Total Fat, 1 g Sat Fat, 188 mg Sod, 28 g Total Carb, 1 g Sugar, 8 g Fib, 12 g Prot. SmartPoints value: 5

SPICY SWEET POTATO OVEN FRIES

SERVES 4
Gluten Free, Vegetarian

2   (½-pound) sweet potatoes, peeled and cut into ½ x 4-inch sticks

2   teaspoons olive oil

1   teaspoon chipotle chile powder

1   teaspoon ground turmeric

¾   teaspoon salt

½   teaspoon sugar

1. Combine potatoes with enough cold water to cover in large bowl. Soak at least 30 minutes or up to 1 hour; drain.

2. Meanwhile, preheat oven to 425°F. Spray large nonstick baking sheet with nonstick spray.

3. Arrange potatoes close together on prepared baking sheet. Drizzle with oil and turn until coated evenly.

4. Stir together chile powder, turmeric, salt, and sugar in cup. Sprinkle half of spice mixture over potatoes; turn until coated evenly. Sprinkle with remaining spice mixture and turn until coated. Spread potatoes to form single layer. Bake, turning once or twice, until tender on inside and crisp on outside, about 30 minutes.

Per serving (½ potato): 123 Cal, 2 g Fat, 0 g Sat Fat, 505 mg Sod, 24 g Total Carb, 5 g Sugar, 4 g Fib, 2 g Prot. SmartPoints value: 4

 Cook's Tip

For spicier fries, substitute a small amount of cayenne for the chipotle chile powder and 1 teaspoon garlic powder for the turmeric.

SPICY SWEET POTATO OVEN FRIES

COFFEE-ALMOND FLANS

SERVES 4

Gluten Free, Vegetarian

⅓ cup + 2 tablespoons sugar

3 tablespoons water

1 cup fat-free half-and-half

2 teaspoons instant espresso powder

2 large eggs

¼ teaspoon almond extract

Pinch cinnamon

2 tablespoons sliced or slivered almonds, toasted

1. Preheat oven to 325°F.

2. Combine ⅓ cup of sugar and the water in small heavy saucepan. Cook over medium heat, stirring occasionally, until sugar is dissolved; bring to boil. Reduce heat and simmer, without stirring, brushing side of saucepan with brush dipped in cool water during first few minutes of cooking time, until syrup turns amber. Cook, swirling saucepan occasionally, until caramel is dark amber. Immediately pour caramel into 4 (6-ounce) ramekins, gently swirl ramekins to coat bottoms and halfway up sides. Refrigerate until caramel is hard, about 10 minutes.

3. Meanwhile, combine half-and-half and espresso powder in medium saucepan and cook over medium heat until bubbles form. Whisk eggs, remaining 2 tablespoons sugar, the almond extract, and cinnamon in bowl. Remove saucepan from heat; whisk hot half-and-half mixture into egg mixture. Return mixture to saucepan and cook over medium-low heat, stirring constantly, until slightly thickened, about 3 minutes. Pour through sieve set over bowl.

4. Divide custard among ramekins. Put ramekins in 9-inch square baking pan. Place pan in oven; add enough hot water to pan to come halfway up sides of ramekins. Bake until flans are just set around edges and jiggle in center, 35–40 minutes. Transfer ramekins to rack; cool 30 minutes. Cover and refrigerate until chilled, at least 4 hours or up to 1 day.

5. To serve, run thin knife around edges of flans to loosen from ramekins. Unmold onto plates; spoon any sauce over flans. Sprinkle with almonds.

Per serving (1 flan and ½ tablespoon almonds): 182 Cal, 5 g Total Fat, 1 g Sat Fat, 122 mg Sod, 30 g Total Carb, 26 g Sugar, 0 g Fib, 5 g Prot. SmartPoints value: 9

COFFEE-ALMOND FLANS

CITRUS WITH SALTED CARAMEL SAUCE

SERVES 4
20 Minutes or Less,
Gluten Free, Vegetarian

2   tablespoons + ¼ cup water

⅓   cup sugar

1   teaspoon unsalted butter

¼   teaspoon coarse sea salt

¼   teaspoon vanilla extract

2   seedless navel oranges

1   large seedless ruby red grapefruit

½   teaspoon finely chopped
    fresh lavender or lemon thyme
    (optional)

1. Pour 2 tablespoons of water into medium saucepan. Sprinkle sugar in even layer in pan. Cook over medium-low heat, without stirring, brushing down side of saucepan with pastry brush dipped in cool water during first few minutes of cooking time. Simmer until caramel begins to turn light golden. Continue to cook, swirling pan occasionally, until syrup turns golden.

2. Remove saucepan from heat. Wearing oven mitts to protect your arms from spatters, carefully pour remaining ¼ cup water down side of pan. Return saucepan to heat. Add butter and salt; cook, stirring constantly, 30 seconds. Remove saucepan from heat. Stir in vanilla and let caramel cool to room temperature.

3. Meanwhile, cut away peel and pith from oranges and grapefruit. Cut ¼-inch slice from stem and blossom ends of oranges and grapefruit and cut into thin rounds. Arrange citrus on 4 plates, dividing evenly, and drizzle with sauce. Sprinkle each serving with pinch of lavender (if using).

Per serving (about 5 slices fruit and 1½ tablespoons sauce): 133 Cal, 1 g Total Fat, 1 g Sat Fat, 118 mg Sod, 32 g Total Carb, 29 g Sugar, 3 g Fib, 1 g Prot. SmartPoints value: 5

PINK GRAPEFRUIT— CAMPARI GRANITA

SERVES 6
Gluten Free, Vegetarian

3   cups pink or ruby red grapefruit juice

1   cup water

½   cup superfine sugar

2   tablespoons Campari

1   tablespoon grated lime zest

1. Whisk together all ingredients in large bowl until sugar is dissolved. Pour mixture into 9 x 13-inch baking pan. Cover and freeze until partially frozen, about 2 hours. Remove from freezer and stir with fork, breaking up ice crystals. Cover pan and return to freezer, stirring mixture every 30 minutes, until completely icy, about 3 hours longer.

2. Scoop granita loosely into airtight container and freeze up to 2 weeks. To serve, scoop into glasses.

Per serving (about ¾ cup): 124 Cal, 0 g Total Fat, 0 g Sat Fat, 3 mg Sod, 30 g Total Carb, 18 g Sugar, 0 g Fib, 1 g Prot. SmartPoints value: 6

 Cook's Tip

For the best results, use freshly squeezed grapefruit juice in this recipe—the flavor will be far superior without the harsh bitterness that store-bought juice sometimes has. One large grapefruit yields about 1 cup of juice.

PEA SOUP WITH SHRIMP AND TARRAGON

SERVES 4
Gluten Free

1 tablespoon butter

2 onions, chopped

1 (10-ounce) package frozen peas

1¾ cups reduced-sodium chicken broth

1 cup low-fat buttermilk

1 tablespoon fresh tarragon leaves + 4 sprigs

½ teaspoon salt

⅛–¼ teaspoon ground pepper, preferably white

12 cooked medium shrimp (about ¼ pound)

2 very thin lemon slices, halved

1. Melt butter in large saucepan over medium heat. Add onions and cook, covered, stirring occasionally until softened, about 8 minutes. Stir in peas and broth; bring to boil. Reduce heat and simmer until peas are tender, about 5 minutes.

2. Remove saucepan from heat; stir in buttermilk, tarragon leaves, salt, and pepper; let cool slightly.

3. Puree soup, in batches, in blender or food processor. Return soup to saucepan and reheat over medium-low heat. Ladle evenly into 4 bowls. Top each serving with 3 shrimp and garnish with tarragon sprig and half slice lemon.

Per serving (1 cup soup and 3 shrimp): 168 Cal, 4 g Total Fat, 2 g Sat Fat, 914 mg Sod, 19 g Total Carb, 10 g Sugar, 5 g Fib, 13 g Prot. SmartPoints value: 5

Cook's Tip

Pretty as a picture, this elegant soup can also be served chilled. White pepper, less potent and "fruitier" than black pepper, is recommended so the soup isn't dotted with black specks.

FRESH FIGS WITH ARUGULA, PROSCIUTTO, AND GOAT CHEESE

SERVES 4
20 Minutes or Less,
Gluten Free

6   cups lightly packed baby arugula

8   fresh green or black mission figs, quartered

½   small fennel bulb, very thinly sliced

2   tablespoons balsamic glaze

1½ teaspoons olive oil

    Pinch salt

4   (½-ounce) slices prosciutto, cut crosswise into ¼-inch strips

1   (3-ounce) log soft goat cheese, coarsely crumbled

¼   teaspoon black pepper

Toss together arugula, figs, fennel, 1 tablespoon of balsamic glaze, the oil, and salt in large bowl. Divide salad evenly among 4 plates; top evenly with prosciutto and goat cheese. Drizzle with remaining 1 tablespoon glaze and sprinkle with pepper.

Per serving (1 salad): 222 Cal, 10 g Total Fat, 5 g Sat Fat, 654 mg Sod, 24 g Total Carb, 18 g Sugar, 4 g Fib, 12 g Prot. SmartPoints value: 5

Cook's Tip

To make this dish vegetarian, omit the prosciutto. This will reduce the per-serving SmartPoints value to 4.

COCONUT SHRIMP

SERVES 4

24 medium shrimp (about ½ pound), peeled, deveined, and butterflied, tails left on

6 tablespoons unsweetened flaked coconut

¼ cup panko bread crumbs

2 tablespoons all-purpose flour

½ teaspoon salt

3 large egg whites

1. Preheat oven to 450°F. Spray baking sheet with nonstick spray.

2. Pat shrimp dry with paper towel. Mix together coconut, panko, flour, and salt on sheet of wax paper. Beat egg whites in medium bowl until frothy; add shrimp and toss until coated evenly. Lift shrimp from egg whites, one at a time, allowing excess to drip back into bowl. Coat shrimp with coconut mixture, pressing gently so it adheres.

3. Arrange shrimp on prepared baking sheet in single layer. Spray lightly with nonstick spray. Bake until golden and opaque in center, 8–10 minutes. Serve hot or warm.

Per serving (6 shrimp): 114 Cal, 4 g Total Fat, 2 g Sat Fat, 433 mg Sod, 8 g Total Carb, 1 g Sugar, 1 g Fib, 11 g Prot. SmartPoints value: 3

 Cook's Tip

Serve this perennial favorite with glasses of chilled white wine, such as sauvignon blanc or pinot grigio, or with prosecco. A 5-ounce glass of dry white wine or prosecco will up the per-serving SmartPoints value by 4.

LEMON-SAGE ROAST TURKEY BREAST

SERVES 8
Gluten Free

3 tablespoons unsalted butter, softened

3 tablespoons chopped fresh sage

1 tablespoon chopped fresh thyme

½ teaspoon grated lemon zest

½ teaspoon kosher salt

½ teaspoon black pepper

1 (2-pound) skinless boneless turkey breast

1½ cups chicken broth

6 large garlic cloves, unpeeled

2 tablespoons lemon juice

1. Preheat oven to 400°F.

2. With fork, mash together 1½ tablespoons of butter, the sage, thyme, lemon zest, salt, and pepper in small bowl; smear all over turkey.

3. Place turkey in small flameproof roasting pan or large ovenproof skillet. Pour ¾ cup of broth around turkey; add garlic to pan.

4. Roast turkey, basting with broth from pan and turning garlic occasionally, until instant-read thermometer inserted into thickest part of breast registers 165°F. Transfer turkey to cutting board; loosely cover with foil and let rest about 10 minutes.

5. Meanwhile, peel garlic. Place roasting pan with drippings on burner over medium-high heat; add garlic, remaining ¾ cup broth, and the lemon juice. Bring to boil, scraping up browned bits from bottom of pan; boil until sauce is slightly reduced, mashing garlic and blending it into sauce, about 3 minutes.

6. Remove roasting pan from heat. Pour sauce through sieve set over small bowl; swirl in remaining 1½ tablespoons butter until melted and smooth. Transfer to sauce boat.

7. Slice turkey and arrange on platter. Serve sauce alongside.

Per serving (about 3 ounces turkey and 1 tablespoon sauce): 179 Cal, 5 g Total Fat, 3 g Sat Fat, 321 mg Sod, 2 g Total Carb, 0 g Sugar, 0 g Fib, 29 g Prot. SmartPoints value: 3

PAN-SEARED DUCK WITH BLUEBERRY SAUCE

SERVES 4
Gluten Free

4   (5-ounce) skinless boneless duck breasts, trimmed

½   teaspoon salt

¼   teaspoon black pepper

2   teaspoons olive oil

1   small onion, finely chopped

⅓   cup dry red wine

⅓   cup no-sugar-added blueberry preserves

1½   teaspoons chopped fresh thyme or ½ teaspoon dried

1. Sprinkle duck with ¼ teaspoon of salt and the pepper. Heat oil in large nonstick skillet over medium heat. Add duck and cook until golden and instant-read thermometer inserted into center of breasts registers 165°F, about 5 minutes per side. Transfer to plate and keep warm.

2. Add onion to skillet and cook, stirring occasionally, until softened, about 4 minutes. Stir in wine, preserves, remaining ¼ teaspoon salt, and any accumulated duck juices. Increase heat and cook, stirring occasionally, until mixture is reduced to ½ cup, about 2 minutes. Stir in thyme.

3. Thinly slice each breast on diagonal and spoon sauce over.

Per serving (1 duck breast and 2 tablespoons sauce): 242 Cal, 11 g Total Fat, 4 g Sat Fat, 394 mg Sod, 9 g Total Carb, 1 g Sugar, 4 g Fib, 16 g Prot. SmartPoints value: 7

 Cook's Tip

Elegant and flavorful, cooked wild rice is the perfect accompaniment to this delectable main dish. One-half cup of cooked wild rice per serving will up the per-serving SmartPoints value by 2.

RACK OF LAMB WITH LEMON-HERB CRUST

SERVES 8

2 garlic cloves, peeled

1½ slices whole wheat bread

2 tablespoons lightly packed fresh mint leaves

2 tablespoons lightly packed fresh flat-leaf parsley leaves

2 teaspoons fresh thyme leaves

Grated zest of 1 lemon

1 tablespoon olive oil

2 (8-rib) racks of lamb (1½ pounds each), trimmed and frenched

1 teaspoon kosher salt

½ teaspoon black pepper

1. Put garlic in food processor and pulse until finely chopped. Add bread, mint, parsley, thyme, and lemon zest; pulse until bread forms coarse crumbs. With machine running, pour oil through feed tube, pulsing until mixed well. Set aside.

2. Spray grill rack with nonstick spray. Preheat grill to medium-high or prepare medium-high fire.

3. Sprinkle lamb with salt and pepper. Place lamb on grill rack and grill until browned, about 5 minutes per side. Transfer to platter. Press crumb mixture onto meaty side of lamb; lightly spray with nonstick spray. Return lamb to grill, crumbed side up. Grill, without turning, until instant-read thermometer inserted into center of rack (not touching bone) registers 145°F, about 10 minutes.

4. With tongs, carefully transfer lamb to cutting board. Let stand 10 minutes. Cut between every other bone, making 8 double chops in all.

Per serving (1 double chop): 275 Cal, 10 g Total Fat, 3 g Sat Fat, 305 mg Sod, 3 g Total Carb, 0 g Sugar, 1 g Fib, 28 g Prot. SmartPoints value: 6

Cook's Tip

When you want to pull out all the stops, rack of lamb is the way to go. Cooking it on the grill makes it easy and adds a tempting layer of smoky goodness. Look for vacuum-packed Australian racks of lamb at your supermarket or big-box store. They are often a good value.

10 TIPS FOR GRACIOUS ENTERTAINING

Whenever you're hosting an event, large or small, simple or elaborate, remember the most basic element of hospitality: sharing yourself and your home with people you care about. Visitors dropping by unannounced was once a normal, joyful part of family and community life. Entertaining often meant greeting guests warmly and offering them refreshment as simple as a cup of coffee or a glass of whatever was on hand. If the conversation flowed and time moved on, sometimes an impromptu meal would be set out.

That said, planning ahead always helps things go more smoothly, and it should be fun and exciting, not stressful, for you as the host. Here are some tried-and-true strategies that will help make your party successful.

1. Take some time with your invite

Whether you're emailing, using an online invitation site, or calling on the phone, communicate excitement about your event and let everyone know you look forward to seeing them. If your party has a theme, like eggnog and caroling, Halloween, or a significant birthday, let guests know how they can contribute to the fun. Perhaps they can dress up for the occasion, come prepared with a toast or anecdote, or bring something special to share. If it's a family event, mentioning traditions from past celebrations can help everyone start to feel connected before the gathering.

2. Ask about dietary needs

You may not be able to accommodate everyone, but asking if anyone is following a gluten-free, vegan, or other special eating plan is gracious. Your guests may offer to contribute a dish of their own that meets their specifications, or you can suggest it as an option if you think they won't find enough to eat otherwise. Either way, your visitors should be pleased to know that their needs are important to you.

3. Pick a play list

The music you select will affect the mood of your party, so give it some thought. If choosing tunes isn't your thing or you already have enough on your plate, assign this task in advance to someone who enjoys playing DJ. Make sure there's enough music to last the duration of the event, and keep tabs on the volume level, so it doesn't hinder conversation.

4. Do as much ahead as possible

Plan a menu that allows you plenty of time to mingle with your guests. It's helpful to include a few dishes you can make entirely in advance, and it's fine to either bring in premade items or accept people's offers to contribute a dish. The day before the party, it's a good idea to go over the house and make sure everything is clean and in order. Check the bathroom that guests will be using, and make sure extra toilet paper and hand towels or guest towels are readily available. Set the table for a sit-down dinner a few hours early or, if you're serving buffet-style, make sure you have all the seating, plates, and utensils for the number you're expecting.

5. Welcome everyone

Try to greet each visitor at the door if you can. If you know you'll be busy in the kitchen or elsewhere, enlist a friend or family member to answer the door and take coats. Make space for outerwear and bags ahead of time, preferably in a front closet (be sure you have enough extra hangers), or, for large parties, designate a bedroom or other area where they can be left safely.

6. Offer guests a drink as soon as they're settled

It's one of the oldest rules of hosting and with good reason: It's your first opportunity to show party goers that you want them to feel taken care of. You can pour the drinks yourself or, for larger get-togethers, point people in the direction of the bar or drinks table so they can help themselves. Make sure you have a few nonalcoholic options, including water, for anyone who's not imbibing. A calorie-free drink like flavored seltzer or unsweetened iced tea is also a good idea for guests who are watching their weight.

7. Make introductions

Once guests are comfortable, try to introduce (or reintroduce) them to as many other party goers as possible, or at least to those standing nearby. If it's a large event, make sure to connect them with at least one new person before you have to circulate. Mentioning something your guests have in common, or simply indicating how you know each of them, can help get the conversation flowing.

8. Stay relaxed

Hosting a soiree can be draining, so remember to make time to sit back and really enjoy your guests. Undoubtedly some of your attention will be focused on keeping things moving smoothly, but don't start cleaning or tidying up when you should be having fun. It's fine to spend a few minutes clearing plates and organizing as long as you set your guests up in another room and make sure they're chatting happily.

9. Keep it as casual as you want

At the end of the day, it's the laughter and friendship you share that makes for great times and wonderful memories. If you're not a fan of traditional entertaining or feel you just don't have the time for the planning, cooking, and cleaning involved, you've still got plenty of options. Potlucks are a terrific way to share a fun meal with friends without overburdening the host. Organizing a picnic in a community park can also be a less stressful way to entertain. Or invite friends and neighbors to drop by for a porch party, back-yard water-balloon fight, or game night. Just don't stand on ceremony—get together and start celebrating!

10. Follow up with thanks the next day

It's important to let everyone know how much you appreci-ated seeing them and to thank them again if they brought a dish. You can contact guests individually if you have time, or send out a group email or text if you don't. If you've taken photos, it's nice to include them, or you can just mention some of the party's highlights.

MIXED VEGETABLES WITH ORANGE GREMOLATA

SERVES 6
Gluten Free, Vegetarian

3   tablespoons chopped fresh flat-leaf parsley

2   tablespoons chopped fresh tarragon

    Grated zest of 1 small orange

1   garlic clove, minced

3   teaspoons extra-virgin olive oil

2   large shallots, chopped (about ⅓ cup)

1½ cups trimmed slender green beans (haricots verts)

2   large carrots, cut into ¼-inch-thick matchstick strips (about 2 cups)

1   yellow squash, cut into ¼-inch-thick matchstick strips (about 2 cups)

1   red bell pepper, cut into ¼-inch-thick matchstick strips

¼   cup vegetable broth

1   tablespoon orange juice

¾   teaspoon salt

¼   teaspoon black pepper

1. To make gremolata, mix together parsley, tarragon, orange zest, garlic, and 1 teaspoon of oil in small bowl. Cover bowl with piece of plastic wrap and set aside. (Can be prepared up to several hours ahead and refrigerated.)

2. Heat remaining 2 teaspoons oil in large nonstick skillet over medium heat. Add shallots and cook, stirring, until softened, about 3 minutes. Add green beans and carrots; cook, stirring occasionally, 2 minutes. Add squash, bell pepper, broth, orange juice, salt, and black pepper; cook, stirring occasionally, until vegetables are just tender, about 4 minutes longer.

3. Add gremolata to vegetables and toss until mixed.

Per serving (¾ cup): 65 Cal, 3 g Total Fat, 0 g Sat Fat, 352 mg Sod, 11 g Total Carb, 3 g Sugar, 3 g Fib, 2 g Prot. SmartPoints value: 1

 Cook's Tip

Gremolata, often sprinkled over osso buco (braised veal shanks), is also excellent over cooked whole baby potatoes, grilled or broiled chicken breasts, or grilled or broiled fish. If you like, use lemon or lime zest, or a combination, instead of the orange zest.

POTATO-CARAWAY ROSTI WITH BACON AND CHIVES

SERVES 6
Gluten Free

3   slices turkey bacon, chopped

2   russet (baking) potatoes
    (1½ pounds), scrubbed, grated,
    and squeezed dry

1   small sweet onion, such as
    Vidalia, grated

1½ tablespoons chopped
    fresh chives

1   teaspoon salt

½   teaspoon caraway seeds

¼   teaspoon black pepper

3   teaspoons olive oil

6   tablespoons fat-free sour cream

1. Cook bacon in medium nonstick skillet over medium heat until browned, about 5 minutes. Transfer to paper towel–lined plate to drain. Wipe skillet clean.

2. Stir together potatoes, onion, bacon, 1 tablespoon of chives, the salt, caraway seeds, and pepper in large bowl until mixed well.

3. Add 1½ teaspoons of oil to same skillet and set over medium heat. Add potato mixture, spreading and pressing it down to form even layer. Cook, without stirring, until potatoes are browned on bottom, about 10 minutes.

4. Invert large plate on top of potato cake and carefully turn skillet over. Add remaining 1½ teaspoons oil to skillet. Slide potato cake back into skillet and cook, without stirring, until browned on second side, about 6 minutes. Cut rosti into 6 wedges. Top each serving with 1 tablespoon sour cream and sprinkle evenly with remaining ½ tablespoon chives.

Per serving (1 garnished wedge): 106 Cal, 3 g Total Fat, 1 g Sat Fat, 488 mg Sod, 16 g Total Carb, 1 g Sugar, 2 g Fib, 3 g Prot. SmartPoints value: 3

 Cook's Tip

Rosti is the Swiss word for "crisp and golden." This dish, similar to hash browns, has long been enjoyed by farmers in Bern, Switzerland, where it originated.

DARK CHOCOLATE AND SEA SALT TARTLETS

MAKES 15

Vegetarian

15 mini phyllo shells, thawed
if frozen

¼ cup low-fat (1%) milk

1 teaspoon salted butter

3½ ounces bittersweet chocolate,
chopped (about ¾ cup)

½ teaspoon vanilla extract

⅛ teaspoon coarse sea salt

5 tablespoons thawed frozen
fat-free whipped topping

1. Preheat oven to 350°F.

2. Place phyllo shells on baking sheet and bake until lightly crisp, about 5 minutes. Transfer to wire rack and let cool.

3. Meanwhile, combine milk and butter in small saucepan and set over high heat; cook, stirring occasionally, until milk bubbles around edge and butter is melted. Reduce heat to low; stir in chocolate and vanilla until chocolate is melted and mixture is smooth.

4. Let chocolate mixture cool 2–3 minutes. Spoon evenly into phyllo shells and sprinkle with salt. Refrigerate until filling is set, about 10 minutes. Top each tartlet with 1 teaspoon whipped topping just before serving.

Per serving (1 tartlet): 54 Cal, 4 g Total Fat, 2 g Sat Fat, 30 mg Sod, 5 g Total Carb, 0 g Sugar, 1 g Fib, 1 g Prot. SmartPoints value: 2

BUTTERMILK SORBET
WITH CRUSHED BLACKBERRY—
MINT SAUCE

BUTTERMILK SORBET WITH CRUSHED BLACKBERRY—MINT SAUCE

SERVES 6
Gluten Free, Vegetarian

3½ cups low-fat buttermilk

⅓ cup honey

4 tablespoons sugar

1 teaspoon vanilla extract

½ teaspoon grated orange zest

2 cups fresh blackberries (about two 6-ounce containers)

1 tablespoon chopped fresh mint + 6 small sprigs

1. Whisk together buttermilk, honey, 3 tablespoons of sugar, the vanilla, and orange zest in medium bowl until sugar is dissolved. Pour buttermilk mixture into ice-cream maker and freeze according to manufacturer's instructions. Transfer sorbet to freezer container and freeze until firm, at least 4 hours or up to 2 days.

2. To make sauce, combine 1½ cups of blackberries and remaining 1 tablespoon sugar in small bowl. With fork, crush berries until very coarse puree is formed; let stand 10 minutes. Stir in remaining ½ cup blackberries and the chopped mint. (Can be made up to 4 hours ahead and refrigerated.)

3. To serve, scoop sorbet into 6 dessert dishes and top with ¼ cup blackberry sauce. Garnish with mint sprigs.

Per serving (about ⅔ cup sorbet with ¼ cup blackberry sauce): 170 Cal, 2 g Total Fat, 1 g Sat Fat, 151 mg Sod, 35 g Total Carb, 33 g Sugar, 3 g Fib, 5 g Prot. SmartPoints value: 8

 Cook's Tip

If you don't have an ice-cream maker, you can freeze the buttermilk mixture in a shallow baking pan until solid, about 4 hours. Let stand at room temperature to slightly soften, then break it into chunks and pulse in food processor until smooth.

CHAPTER 3
THEME NIGHT
Fun Times with Great Friends

Sharing good times with friends is one of life's special pleasures. Filling your home with laughter and delicious food makes it even better. Creating a theme-inspired meal is an easy way to guarantee fun for everyone. Here you'll find eight great themes chosen especially with you in mind. Since we know what matters most is having a good time—not spending countless hours in the kitchen—our easy-to-prepare recipes are a joy to make. To get started, mix and match the recipes within any section to create your menu.

ITALIAN NIGHT!
Starters, Mains, Sides, and Desserts from the "Boot"

ASIAN FUSION
Light and Luscious Apps, Mains, Sides, and Desserts

MEXICAN FIESTA TIME
South-of-the-Border Drinks, Apps, Mains, and Sweets

GO GREEK!
Apps, Mains, Sides, and Dessert from the Greek Isles

ROSEMARY AND POTATO FLATBREAD

SERVES 10
Vegetarian

2½ pounds Yukon Gold potatoes, peeled

4 cups water

1 teaspoon table salt

1 pound refrigerated whole wheat pizza dough, at room temperature

½ cup chopped red onion

1 tablespoon + 1 teaspoon chopped fresh rosemary

2¾ teaspoons extra-virgin olive oil

¼ teaspoon black pepper

2 cups very thinly sliced white or cremini mushrooms

½ teaspoon coarse sea salt or kosher salt

1. With vegetable slicer or sharp knife, cut potatoes into ¹⁄₁₆-inch slices. Stir together water and fine salt in large bowl until salt is dissolved. Add potatoes and let stand 15 minutes. Drain. Pat potatoes dry with paper towels. Rinse bowl and wipe dry; return potatoes to bowl.

2. Preheat oven to 475°F.

3. On lightly floured work surface with lightly floured rolling pin, roll dough into 12-inch round; transfer to 14½-inch pizza pan and gently stretch dough to fit pan.

4. Add onion, 1 tablespoon of rosemary, 2 teaspoons of oil, and the pepper to potatoes. Toss until mixed well and potatoes are coated evenly. Arrange potatoes in concentric circles over dough, overlapping them. Scatter mushrooms over potatoes, leaving border of potatoes exposed around edge.

5. Bake until potatoes are tender and golden and crust is browned along edge, about 20 minutes. Drizzle with remaining ¾ teaspoon oil and sprinkle with remaining 1 teaspoon rosemary and the coarse salt. Cut into 10 pieces.

Per serving (1 piece): 193 Cal, 3 g Total Fat, 0 g Sat Fat, 566 mg Sod, 38 g Total Carb, 3 g Sugar, 5 g Fib, 6 g Prot. SmartPoints value: 6

 Cook's Tip

If the pizza dough springs back when you try to stretch it, cover it with a clean kitchen towel and let it rest for about 10 minutes. This will give the gluten in the dough time to relax, making it easy to stretch.

ROSEMARY AND
POTATO FLATBREAD

CELERY-PARMESAN SALAD WITH LEMON-ANCHOVY DRESSING

SERVES 4
20 Minutes or Less,
Gluten Free

4   cups very thin diagonally
    sliced celery

1   red apple, unpeeled and cut into
    ¼-inch matchstick strips

⅓   cup firmly packed fresh flat-leaf
    parsley leaves

2   tablespoons chopped fresh chives

    Grated zest and juice of 1 lemon

1   tablespoon extra-virgin olive oil

2   teaspoons Dijon mustard

¾   teaspoon salt

½   teaspoon anchovy paste

¼   teaspoon black pepper

⅓   cup Parmesan cheese shavings

1. Combine celery, apple, parsley, and chives in large bowl.

2. To make dressing, whisk together lemon zest and juice, oil, mustard, salt, anchovy paste, and pepper in small bowl.

3. Pour dressing over celery-apple mixture and toss until coated evenly. Divide salad evenly among 4 plates and top evenly with Parmesan shavings.

Per serving (about 1¼ cups): 118 Cal, 7 g Total Fat, 2 g Sat Fat, 787 mg Sod, 11 g Total Carb, 7 g Sugar, 3 g Fib, 5 g Prot. SmartPoints value: 3

 Cook's Tip

Loaded with flavor and crunch, this salad is sure to become part of your recipe repertoire. Don't hesitate to add the anchovy paste. You can't taste it, but the anchovy adds complexity to the overall flavor. Anchovy paste is sold in small tubes, usually in the same aisle as canned tomato products.

SUPER-EASY SPAGHETTI AND MEATBALLS

SERVES 6

1 pound ground lean beef (7% fat or less)

¼ cup plain dried bread crumbs

¼ cup grated Parmesan cheese

1 large egg

1½ teaspoons dried Italian seasoning

1½ teaspoons kosher salt

12 ounces whole wheat spaghetti

1 (24-ounce) jar fat-free tomato sauce

¼ cup chopped fresh basil

1. Preheat oven to 350°F. Line large rimmed baking sheet with parchment paper.

2. Mix together beef, bread crumbs, Parmesan, egg, Italian seasoning, and salt in large bowl until blended well but not overmixed. With damp hands, shape into 30 (1¼-inch) meatballs and place on prepared baking sheet. Bake, shaking baking sheet every 5 minutes for even browning, until cooked through, about 15 minutes. Keep warm.

3. Meanwhile, cook spaghetti according to package directions. Drain and keep warm.

4. Heat tomato sauce in large pot over medium-low heat. Add meatballs and spaghetti; toss until coated evenly with sauce. Transfer to serving bowl and sprinkle with basil.

Per serving (5 meatballs and 1 cup spaghetti with sauce): 401 Cal, 7 g Total Fat, 3 g Sat Fat, 870 mg Sod, 56 g Total Carb, 5 g Sugar, 7 g Fib, 30 g Prot. SmartPoints value: 11

 Cook's Tip

The best Italian cooks know that Parmesan cheese is the secret to the best-tasting meatballs. Now you know it too.

LEMONY PORK PICCATA

SERVES 4
20 Minutes or Less

2   tablespoons all-purpose flour

1¼ teaspoons kosher salt

¼   teaspoon black pepper

4   (¼-pound) lean boneless pork loin chops, trimmed and pounded to scant ¼-inch thickness

3   teaspoons unsalted butter

2   teaspoons olive oil

½   cup chicken broth

¼   cup minced shallots (about 2 large)

2   tablespoons lemon juice

1   tablespoon capers, chopped

1   garlic clove, minced

2   tablespoons chopped fresh flat-leaf parsley

1   tablespoon grated Parmesan cheese

1   teaspoon grated lemon zest

1. **Mix together flour, 1 teaspoon of salt, and the pepper in large shallow bowl. Coat pork with seasoned flour, shaking off excess.**

2. **Heat 2 teaspoons of butter and the oil in large heavy nonstick skillet over medium-high heat. Add pork and cook until browned and cooked through, about 3 minutes per side. Transfer to plate and keep warm.**

3. **Add broth, shallots, lemon juice, capers, and garlic to skillet. Bring to boil over high heat, scraping up browned bits from bottom of skillet. Reduce heat to medium and cook, stirring occasionally, until sauce is slightly thickened, about 4 minutes. Season with remaining ¼ teaspoon salt and whisk in remaining 1 teaspoon butter until melted and sauce is smooth.**

4. **Return pork to skillet, turning to coat with sauce until heated through. Place pork on 4 plates and spoon sauce evenly over. Stir together parsley, Parmesan, and lemon zest in cup; sprinkle over pork.**

Per serving (1 piece pork and about 2 tablespoons sauce): 257 Cal, 13 g Total Fat, 5 g Sat Fat, 837 mg Sod, 6 g Total Carb, 0 g Sugar, 0 g Fib, 27 g Prot. SmartPoints value: 6

 Cook's Tip

This recipe, a riff on the classic veal piccata, is a mainstay in Italian cuisine. Quick, easy, and piquant, piccata is great for company, as it cooks in just minutes. Serve it over angel hair pasta to capture all the sauce, if you like. A cup of cooked angel hair pasta per serving will up the SmartPoints value by 5.

SPINACH WITH PARMESAN BREAD CRUMBS

SERVES 4
20 Minutes or Less,
Vegetarian

1½ teaspoons olive oil

½ cup coarse fresh bread crumbs
   (from firm-textured bread)

1 tablespoon grated
   Parmesan cheese

1 small garlic clove, minced

1½ pounds regular spinach,
   stemmed and torn, or baby
   spinach, rinsed under cold
   water and spun dry

½ teaspoon salt

1. Heat 1 teaspoon of oil in large nonstick skillet over medium heat; add bread crumbs and cook, stirring, until golden, about 3 minutes. Remove skillet from heat; stir in Parmesan. Transfer to small bowl; set aside.

2. Add ¼ teaspoon oil to skillet. Add garlic and cook, stirring, until fragrant, about 30 seconds. Add half of spinach, in batches, tossing and adding more spinach as each batch wilts. Continue cooking and tossing, until spinach is tender, about 3 minutes. Transfer spinach to bowl. Repeat with remaining ¼ teaspoon oil and spinach.

3. Return spinach to skillet and sprinkle with salt. Cook, stirring over low heat, until spinach is heated through. Transfer to serving bowl and sprinkle with seasoned crumbs.

Per serving (about ¾ cup): 77 Cal, 3 g Total Fat, 1 g Sat Fat, 487 mg Sod, 9 g Total Carb, 1 g Sugar, 4 g Fib, 6 g Prot. SmartPoints value: 1

Cook's Tip

Here's a quick and easy way to make coarse bread crumbs: Grate the bread on the large holes of a box grater.

FETTUCCINE WITH CHICKEN SAUSAGE AND ARTICHOKES

SERVES 6

1   (12-ounce) package whole wheat fettuccine

1   teaspoon olive oil

¾ pound fully cooked chicken sausage, sliced

3   garlic cloves, minced

1   (24- to 26-ounce) jar marinara sauce

1   (14-ounce) can artichoke hearts (water packed), drained and quartered if large

⅛ teaspoon red pepper flakes

2   tablespoons thinly sliced fresh basil

1. Cook fettuccine according to package directions. Drain and keep warm.

2. Meanwhile, to make sauce, heat oil in large skillet over medium-high heat. Add sausage and cook, stirring frequently, until browned, about 5 minutes. Add garlic and cook, stirring, until fragrant, about 30 seconds. Add marinara sauce, artichokes, and pepper flakes; bring to boil. Reduce heat and simmer until flavors are blended, about 10 minutes longer.

3. Divide pasta evenly among 6 large shallow bowls. Top evenly with sausage mixture and sprinkle with basil.

Per serving (1 cup fettuccine and 1 cup sausage with sauce): 356 Cal, 7 g Total Fat, 1 g Sat Fat, 1,081 mg Sod, 57 g Total Carb, 8 g Sugar, 10 g Fib, 20 g Prot. SmartPoints value: 10

Cook's Tip

Pump up the veggies by adding a thinly sliced green or yellow bell pepper along with the garlic in step 2.

STUFFED WHOLE ARTICHOKES

SERVES 4
Vegetarian

4   artichokes

½   lemon

1   light English muffin, split
     and toasted

½   cup grated Parmesan cheese

2   tablespoons pine nuts,
     coarsely chopped

1   tablespoon dried currants or
     chopped raisins

1   large garlic clove, minced

2   teaspoons extra-virgin olive oil

¼   teaspoon salt

¼   teaspoon black pepper

½   cup vegetable broth or water

1. Working with one artichoke at a time, bend back and snap off dark green leaves from around base of artichoke. With kitchen scissors, trim thorny tops from remaining leaves, rubbing cut surfaces with cut side of lemon to prevent browning. Lay artichoke on its side and cut off stem level with base of artichoke. Slice 1 inch off top of artichoke and discard. With small knife, peel tough skin from stem. Rub with lemon and reserve.

2. Stand artichokes on wire rack in large pot over simmering water. Scatter stems around artichokes. Cover and steam until small knife inserted into bottom of artichoke goes in easily, about 30 minutes. Lift out artichokes and stems and let cool on cutting board.

3. Preheat oven to 425°F. Spray 7 x 11-inch baking dish with olive oil nonstick spray.

4. When cool enough to handle, with small spoon, scoop out and discard fuzzy choke and any violet-tipped leaves from artichokes (do not cut into base).

5. Tear English muffin into pieces and put in food processor. Pulse until crumbs form; transfer to small bowl. Put stems in food processor and pulse until finely chopped; add to crumbs along with Parmesan, pine nuts, currants, garlic, oil, salt, and pepper, stirring to combine. Spoon bread mixture into cavity and between leaves of artichokes; lightly spray with nonstick spray. Stand artichokes in prepared baking dish and pour broth into dish around artichokes. Bake until heated through and filling is golden, about 20 minutes.

Per serving (1 stuffed artichoke): 193 Cal, 8 g Total Fat, 3 g Sat Fat, 630 mg Sod, 23 g Total Carb, 3 g Sugar, 9 g Fib, 11 g Prot. SmartPoints value: 4

STUFFED WHOLE
ARTICHOKES

SAUTÉED ARUGULA AND TOMATOES WITH CHEESE AND PINE NUTS

SERVES 6
20 Minutes or Less,
Gluten Free, Vegetarian

¼   cup pine nuts

2   teaspoons olive oil

2   pints grape tomatoes

1   large garlic clove, minced

2   (5-ounce) containers baby arugula

⅛   teaspoon salt

⅛   teaspoon black pepper

½   cup crumbled soft goat cheese (about 2 ounces)

1. Cook pine nuts in large, heavy nonstick skillet over medium heat, tossing occasionally, until golden, about 2 minutes. Transfer to cup and set aside.

2. Heat oil in large skillet over medium-high heat. Add tomatoes and cook, tossing occasionally, until skins are lightly charred and begin to split, about 5 minutes, gently pressing down on tomatoes with back of spoon once or twice. Add garlic and cook, stirring, until fragrant, about 30 seconds longer.

3. Add arugula to tomato mixture; cook, stirring, just until wilted, about 1 minute. Sprinkle with salt and pepper and stir to mix well. Spoon arugula-tomato mixture into serving bowl; sprinkle with goat cheese and pine nuts.

Per serving (about ⅔ cup): 102 Cal, 7 g Total Fat, 2 g Sat Fat, 100 mg Sod, 7 g Total Carb, 4 g Sugar, 2 g Fib, 5 g Prot. SmartPoints value: 3

LEMON BARS

SERVES 24
Vegetarian

1⅓ cups all-purpose flour

5 tablespoons light brown sugar

½ cup (1 stick) cold butter, cut into pieces

4 large eggs

1½ cups confectioners' sugar

2 teaspoons grated lemon zest

½ teaspoon vanilla extract

¾ cup lemon juice (about 3 large lemons)

1. Preheat oven to 350°F.

2. To make crust, combine flour and brown sugar in food processor; pulse until combined well. Scatter cold butter on top of flour mixture; pulse until butter is size of baby peas and mixture resembles coarse crumbs. Transfer crumb mixture to 9 x 13-inch baking pan; with spatula, press down firmly to form crust. Bake until golden, about 20 minutes.

3. Meanwhile, to make lemon filling, with electric mixer on medium-high speed, beat eggs in medium bowl until blended well. Reduce mixer speed to medium. Beat in ¾ cup of confectioners' sugar, the lemon zest, and vanilla. Beat in lemon juice and remaining ¾ cup confectioners' sugar until blended well.

4. As soon as crust is baked, remove from oven and reduce oven temperature to 300°F. Immediately pour lemon mixture over hot crust. Bake until filling is set, about 30 minutes. Let cool completely in pan on wire rack. Cut lengthwise into 3 strips, then cut each strip crosswise into 8 bars, making total of 24 bars.

Per serving (1 bar): 114 Cal, 5 g Total Fat, 3 g Sat Fat, 45 mg Sod, 16 g Total Carb, 10 g Sugar, 0 g Fib, 2 g Prot. SmartPoints value: 5

 Cook's Tip

The crust *must* be hot when you pour on the lemon mixture.

CHOCOLATE CHIP BISCOTTI

MAKES 20
Vegetarian

2 cups all-purpose flour

1 teaspoon baking powder

½ teaspoon salt

3 tablespoons mini semisweet chocolate chips

1 cup sugar

2 large eggs

1 teaspoon canola oil

1 teaspoon vanilla extract

1. Preheat oven to 325°F. Lightly spray large baking sheet with nonstick spray.

2. Whisk together flour, baking powder, and salt in medium bowl; stir in chocolate chips.

3. With electric mixer on medium-high speed, beat sugar, eggs, oil, and vanilla until frothy, about 2 minutes. Make well in center of flour mixture and pour in egg mixture; stir just until it comes together and forms dough.

4. Shape dough into 3 x 13-inch log on prepared baking sheet. Bake 30 minutes. With two spatulas, transfer log to wire rack and let cool 10 minutes.

5. Meanwhile, reduce oven temperature to 300°F.

6. With serrated bread knife, cut log on slight diagonal into ½-inch slices, making total of 20 biscotti. Stand slices, about 1 inch apart, on baking sheet; bake 12 minutes. Transfer to rack and let cool completely.

Per serving (1 biscotti): 102 Cal, 1 g Total Fat, 0 g Sat Fat, 89 mg Sod, 21 g Total Carb, 11 g Sugar, 0 g Fib, 2 g Prot. SmartPoints value: 4

 Cook's Tip

Biscotti are beloved Italian cookies that have been embraced here as the go-to dunker for espresso and cappuccino. Our delicious chocolate chip–laden version will be soft when baked but hardens as it cools.

CHOCOLATE CHIP BISCOTTI

ASIAN BEEF AND SCALLION BITES

SERVES 8

3 tablespoons reduced-sodium soy sauce

1 teaspoon honey

1 small garlic clove, minced

1 teaspoon grated peeled fresh ginger

¾ pound lean sirloin steak, trimmed and cut into 24 chunks

2 teaspoons canola oil

8 scallions (white and light green parts only), each cut into 3 pieces

1. Stir together soy sauce, honey, garlic, and ginger in cup. Put all but 1 tablespoon of soy-sauce mixture in large zip-close plastic bag and add beef; refrigerate remaining marinade. Squeeze out air and seal bag; turn to coat beef. Refrigerate at least 6 hours or up to 1 day.

2. Heat oil in medium heavy nonstick skillet over medium heat. Add scallions and increase heat to medium-high; cook, tossing gently, until light golden in spots, but still bright green, about 3 minutes. Transfer scallions to plate; drizzle with reserved marinade and set aside.

3. Spray skillet with nonstick spray and add beef; discard marinade. Cook over medium-high heat, turning beef occasionally, until lightly browned and cooked through, about 4 minutes.

4. Thread 1 piece of beef and 1 piece of scallion on each of 24 toothpicks or small bamboo picks. Serve warm.

Per serving (3 skewers): 76 Cal, 3 g Total Fat, 1 g Sat Fat, 227 mg Sod, 2 g Total Carb, 1 g Sugar, 0 g Fib, 10 g Prot. SmartPoints value: 2

EDAMAME HUMMUS

SERVES 10
20 Minutes or Less,
Vegetarian

3   cups frozen shelled edamame

4   scallions, thinly sliced

1   garlic clove, quartered

¼   cup reduced-sodium soy sauce

¼   cup rice vinegar

2   tablespoons mirin or dry sherry

1   tablespoon tahini

1   teaspoon wasabi powder

1   tablespoon Asian (dark) sesame oil

½   teaspoon salt

1. Cook edamame according to package directions. Drain in colander and rinse under cold water to stop cooking. Drain again.

2. Combine edamame, scallions, garlic, soy sauce, vinegar, mirin, tahini, wasabi powder, sesame oil, and salt in food processor; pulse until smooth. Scrape hummus into serving bowl. Serve or cover and refrigerate up to 4 days; bring to room temperature for best flavor.

Per serving (¼ cup): 99 Cal, 5 g Total Fat, 1 g Sat Fat, 334 mg Sod, 7 g Total Carb, 2 g Sugar, 2 g Fib, 6 g Prot. SmartPoints value: 3

 Cook's Tip

Serve the hummus spooned into halved sweet baby peppers or with fresh vegetable dippers or baked tortilla chips. Eight baked tortilla chips per serving will up the SmartPoints value by 2.

VEGETABLE DUMPLINGS
WITH SOY DIPPING SAUCE

VEGETABLE DUMPLINGS WITH SOY DIPPING SAUCE

SERVES 6
Vegetarian

2   teaspoons olive oil

1½ cups firmly packed shredded green cabbage or coleslaw mix

½   cup shredded carrot

2   scallions, finely chopped

2   garlic cloves, minced

¼   cup + 2 teaspoons reduced-sodium soy sauce

24   wonton wrappers (half of 12-ounce package)

1   teaspoon Asian (dark) sesame oil

1. Preheat oven to 350°F. Spray large baking sheet with nonstick spray.

2. Heat olive oil in large skillet over medium-high heat. Add cabbage, carrot, half of scallions, and the garlic; cook, stirring, until cabbage is wilted, about 2 minutes. Remove skillet from heat and stir in 2 teaspoons of soy sauce.

3. Lay wonton wrappers on work surface. Place 1 teaspoon cabbage mixture in center of each wrapper. With wet finger, moisten edges of wrappers, one at a time. Fold one corner over to meet opposite corner forming triangle; firmly press edges together to make tight seal. Repeat, transferring dumplings to prepared baking sheet; spray with nonstick spray.

4. Bake until dumplings are golden brown, about 15 minutes.

5. Meanwhile, stir together remaining ¼ cup soy sauce, remaining scallions and the sesame oil in serving bowl. Serve with dumplings.

Per serving (4 dumplings and 1 tablespoon sauce): 132 Cal, 3 g Total Fat, 0 g Sat Fat, 610 mg Sod, 23 g Total Carb, 2 g Sugar, 2 g Fib, 4 g Prot. SmartPoints value: 3

GRILLED HOISIN-GINGER FLANK STEAK

SERVES 4

¼ cup hoisin sauce

1 tablespoon white wine vinegar

1 tablespoon grated peeled
 fresh ginger

1 shallot, finely chopped

2 garlic cloves, minced

1½ teaspoons grated orange zest

1 pound lean flank steak, trimmed

¼ teaspoon kosher salt

1. Combine hoisin sauce, vinegar, ginger, shallot, garlic, and orange zest in large zip-close plastic bag; add steak. Squeeze out air and seal bag; turn to coat steak. Refrigerate, turning bag occasionally, at least 2 hours or up to 2 days.

2. Spray grill rack with nonstick spray. Preheat grill to medium or prepare medium fire.

3. Remove steak from marinade; discard marinade. Pat steak dry with paper towels. Place steak on grill rack and grill until instant-read thermometer inserted into side of steak registers 145°F, about 5 minutes per side. Transfer steak to cutting board and let stand 10 minutes. Cut against grain into 12 slices. Serve sprinkled with salt.

Per serving (3 slices steak): 206 Cal, 7 g Total Fat, 2 g Sat Fat, 441 mg Sod, 9 g Total Carb, 4 g Sugar, 0 g Fib, 25 g Prot. SmartPoints value: 5

 Cook's Tip

While the steak rests, cut ¾ pound small zucchini lengthwise in half; sprinkle with salt and pepper and spray on both sides with olive oil nonstick spray. Place on the grill rack and grill, turning once, until tender, 6 to 8 minutes.

SPICY CHICKEN-ASPARAGUS STIR-FRY

SERVES 4

3   teaspoons canola oil

1   pound skinless boneless chicken breasts, cut into strips

¼   teaspoon salt

1   tablespoon grated peeled fresh ginger

2   garlic cloves, minced

½   pound asparagus, trimmed and cut into 2-inch lengths

1½ cups matchstick-cut carrots

1   small red bell pepper, cut into thin strips

1   small yellow bell pepper, cut into thin strips

2   tablespoons water

3   tablespoons black bean sauce

1   tablespoon reduced-sodium soy sauce

1½ teaspoons hot chili oil

2   teaspoons toasted sesame seeds

1. Heat wok or large deep skillet over medium-high heat until drop of water sizzles in it. Add 1½ teaspoons of canola oil and swirl to coat pan. Sprinkle chicken with salt; add to wok and stir-fry until lightly browned and cooked through, about 5 minutes. Transfer to plate.

2. Add remaining 1½ teaspoons canola oil to wok and swirl to coat pan. Add ginger and garlic; stir-fry until fragrant, about 30 seconds. Add asparagus, carrots, bell peppers, and water; cook, covered, until vegetables are crisp-tender, 4–5 minutes.

3. Return chicken to wok along with black bean sauce, soy sauce, and chili oil. Stir-fry until chicken is heated through, about 2 minutes. Sprinkle with sesame seeds.

Per serving (about 1⅔ cups): 250 Cal, 10 g Total Fat, 2 g Sat Fat, 712 mg Sod, 12 g Total Carb, 5 g Sugar, 4 g Fib, 28 g Prot. SmartPoints value: 4

 Cook's Tip

Brown rice is a natural for serving with this easy stir-fry. One-half cup of cooked brown rice per serving will up the SmartPoints value by 3.

FABULOUS FINGER FOODS PERFECT FOR ANY PARTY

Treating your guests (and yourself!) to delicious appetizers or hors d'oeuvres can be one of the highlights of entertaining. And putting tasty, healthful dishes together doesn't have to be difficult. You'll find many great finger-food recipes right here in this chapter, but we can't help ourselves: We love appetizers, and we want to give you more healthy options to delight your friends and family. So we've also included a list of terrific ideas you'll find elsewhere in this book, plus a dozen more tasty suggestions that are almost too easy for a recipe. Cheers!

Salmon with Tzatziki

SERVES 12

Top **12 butter crackers** with **¼ cup prepared tzatziki-style yogurt dip**. Cut **6 (½-ounce) slices smoked salmon** in half; fold each piece in half and place on cracker. Sprinkle evenly with **1 tablespoon chopped fresh chives**.

Per serving (1 garnished cracker) SmartPoints value: 1

Shrimp with Spicy Coconut-Mango Dip

SERVES 12

Pulse **1 cup prepared mango salsa**, **¼ cup sweetened coconut flakes**, and **¼ teaspoon red pepper flakes** in food processor until finely chopped; transfer to serving dish. Serve with **24 peeled and cooked extra-large shrimp (about 1 pound)**.

Per serving (2 shrimp and 4 teaspoons dip) SmartPoints value: 2

Fresh Figs with Boursin

SERVES 24

Halve **12 fresh figs** through stem end. Place **1 teaspoon room temperature light Boursin cheese** on top of each fig half. Drizzle each with **few drops aged balsamic vinegar**.

Per serving (1 stuffed fig half) SmartPoints value: 1

Mussels Vinaigrette

SERVES 24

Bring **¾ cup dry white wine** to boil in large pot over high heat. Add **24 scrubbed and debearded mussels**; cook, covered, just until mussels open. Discard any mussels that do not open. Remove and discard top half of mussel shells. Drizzle **½ cup low-fat Italian vinaigrette** over mussels; sprinkle with **¼ cup minced red bell pepper**. Refrigerate until chilled.

Per serving (1 garnished mussel) SmartPoints value: 1

Gazpacho and Egg Shooters

SERVES 14

Pulse **1 (14½-ounce) can petite-diced tomatoes**, **1 cup tomato juice**, **½ chopped English (seedless) cucumber**, **½ seeded and chopped jalapeño**, **1½ tablespoons chopped red onion**, **1½ teaspoons red wine vinegar**, and **⅛ teaspoon salt** in food processor until well chopped. Chill. Divide evenly among 14 (2-ounce) glasses. Sprinkle with **1 finely chopped hard-cooked large egg** and **1 tablespoon finely chopped fresh parsley**.

Per serving (1 shooter) SmartPoints value: 1

Endive with Chipotle Cream Cheese

SERVES 8

Stir together **¼ cup softened fat-free cream cheese**, **¼ cup finely diced water-packed roasted red pepper**, **3 tablespoons thinly sliced scallion**, **3 tablespoons chopped fresh cilantro**, **2 teaspoons canned chipotle sauce**, **¼ teaspoon cumin**, and **¼ teaspoon salt** in small bowl until mixed well. Spoon about 1 teaspoon cheese mixture on wide end of each of **24 Belgian endive leaves**. Garnish with **fresh cilantro leaves** and arrange on platter.

Per serving (3 stuffed endive leaves) SmartPoints value: 0

Herbed Parmesan Crisps

SERVES 12

Line two baking sheets with parchment paper. Drop **1½ cups grated Parmesan cheese** by scant tablespoonfuls, 2 inches apart, onto prepared baking sheets. Flatten mounds; sprinkle evenly with **2 tablespoons finely chopped fresh chives, 2 tablespoons minced fresh parsley,** and **½ teaspoon black pepper.** Bake at 425°F until crisp and golden, 5–6 minutes. Let cool on baking sheets.

Per serving (2 crisps) SmartPoints value: 2

Honey-and-Cheese-Stuffed Figs

SERVES 8

Arrange **16 halved fresh figs,** cut side up, on platter. Stir together **6 tablespoons part-skim ricotta cheese, 2 tablespoons soft goat cheese,** and **2 tablespoons fresh thyme leaves** in small bowl until mixed well. Spoon about ¾ teaspoon cheese mixture on each fig half. Drizzle evenly with **2 tablespoons honey** and sprinkle with **½ teaspoon black pepper.**

Per serving (4 stuffed fig halves) SmartPoints value: 2

Beet Hummus on Cucumber Rounds

SERVES 24

Pulse **1 cooked small beet** in food processor until chopped. Add **1 cup prepared hummus** and process until smooth. Place 1 tablespoon of beet mixture on each of **24 slices English (seedless) cucumber.** Just before serving, garnish with **24 small fresh dill sprigs.**

Per serving (1 garnished cucumber slice) SmartPoints value: 1

Mini Antipasto Sticks

SERVES 12

Wrap **12 (⅓-ounce) slices prosciutto** around **12 (1-ounce) sticks part-skim string cheese.**

Per serving (1 piece) SmartPoints value: 3

Pimiento Cocktail Toasts

SERVES 12

Place **12 slices cocktail rye bread** on broiler rack and broil until just toasted. Turn and toast on other side. Stir together **6 tablespoons whipped cream cheese, 3 tablespoons shredded reduced-fat Cheddar cheese, 3 tablespoons drained and chopped roasted red pepper (not oil packed),** and **⅛ teaspoon cayenne.** Spread evenly on toasts.

Per serving (1 garnished toast) SmartPoints value: 2

Ricotta and Tapenade Pita Crisps

SERVES 24

Cut each of **2 large whole wheat pitas** into 6 wedges; separate each wedge into 2 pieces at fold. Arrange on baking sheet and spray with nonstick spray. Broil, turning once, until crisp. Spread **¾ cup part-skim ricotta cheese** on pita wedges; top with **¼ cup tapenade.** Sprinkle with **6 chopped cherry tomatoes** and **2 tablespoons sliced fresh basil.**

Per serving (1 garnished pita wedge) SmartPoints value: 1

ELSEWHERE IN FAMILY MEALS

Beef and Blue Cheese Pickups, page 339

Bloody Mary Shrimp Cocktail, page 343

Cherry Tomatoes Stuffed with Blue Cheese and Bacon, page 348

Coconut Shrimp, page 164

Creamy Spinach-Parmesan Dip, page 104

Homemade Vegetable Pickles, page 132

Provençal Baked Mussels, page 344

Smoked Duck on Cranberry Corn Bread, page 340

MISO-GLAZED SALMON

SERVES 4

2 tablespoons white miso

1 tablespoon reduced-sodium soy sauce

1 tablespoon lime juice

1 tablespoon grated peeled fresh ginger

1 garlic clove, minced

Pinch cayenne

4 (5-ounce) skinless salmon fillets

3 scallions (white and light green parts only), thinly sliced on diagonal

1. Whisk together miso, soy sauce, lime juice, ginger, garlic, and cayenne in small bowl. Pour mixture into large zip-close plastic bag; add salmon. Squeeze out air and seal bag; turn to coat salmon. Refrigerate, turning bag occasionally, at least 20 minutes or up to 1 hour.

2. Preheat broiler. Line broiler pan with foil.

3. Remove salmon from marinade; reserve marinade. Place salmon on broiler rack and broil 5 inches from heat 5 minutes. Turn and brush with reserved marinade. Broil just until salmon is opaque in center, 3–4 minutes longer. Discard any remaining marinade. Sprinkle salmon with scallions.

Per serving (1 salmon fillet): 231 Cal, 9 g Total Fat, 2 g Sat Fat, 512 mg Sod, 5 g Total Carb, 1 g Sugar, 1 g Fib, 32 g Prot. SmartPoints value: 4

 Cook's Tip

If you have a choice between purchasing wild salmon and farm-raised salmon, opt for wild: It's lower in fat than farmed salmon, and it's recommended by Seafood Watch and the Environmental Defense Fund.

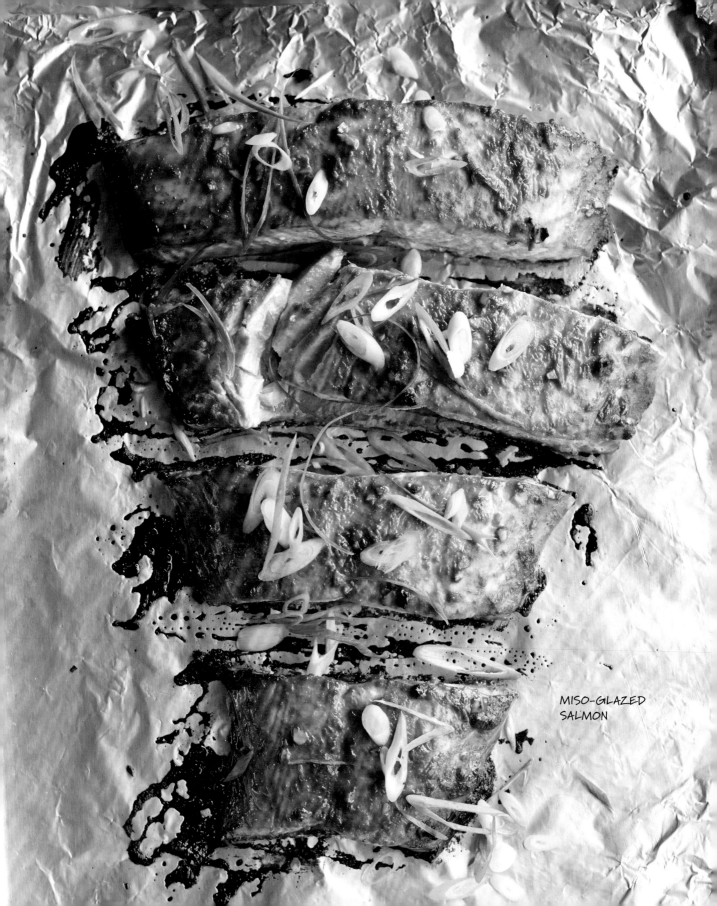

MISO-GLAZED
SALMON

SPICY SCALLION SALAD

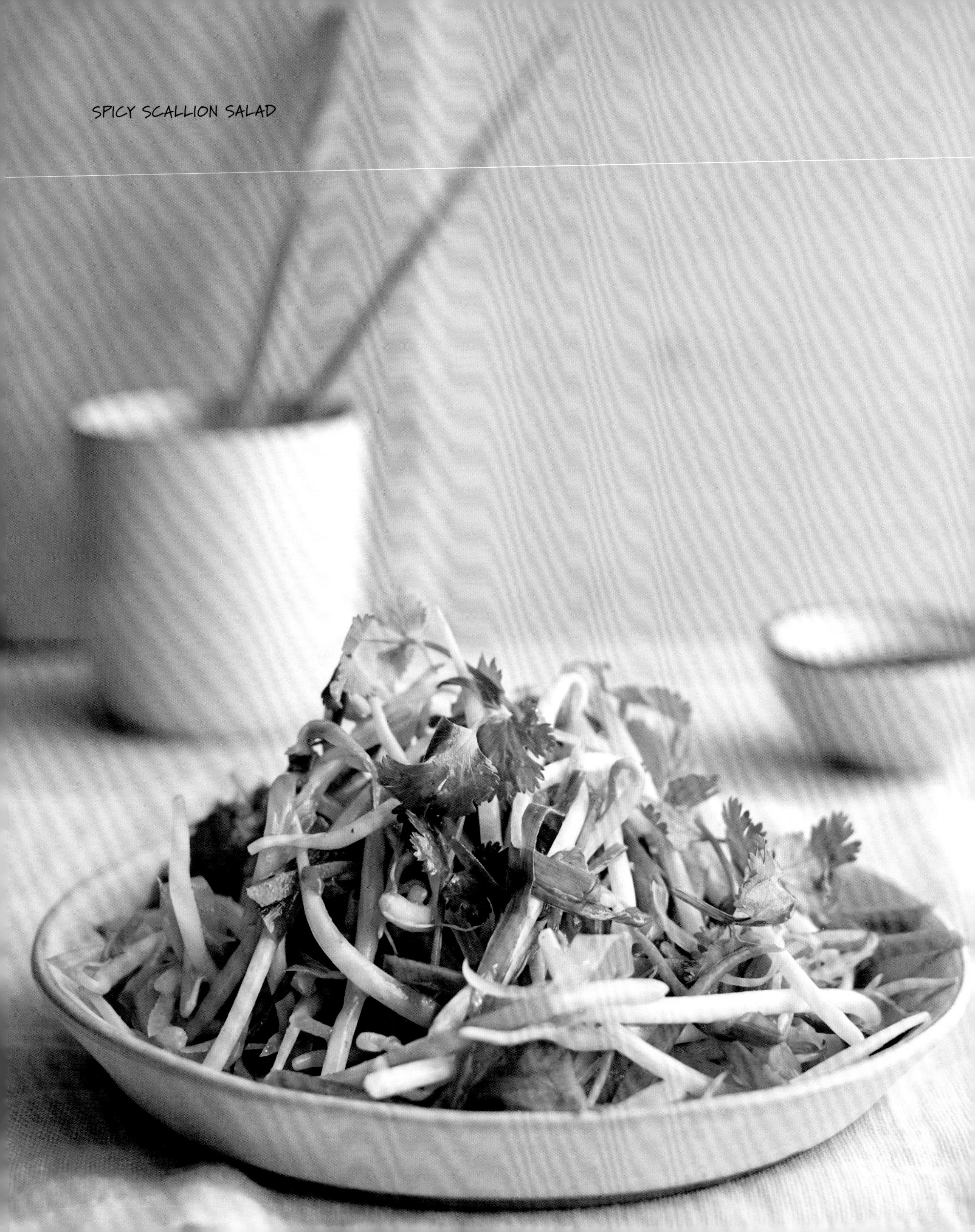

SPICY SCALLION SALAD

SERVES 6
20 Minutes or Less,
Gluten Free, Vegetarian

8 large scallions

1 (2-inch) piece ginger, unpeeled

2 tablespoons rice vinegar

1 tablespoon + ½ teaspoon Asian
   (dark) sesame oil

2 teaspoons honey

½ teaspoon red curry paste

½ teaspoon salt

4 cups lightly packed bean sprouts

2 cups lightly packed fresh cilantro
   leaves and trimmed tender stems

1 cup matchstick-cut carrots

1. Cut scallions crosswise in thirds, then slice lengthwise into thin strips. Have bowl of ice water ready.

2. Bring medium saucepan of water to boil. Add scallions to boiling water, then immediately drain in colander. Plunge scallions into ice water to stop cooking. Drain, then gently pat dry with paper towels. Set aside.

3. On small holes of box grater or with microplane grater, grate ginger into medium bowl. With your hands, squeeze ginger, allowing juice to fall into large bowl. Discard pulp.

4. To make dressing, add vinegar, sesame oil, honey, curry paste, and salt to ginger juice in bowl. Whisk until blended well. Add bean sprouts, cilantro, carrots, and scallions; toss until coated evenly.

Per serving (about 1½ cups): 74 Cal, 3 g Total Fat, 0 g Sat Fat, 227 mg Sod, 11 g Total Carb, 5 g Sugar, 3 g Fib, 3 g Prot. SmartPoints value: 1

Cook's Tip

Bean sprouts are also called mung bean sprouts. If you have the time, trim off the delicate threadlike ends.

BABY BOK CHOY WITH MISO-GINGER DRESSING

SERVES 4
Gluten Free, Vegetarian

⅓ cup water

1 tablespoon canola oil

3 large garlic cloves, thinly sliced

1 pound baby bok choy, halved lengthwise

¼ teaspoon salt

2½ tablespoons rice vinegar

2 tablespoons white miso

2 tablespoons mirin

2 teaspoons Asian (dark) sesame oil

2 teaspoons grated peeled fresh ginger

1. Combine water, canola oil, and garlic in large skillet; bring to simmer over low heat. Add bok choy and salt; cook, covered, until tender, 12–15 minutes. Drain well, leaving bok choy in skillet.

2. Meanwhile, to make dressing, whisk together vinegar, miso, mirin, sesame oil, and ginger in small bowl.

3. When bok choy is drained, add vinegar mixture and bring to simmer; cook, stirring, until syrupy, about 2 minutes. Serve hot, warm, or at room temperature.

Per serving (¾ cup): 91 Cal, 6 g Total Fat, 1 g Sat Fat, 572 mg Sod, 6 g Total Carb, 3 g Sugar, 2 g Fib, 3 g Prot. SmartPoints value: 3

 Cook's Tip

There are three types of miso: white, yellow, and red. White miso, also known as sweet miso, is fermented for the shortest amount of time, making it mild and delicate. It is best used for dressings, soups, and sauces. Yellow miso is fermented a bit longer, so its flavor is bolder and is mostly used in cooking. Red miso is fermented the longest and has a bold, assertive flavor. It is best suited for hearty dishes like braises and marinades.

GREEN TEA–HONEYDEW GRANITA

SERVES 6
Gluten Free, Vegetarian

⅔ cup water
5   green tea bags
½   cup sugar
6   cups ripe honeydew chunks
    Grated zest of 1 lime
3   tablespoons lime juice
6   fresh mint sprigs (optional)

1. Bring water to boil in small saucepan. Add tea bags; cover and steep 4 minutes. Remove tea bags, squeezing out as much liquid as possible. Stir in sugar until dissolved. Let cool completely.

2. Puree honeydew, in batches, in food processor; transfer to large bowl. Stir in tea and lime zest and juice.

3. Pour honeydew mixture into 8-inch square baking pan. Cover pan with foil and freeze until frozen along edges, about 1 hour. With fork, scrape ice along edges in towards center. Repeat every 30 minutes until granita is semifirm, about 2 hours.

4. To serve, use fork to scrape across surface of granita, transferring ice shards to 6 dessert dishes. Garnish with mint sprigs (if using).

Per serving (⅔ cup): 129 Cal, 0 g Total Fat, 0 g Sat Fat, 19 mg Sod, 34 g Total Carb, 28 g Sugar, 1 g Fib, 1 g Prot. SmartPoints value: 4

Cook's Tip

Make sure you use a very ripe melon for the most flavorful granita. When choosing honeydew, lightly press the stem end. When ripe, it will give very slightly and the melon will have a floral aroma. Honeydew continues to ripen after being picked, so leave it on the counter for a few days if it seems under ripe.

MANGO-BERRY SALAD WITH GINGER GLAZE

SERVES 6
20 Minutes or Less,
Gluten Free, Vegetarian

½   cup warm water

¼   cup apricot preserves

1   teaspoon ground ginger

3   cups diced ripe mango
     (about 2 mangoes)

2½ cups fresh blueberries

½   cup fresh raspberries

1. Stir together water, preserves, and ginger in small saucepan, mashing large pieces of apricot with fork; bring to boil. Boil, stirring occasionally, until mixture is syrupy, about 6 minutes. Remove saucepan from heat and let cool to room temperature.

2. Combine mango and blueberries in serving bowl; drizzle with apricot glaze and toss until coated evenly. Add raspberries and gently toss to combine.

Per serving (about 1 cup): 127 Cal, 1 g Total Fat, 0 g Sat Fat, 8 mg Sod, 33 g Total Carb, 25 g Sugar, 4 g Fib, 1 g Prot. SmartPoints value: 2

 Cook's Tip

Top each serving with a generous dollop of plain Greek yogurt. One-quarter cup of plain fat-free Greek yogurt per serving will up the SmartPoints value by 1.

FROZEN WATERMELON VIRGIN MOJITOS

SERVES 8
Gluten Free, Vegetarian

9   cups cubed seedless watermelon

2   cups diet lemon-lime soda

12 tablespoons lime juice
    (about 5 limes)

2   tablespoons rum extract

3   tablespoons chopped fresh mint

1. Puree watermelon, in batches, in blender (you need about 6 cups puree). Pour 2 cups of puree into each of 2 standard-size ice-cube trays (16 cubes each); freeze until solid, about 4 hours or up to overnight. Chill remaining 2 cups watermelon puree in refrigerator.

2. When ready to make mojitos, put one tray of watermelon cubes, 1 cup of chilled watermelon puree, 1 cup of soda, 6 tablespoons of lime juice, and 1 tablespoon of rum extract in blender; process until smooth.

3. Stir 1½ tablespoons of mint into mojito mixture; pour into 4 glasses. Repeat with remaining ingredients to make total of 8 mojitos.

Per serving (1 cup): 68 Cal, 1 g Total Fat, 0 g Sat Fat, 8 mg Sod, 15 g Total Carb, 12 g Sugar, 1 g Fib, 1 g Prot. SmartPoints value: 3

 Cook's Tip

You'll need about 7½ pounds of watermelon to get 9 cups of cubes.

WINTER-SPICED POMEGRANATE
AND CLEMENTINE SANGRIA

WINTER-SPICED POMEGRANATE AND CLEMENTINE SANGRIA

SERVES 8
Gluten Free, Vegetarian

1 (750-ml) bottle dry red wine, such as Grenache

1 cup reduced-calorie cranberry-juice cocktail

1 cup pure pomegranate juice

¼ cup orange liqueur, such as Grand Marnier or Cointreau

2 clementines, halved and thinly sliced into half-rounds

1 lemon, thinly sliced

4 (3-inch) cinnamon sticks

5 star anises

1 cup diet lemon-lime soda

½ cup pomegranate seeds

1. Combine wine, cranberry juice, pomegranate juice, orange liqueur, clementines, lemon, cinnamon sticks, and star anise in large pitcher.

2. Refrigerate at least several hours or up to overnight to allow flavors to blend.

3. When ready to serve, discard cinnamon sticks and star anises, and pour in soda. Fill 8 wineglasses or other glasses with ice and top with sangria. Sprinkle with pomegranate seeds.

Per serving (½ cup): 155 Cal, 0 g Total Fat, 0 g Sat Fat, 11 mg Sod, 19 g Total Carb, 13 g Sugar, 2 g Fib, 1 g Prot. SmartPoints value: 6

 Cook's Tip

Let guests top off their sangria with a splash of seltzer, which will lighten the drinks and give them extra fizz. Pomegranate seeds are sold in small plastic containers in supermarkets and specialty food stores.

CITRUS PUNCH

SERVES 8
20 Minutes or Less,
Gluten Free, Vegetarian

32 ounces diet ginger ale

2 cups grapefruit juice

2 cups mango nectar

3 tablespoons frozen orange juice concentrate, thawed

½ cup white rum

1 tablespoon lime juice, or to taste

1 small seedless orange, thinly sliced

Combine ginger ale, grapefruit juice, mango nectar, orange juice concentrate, rum, and lime juice in large pitcher. Add orange slices. Fill glasses with ice and add punch.

Per serving (1 cup): 107 Cal, 0 g Total Fat, 0 g Sat Fat, 10 mg Sod, 18 g Total Carb, 16 g Sugar, 1 g Fib, 1 g Prot. SmartPoints value: 5

 Cook's Tip

For a more festive approach, fill a punch bowl with a decorative ice ring and add the punch and orange slices.

BLUE CORN NACHOS

SERVES 6
Gluten Free, Vegetarian

36 baked blue corn tortilla chips

1 (15½-ounce) can pinto beans, rinsed and drained

2 plum tomatoes, chopped

2 scallions, thinly sliced

1 jalapeño pepper, seeded and minced

1 cup shredded reduced-fat Monterey Jack cheese

¼ cup chopped fresh cilantro

½ lime

1. Preheat oven to 400°F. Spray 9 x 13-inch baking dish or 11-inch deep-dish pizza pan with nonstick spray.

2. Arrange 24 tortilla chips in single layer in prepared pizza pan. Top evenly with beans, tomatoes, scallions, and jalapeño.

3. Crush remaining 12 tortilla chips and sprinkle on top; sprinkle evenly with Monterey Jack. Bake until heated through and cheese is melted, about 20 minutes. Sprinkle with cilantro and squeeze lime juice over.

Per serving (⅙ of nachos): 199 Cal, 6 g Total Fat, 3 g Sat Fat, 387 mg Sod, 27 g Total Carb, 2 g Sugar, 6 g Fib, 11 g Prot. SmartPoints value: 6

BLUE CORN NACHOS

GRILLED STUFFED JALAPEÑOS

SERVES 12
Gluten Free, Vegetarian

12 large jalapeño peppers

½ cup light cream cheese
(Neufchâtel), softened

6 tablespoons reduced-fat
shredded Cheddar or Cheddar
Jack cheese

2 tablespoons sliced scallion

2 tablespoons chopped fresh
cilantro

¼ teaspoon minced garlic

¼ teaspoon smoked paprika
+ additional for sprinkling

¼ teaspoon salt

1. Spray grill rack with nonstick spray. Preheat grill to medium-high or prepare medium-high fire.

2. Cut jalapeños lengthwise in half, leaving stems intact; cut thin slice from bottom of each pepper half so it can stand securely. With grapefruit spoon or melon baller, scoop out seeds. Set peppers aside.

3. Stir together cream cheese, 3 tablespoons of Cheddar, the scallion, cilantro, garlic, ¼ teaspoon of paprika, and the salt in small bowl until blended.

4. Fill each pepper half with about 2 teaspoons of cheese mixture; sprinkle evenly with remaining 3 tablespoons Cheddar. Lightly sprinkle with paprika.

5. Reduce grill heat to medium; place peppers on grill rack and grill, covered, until tender, lightly charred on bottom, and cheese is melted, about 8 minutes. Let cool slightly before serving.

Per serving (2 stuffed pepper halves): 42 Cal, 2 g Total Fat, 2 g Sat Fat, 110 mg Sod, 3 g Total Carb, 2 g Sugar, 1 g Fib, 2 g Prot. SmartPoints value: 1

Cook's Tip

The peppers can be stuffed up to 1 day ahead; refrigerate, covered, until ready to grill.

CHICKEN FAJITAS

SERVES 4

Juice of 2 limes

1 large garlic clove, crushed with side of large knife

1 teaspoon chili powder

¼ teaspoon red pepper flakes

¼ teaspoon salt

¼ teaspoon black pepper

1 pound skinless boneless chicken breasts, cut lengthwise into wide strips

1 pint cherry tomatoes, coarsely chopped

½ cup chopped scallions

1 small jalapeño pepper, seeded and minced

2 teaspoons canola oil

1 red onion, thinly sliced

1 small red bell pepper, cut into thin strips

1 small green bell pepper, cut into thin strips

4 (8-inch) whole wheat tortillas, warmed

1. Mix together 2 tablespoons of lime juice, the garlic, chili powder, pepper flakes, ⅛ teaspoon of salt, and ⅛ teaspoon of black pepper in medium bowl; add chicken and stir until coated evenly. Cover and refrigerate at least 1 hour or up to 4 hours.

2. Meanwhile, to make salsa, combine tomatoes, scallions, jalapeño, remaining lime juice, and remaining ⅛ teaspoon salt and ⅛ teaspoon black pepper in another medium bowl. Set aside to allow flavors to blend.

3. Heat 1 teaspoon of oil in large heavy nonstick skillet over medium-high heat. Add onion and bell peppers; cook, stirring frequently, until softened, about 5 minutes. Transfer vegetables to medium bowl and keep warm.

4. Add remaining 1 teaspoon oil to skillet and heat over medium-high heat. Add chicken and any marinade remaining in bowl, but discard garlic (juices will sizzle so be careful of splattering liquid). Cook, turning occasionally, until chicken is browned and cooked through, about 6 minutes.

5. To serve, put one-fourth of chicken on each tortilla; top each with about ½ cup of vegetables and ½ cup of salsa.

Per serving (1 fajita): 271 Cal, 6 g Total Fat, 1 g Sat Fat, 469 mg Sod, 32 g Total Carb, 6 g Sugar, 5 g Fib, 29 g Prot. SmartPoints value: 5

 Cook's Tip

Top the fajitas with light sour cream, guacamole, and fresh cilantro leaves. A 1-tablespoon dollop each of light sour cream and guacamole per serving will up the SmartPoints value by 2.

SOUTHWESTERN GREEN CHILE CHEESEBURGERS

SERVES 4

20 Minutes or Less

1   pound ground lean beef (7% fat or less)

¼   cup fat-free salsa verde

1½   teaspoons chili powder

½   teaspoon salt

4   (½-ounce) slices reduced-fat Swiss cheese

4   small green leaf lettuce leaves

4   light whole wheat English muffins, split and toasted

8   thin tomato slices

8   thin slices sweet onion, such as Vidalia

1. Mix together beef, salsa, chili powder, and salt in large bowl just until combined well. With damp hands, shape mixture into 4 (½-inch-thick) patties.

2. Spray grill pan with nonstick spray and set over medium heat. Put patties in grill pan and grill until browned. Turn burgers; top with Swiss cheese and grill until cheese is melted and instant-read thermometer inserted into side of burger registers 160°F, about 5 minutes longer.

3. Place lettuce and burgers on bottoms of English muffins. Top each with 2 tomato slices, 2 onion slices, and tops of muffins.

Per serving (1 garnished burger): 318 Cal, 7 g Total Fat, 3 g Sat Fat, 775 mg Sod, 29 g Total Carb, 7 g Sugar, 6 g Fib, 35 g Prot. SmartPoints value: 6

 Cook's Tip

For a touch of smokiness, use chipotle chile powder instead of regular chili powder. Chipotles are jalapeños that have been dried and smoked over a fire.

CHICKEN AND TOMATILLO ENCHILADA CASSEROLE

SERVES 6
Gluten Free

2   pounds tomatillos, husked and rinsed

1   cup chopped scallions (about 8)

½   cup chopped fresh cilantro

1 or 2 jalapeño peppers, seeded and minced

2   large garlic cloves, minced

¾   teaspoon salt

¼   teaspoon black pepper

12   (6-inch) corn tortillas

3   cups shredded cooked skinless chicken breast

12   tablespoons shredded reduced-fat Mexican cheese blend

12   tablespoons fat-free sour cream

1. Preheat oven to 350°F. Spray 9 x 13-inch baking dish or casserole dish with nonstick spray.

2. Put tomatillos in food processor and process until finely chopped. Stir together tomatillos, scallions, cilantro, jalapeño, garlic, salt, and black pepper in large shallow bowl.

3. Dip both sides of 1 tortilla into tomatillo mixture. Place tortilla on foil on work surface; top with about ¼ cup of chicken, ½ tablespoon of Mexican cheese blend, and 1 tablespoon of sour cream. Fold two opposite sides of tortilla over to enclose filling. Place enchilada, seam side down, in prepared baking dish. Repeat with remaining tortillas, chicken, 5½ tablespoons of cheese, and sour cream, making total of 12 enchiladas. Pour remaining tomatillo mixture over enchiladas and sprinkle with remaining 6 tablespoons cheese.

4. Cover baking dish with foil. Bake 20 minutes; uncover and bake until heated through, about 10 minutes longer.

Per serving (2 enchiladas): 343 Cal, 8 g Total Fat, 3 g Sat Fat, 492 mg Sod, 37 g Total Carb, 7 g Sugar, 7 g Fib, 31 g Prot. SmartPoints value: 7

 Cook's Tip

Tomatillos, also called Mexican green tomatoes, belong to the tomato family. They look like small tomatoes except for their papery husk, which is a clue to the fact that tomatillos are also related to the cape gooseberry. This slightly tart, firm vegetable is available year-round. Tomatillos can be eaten raw or cooked.

CHOCOLATE-CINNAMON QUESADILLAS

SERVES 4
20 Minutes or Less,
Vegetarian

2   tablespoons grated or finely chopped semisweet chocolate

1   tablespoon granulated sugar

½   teaspoon cinnamon, or to taste

2   (8-inch) whole wheat tortillas

1   teaspoon confectioners' sugar

1. Sprinkle 1 tablespoon of chocolate, ½ tablespoon of granulated sugar, and ¼ teaspoon of cinnamon over one half of each tortilla; fold unfilled half of tortillas over to enclose filling.

2. Set dry large skillet over medium heat; place quesadillas in pan and cook, turning once, until speckled and chocolate is melted, about 2 minutes per side.

3. Transfer quesadillas to cutting board. Cut each quesadilla in half and dust with confectioners' sugar. Serve warm.

Per serving (½ quesadilla): 78 Cal, 2 g Total Fat, 1 g Sat Fat, 89 mg Sod, 18 g Total Carb, 7 g Sugar, 1 g Fib, 2 g Prot. SmartPoints value: 3

CHOCOLATE-CHILE
GRANITA

CHOCOLATE-CHILE GRANITA

SERVES 8
Gluten Free, Vegetarian

1½ cups unsweetened almond milk

½ cup sugar

⅓ cup unsweetened Dutch process cocoa

1 ounce unsweetened chocolate, coarsely chopped

Generous ¼ teaspoon ancho chile powder, or to taste

¼ teaspoon cinnamon

¼ teaspoon salt

⅛ teaspoon nutmeg

1½ cups pure coconut water

1 teaspoon vanilla extract

¼ cup sliced almonds

1 ounce bittersweet or semisweet chocolate, made into shavings

1. Stir together almond milk, sugar, cocoa, unsweetened chocolate, chile powder, cinnamon, salt, and nutmeg in medium saucepan and set over medium heat. Bring to simmer, stirring until sugar and cocoa are dissolved and chocolate is melted. Remove saucepan from heat; stir in coconut water and vanilla.

2. Pour cocoa mixture into 9-inch square baking pan. Cover pan with foil; freeze until mixture is frozen along edges, about 2 hours. With fork, scrape icy edges in towards center. Repeat every 45 minutes or until granita is firm and texture is flaky, 2–3 hours longer. Granita can be frozen up to 3 days.

3. To serve, use fork to scrape across surface of ice. Transfer ice shards to 8 dessert dishes. Garnish each serving with ½ tablespoon almonds and one-eighth of chocolate shavings.

Per serving (about ½ cup granita, ½ tablespoon almonds, and about 2 teaspoons chocolate shavings): 130 Cal, 5 g Total Fat, 2 g Sat Fat, 149 mg Sod, 21 g Total Carb, 16 g Sugar, 3 g Fib, 2 g Prot. SmartPoints value: 6

 Cook's Tip

If you like, pour the cocoa mixture into an ice-cream maker and make sorbet instead of granita.

SKORDALIA

SERVES 8
Gluten Free, Vegetarian

1   pound Yukon Gold potatoes, peeled and cut into 1-inch chunks

4   garlic cloves, minced (about 1 tablespoon)

¾   teaspoon salt

4   teaspoons lemon juice

3   tablespoons extra-virgin olive oil

1   tablespoon walnuts, toasted and finely chopped

1   tablespoon thinly sliced fresh flat-leaf parsley

1. Combine potatoes with enough water to cover in medium saucepan; cover and bring to boil. Reduce heat and simmer, partially covered, until potatoes are fork-tender, about 15 minutes; drain. With potato ricer or food mill, press potatoes into large bowl.

2. Meanwhile, with flat side of large knife, mash garlic with salt until paste forms.

3. With electric mixer on high speed, beat potatoes with lemon juice until smooth. Reduce speed to low and gradually add oil in thin, steady stream until potatoes are very smooth. Beat in garlic paste. Transfer skordalia to serving bowl; sprinkle with walnuts and parsley. Serve warm or at room temperature.

Per serving (about ⅓ cup): 92 Cal, 6 g Total Fat, 1 g Sat Fat, 228 mg Sod, 10 g Total Carb, 1 g Sugar, 1 g Fib, 1 g Prot. SmartPoints value: 3

 Cook's Tip

Skordalia is to Greece what hummus is to Israel. Whipped until creamy, this popular dip is sure to please. Skordalia is excellent served with vegetable dippers like cucumber sticks, sliced fennel, red bell pepper chunks, and endive leaves.

ROASTED EGGPLANT DIP

SERVES 8
Gluten Free, Vegetarian

1   large eggplant (about 1½ pounds)

3   large garlic cloves, peeled

¼   cup plain fat-free Greek yogurt

8   sun-dried tomatoes (not oil packed), finely chopped

1½ teaspoons grated lemon zest

2   teaspoons lemon juice

1   teaspoon harissa

¾ + ⅛ teaspoon salt

1. Preheat oven to 425°F. Line small baking sheet with foil and spray with nonstick spray.

2. With fork, pierce eggplant several times. Spray garlic with nonstick spray and wrap in foil. Place eggplant and garlic on prepared baking sheet. Roast, turning once or twice, until eggplant is very soft, skin is lightly charred, and garlic is very soft, about 45 minutes. Remove from oven; let eggplant stand until cool enough to handle.

3. Cut eggplant lengthwise in half; scoop out flesh and transfer to food processor. Unwrap garlic and add to processor along with yogurt, sun-dried tomatoes, lemon zest and juice, harissa, and salt. Pulse until smooth. Can be refrigerated up to 3 days.

Per serving (¼ cup): 32 Cal, 0 g Total Fat, 0 g Sat Fat, 303 mg Sod, 7 g Total Carb, 3 g Sugar, 2 g Fib, 2 g Prot. SmartPoints value: 0

GREEK-STYLE CHICKEN AND VEGETABLES

SERVES 4
Gluten Free

5   teaspoons extra-virgin olive oil

3   garlic cloves, chopped

2   teaspoons lemon zest

1   tablespoon lemon juice

1½   teaspoons dried oregano

½   teaspoon salt

¼   teaspoon black pepper

2   small or 1 large zucchini, cut into ¼-inch rounds

1   pint grape tomatoes, halved

1   (14-ounce) can artichoke hearts (water packed), drained well and halved

4   (5-ounce) skinless boneless chicken breasts

1. Preheat oven to 450°F. Spray large baking dish or casserole dish with olive oil nonstick spray.

2. Stir together 4 teaspoons of oil, the garlic, 1 teaspoon of lemon zest, the lemon juice, oregano, salt, and pepper in large bowl; add zucchini, tomatoes, and artichoke hearts, tossing until coated evenly. With slotted spoon, transfer vegetables to one side of prepared baking dish, leaving enough room for chicken. Add chicken to bowl and turn until coated with garlic mixture; arrange in baking dish alongside vegetables.

3. Roast, stirring vegetables once, until vegetables are tender and chicken is cooked through, 15–20 minutes. Drizzle vegetables with remaining 1 teaspoon oil and sprinkle with remaining 1 teaspoon lemon zest, tossing until coated. Drizzle chicken with pan juices.

Per serving (1 chicken breast and 1 cup vegetables): 266 Cal, 10 g Total Fat, 2 g Sat Fat, 749 mg Sod, 14 g Total Carb, 5 g Sugar, 5 g Fib, 34 g Prot. SmartPoints value: 4

Cook's Tip

For even more delectable Greek flavor, sprinkle the roasted vegetables with ½ cup crumbled reduced-fat feta cheese before serving for 1 additional SmartPoints value per serving.

GREEK-STYLE CHICKEN
AND VEGETABLES

BULGUR-BEEF MEATBALLS IN
CINNAMON-SCENTED TOMATO SAUCE

BULGUR-BEEF MEATBALLS IN CINNAMON-SCENTED TOMATO SAUCE

SERVES 6

1   pound ground lean beef (7% fat or less)

¾   cup + 2 tablespoons finely chopped fresh flat-leaf parsley

½   cup coarse bulgur

4   scallions, finely chopped

¼   cup fat-free egg substitute

4   garlic cloves, finely chopped

4   teaspoons extra-virgin olive oil

1   teaspoon ground cumin

1   teaspoon kosher salt

½   teaspoon black pepper

1   large red onion, chopped (about 1⅓ cups)

⅛   teaspoon cinnamon

⅓   cup dry red wine

1   (14½-ounce) can diced tomatoes

2   cups reduced-sodium chicken broth

1. **Mix together beef, ¾ cup of parsley, the bulgur, scallions, egg substitute, 2 teaspoons of garlic, 2 teaspoons of oil, the cumin, ½ teaspoon of salt, and ¼ teaspoon of pepper in large bowl. With damp hands, shape beef-bulgur mixture into 24 (1½-inch) meatballs.**

2. **Heat remaining 2 teaspoons oil in large Dutch oven over medium-high heat. Add onion and cook, covered, stirring, until golden, about 6 minutes. Add remaining garlic, ½ teaspoon salt, and ¼ teaspoon pepper, and the cinnamon; cook, stirring constantly, until fragrant, about 30 seconds. Add wine and boil 1 minute; stir in tomatoes. Add meatballs and broth and return to boil. Reduce heat and simmer, covered, until meatballs are cooked through, about 20 minutes.**

3. **With slotted spoon, transfer meatballs to platter; keep warm. Bring sauce to boil. Cook, stirring occasionally, until reduced to 2½ cups, 5–6 minutes. Remove Dutch oven from heat; return meatballs to pot and gently stir until coated with sauce. Sprinkle with remaining 2 tablespoons parsley.**

Per serving (4 meatballs and generous ⅓ cup sauce): 224 Cal, 7 g Total Fat, 2 g Sat Fat, 559 mg Sod, 17 g Total Carb, 4 g Sugar, 4 g Fib, 20 g Prot. SmartPoints value: 5

Cook's Tip

To get a head start on making this Mediterranean-style main dish, prepare the beef mixture as directed in step 1, but do not shape the meatballs. Transfer to a zip-close plastic bag. Squeeze out the air and seal the bag; refrigerate up to 1 day.

QUICK BEEF WITH GREEK YOGURT SAUCE

SERVES 4
20 Minutes or Less,
Gluten Free

2   teaspoons olive oil

1   pound ground lean beef
     (7% fat or less)

1   large garlic clove, minced

1¼   teaspoons ground cumin

¾   teaspoon salt

¼   teaspoon black pepper

1   cup plain low-fat Greek yogurt

½   cup (¼-inch) diced English
     (seedless) cucumber

2   tablespoons chopped fresh mint

1. Heat oil in large heavy nonstick skillet over medium-high heat. Add beef, garlic, cumin, ½ teaspoon of salt, and ⅛ teaspoon of pepper; cook, stirring, until beef is browned, about 4 minutes.

2. Meanwhile, to make sauce, stir together yogurt, cucumber, and remaining ¼ teaspoon salt and ⅛ teaspoon pepper in small bowl.

3. Divide beef evenly among 4 plates; top evenly with yogurt sauce and sprinkle with mint.

Per serving (1 cup beef and ¼ cup yogurt sauce): 222 Cal, 9 g Total Fat, 4 g Sat Fat, 534 mg Sod, 4 g Total Carb, 1 g Sugar, 0 g Fib, 31 g Prot. SmartPoints value: 5

 **Cook's Tip**

Start your meal with a Greek-style salad of romaine lettuce hearts, pepperoncini, tomato wedges, thinly sliced red onion, and pitted Kalamata olives dressed with red wine vinegar, dried oregano, salt, and pepper. Sixteen Kalamata olives will up the per-serving SmartPoints value by 2.

MINTED GREEN BEAN SALAD

SERVES 6
20 Minutes or Less,
Gluten Free, Vegetarian

2   teaspoons grated lemon zest

1   tablespoon lemon juice

1   tablespoon extra-virgin olive oil

½   teaspoon salt

⅛   teaspoon black pepper

1   pound green beans, trimmed

½   pound plum tomatoes, chopped

½   English (seedless) cucumber, halved lengthwise and thinly sliced

1   small red onion, thinly sliced

½   cup crumbled reduced-fat feta cheese

2   tablespoons chopped fresh mint

1. To make dressing, whisk together lemon zest and juice, oil, salt, and pepper in small bowl. Set aside.

2. Meanwhile, bring large pot of lightly salted water to boil. Add green beans; return to boil and cook until crisp-tender, about 5 minutes. Drain beans in colander; rinse under cold water to stop cooking. Drain again. Transfer beans to serving bowl. Add tomatoes, cucumber, onion, feta, mint, and dressing; toss until mixed well and coated evenly with dressing.

Per serving (1 cup): 80 Cal, 4 g Fat, 1 g Sat Fat, 325 mg Sod, 10 g Total Carb, 3 g Sugar, 3 g Fib, 4 g Prot. SmartPoints value: 1

 Cook's Tip

The salad can be prepared up to 1 hour ahead. For a more subtle onion flavor, soak the onion in red wine vinegar for about 30 minutes, then drain well and add to the salad.

BAKED SHRIMP WITH TOMATO AND FETA

SERVES 6
Gluten Free

4   teaspoons extra-virgin olive oil

3   shallots, finely chopped

1   pint grape tomatoes or cherry
      tomatoes, halved

1½   pounds large shrimp, peeled and
      deveined, tails left on if desired

½   teaspoon red pepper flakes

¾   teaspoon kosher salt

⅓   cup crumbled reduced-fat
      feta cheese

2   tablespoons chopped fresh dill

1. Preheat oven to 400°F.

2. Heat oil in large skillet over medium-high heat. Add shallots and cook, stirring, until golden, about 4 minutes. Add tomatoes and cook, stirring occasionally, until softened and beginning to burst, about 4 minutes. Add shrimp and pepper flakes; cook, stirring constantly, just until shrimp start to become firm, 1½–2 minutes. Stir in salt.

3. Transfer shrimp mixture to 9 x 13-inch baking dish or casserole dish. Bake until shrimp are just opaque in center, about 8 minutes. Sprinkle feta on top. Bake until cheese is softened, about 2 minutes longer. Sprinkle with dill.

Per serving (about 1 cup): 184 Cal, 6 g Total Fat, 1 g Sat Fat, 494 mg Sod, 6 g Total Carb, 2 g Sugar, 1 g Fib, 25 g Prot. SmartPoints value: 7

Cook's Tip

Oftentimes this classic Greek dish is prepared with a very generous amount of tomato sauce. Using grape tomatoes instead of tomato sauce adds just the right amount of tomato flavor to complement—not overwhelm—the shrimp and feta.

BAKED SHRIMP WITH TOMATO AND FETA

ROASTED VEGETABLE
AND ORZO SALAD

ROASTED VEGETABLE AND ORZO SALAD

SERVES 6
Vegetarian

- 2   any-color bell peppers, cut into 1-inch pieces
- 1   red onion, cut into 1-inch pieces
- 1   teaspoon kosher salt
- ¼   teaspoon black pepper
- 1   (¾-pound) zucchini, quartered lengthwise and cut into 1-inch chunks
- 2   large garlic cloves, minced
- 1   cup orzo
-      Grated zest of ½ lemon
- 3   tablespoons lemon juice
- 4   teaspoons extra-virgin olive oil
- 1   tablespoon chopped fresh oregano or fresh flat-leaf parsley
- 10   pitted Kalamata olives, chopped

1. Preheat oven to 425°F. Line large rimmed baking sheet with nonstick foil.

2. Spread bell peppers and onion on prepared baking sheet to form single layer; sprinkle with ½ teaspoon of salt and ⅛ teaspoon of black pepper; lightly spray with olive oil nonstick spray. Roast until vegetables are lightly browned, about 15 minutes. Scatter zucchini and garlic on top of vegetables; spray zucchini with nonstick spray and roast until tender, about 15 minutes.

3. Meanwhile, cook orzo according to package directions. Drain in colander and briefly rinse under cool water. Drain again.

4. To make dressing, whisk together lemon zest and juice, oil, oregano, and remaining ½ teaspoon salt and ⅛ teaspoon black pepper in serving bowl. Add orzo, roasted vegetables, and olives. Gently toss until mixed well. Serve warm or at room temperature.

Per serving (about ¾ cup): 168 Cal, 4 g Total Fat, 1 g Sat Fat, 384 mg Sod, 28 g Total Carb, 4 g Sugar, 3 g Fib, 5 g Prot. SmartPoints value: 4

Cook's Tip

Serve this salad on a bed of baby arugula or spinach for a dose of vitamins K, A, B2, B6, and C, as well as manganese, folate, magnesium, iron, copper, calcium, and potassium.

GREEK-STYLE GRILLED EGGPLANT

SERVES 6
Gluten Free, Vegetarian

2   tablespoons extra-virgin olive oil

2   teaspoons chopped fresh oregano + additional for sprinkling

1½ teaspoons balsamic vinegar

½   teaspoon salt

⅛   teaspoon red pepper flakes

⅛   teaspoon garlic powder

1   small eggplant (about 1 pound), unpeeled and cut into ½-inch rounds

6   tablespoons crumbled feta cheese

1. Preheat grill to medium-high or prepare medium-high fire.

2. Meanwhile, to make dressing, whisk together oil, oregano, vinegar, ¼ teaspoon of salt, the pepper flakes, and garlic powder in small bowl. Set aside.

3. Spray eggplant on both sides with olive oil nonstick spray; sprinkle with remaining ¼ teaspoon salt. Place eggplant on grill rack and grill, turning once, until lightly charred and tender, about 10 minutes. Arrange eggplant on platter; brush dressing over eggplant. Sprinkle with feta and additional oregano.

Per serving (2 slices eggplant and 1 tablespoon feta): 81 Cal, 7 g Fat, 2 g Sat Fat, 300 mg Sod, 4 g Total Carb, 2 g Sugar, 1 g Fib, 2 g Prot. SmartPoints value: 2

YOGURT WITH POMEGRANATE-ORANGE SYRUP

SERVES 4
20 Minutes or Less,
Gluten Free, Vegetarian

¾ cup orange juice

2 tablespoons pomegranate molasses

1 tablespoon honey

½ (3-inch) cinnamon stick

½ cup dried apricots, cut into ¼-inch dice

¼ cup dried tart cherries

2 cups vanilla fat-free Greek yogurt

4 tablespoons pistachios, chopped

1. To make sauce, combine orange juice, pomegranate molasses, honey, and cinnamon stick in small saucepan; bring to boil. Reduce heat and cook, swirling pan occasionally, until reduced and syrupy, about 10 minutes. Remove pan from heat and let cool. Remove cinnamon stick and discard.

2. Combine apricots and dried cherries in small bowl.

3. Put ½ cup yogurt in each of 4 wineglasses or dessert dishes. Drizzle each with 2 teaspoons sauce, 2 tablespoons dried fruit mixture, and 1 tablespoon pistachios.

Per serving (1 dessert): 177 Cal, 3 g Total Fat, 0 g Sat Fat, 37 mg Sod, 33 g Total Carb, 27 g Sugar, 3 g Fib, 9 g Prot. SmartPoints value: 8

 Cook's Tip

Pomegranate molasses is not molasses at all but a syrup made from concentrated pomegranate juice and sugar. It is popular in Middle Eastern cuisine. Its intense flavor is sometimes compared to balsamic vinegar and, just like balsamic, a little goes a long way. Pomegranate molasses can be found in specialty food stores, big-box stores, and Middle Eastern groceries.

JALAPEÑO POPPERS

SERVES 8

Vegetarian

½ cup shredded reduced-fat sharp Cheddar cheese

¼ cup light cream cheese (Neufchâtel), softened

1 tablespoon fat-free mayonnaise

8 small jalapeño peppers

¼ cup fat-free egg substitute

½ cup cornflake crumbs

1. Preheat oven to 350°F. Spray baking sheet with nonstick spray.

2. Mix together Cheddar, cream cheese, and mayonnaise in small bowl until blended well; set aside. Halve peppers lengthwise and remove seeds; fill peppers evenly with cheese mixture.

3. Pour egg substitute into small bowl. Spread cornflake crumbs on sheet of wax paper. Dip stuffed peppers into egg substitute, one at a time, then roll in cornflake crumbs until coated, transferring stuffed peppers to prepared baking sheet; spray with nonstick spray. Bake until filling is bubbly and lightly browned, about 30 minutes. Serve hot or warm.

Per serving (2 poppers): 59 Cal, 2 g Total Fat, 1 g Sat Fat, 156 mg Sod, 6 g Total Carb, 1 g Sugar, 0 g Fib, 4 g Prot. SmartPoints value: 2

WARM MEXICAN CHILI DIP

SERVES 6
Vegetarian,
20 Minutes or Less

1   (8-ounce) package fat-free cream cheese, softened

1   (15-ounce) can low-fat or fat-free vegetarian chili

1   cup reduced-fat shredded sharp Cheddar cheese or Mexican cheese blend

½   cup finely diced red bell pepper

3   scallions, chopped

1. Preheat oven to 350°F.

2. Spread cream cheese in bottom of casserole dish measuring about 6 x 10 inches; spoon chili on top and sprinkle with Cheddar. Bake until heated through and cheese is melted, 10–15 minutes. Sprinkle with bell pepper and scallions. Serve hot or warm.

Per serving (about 1¼ cups): 125 Cal, 2 g Total Fat, 1 g Sat Fat, 605 mg Sod, 15 g Total Carb, 4 g Sugar, 2 g Fib, 14 g Prot. SmartPoints value: 3

 Cook's Tip

This dip is easy to double—just use a larger casserole dish. It can also be made up to 3 days ahead and refrigerated. Simply reheat when ready to serve. Add some heat by stirring in chopped pickled jalapeño peppers, if you like.

CRUNCHY PARMESAN KALE CHIPS

SERVES 8
Gluten Free, Vegetarian

2   bunches curly kale, tough stems removed and leaves torn into 2-inch pieces

4   teaspoons olive oil

1   teaspoon garlic powder

½   teaspoon kosher salt

2   tablespoons grated Parmesan cheese

1. Preheat oven to 350°F. Spray two large baking sheets with nonstick spray.

2. Toss together kale and oil in very large bowl until coated evenly, using your fingers to "massage" in the oil. Sprinkle with garlic powder and salt; toss to coat evenly.

3. Divide kale evenly between prepared baking sheets, spreading to form single layer. Bake until crisp, 20–25 minutes. Let cool slightly; sprinkle evenly with Parmesan.

Per serving (about 1¼ cups): 85 Cal, 3 g Total Fat, 1 g Sat Fat, 193 mg Sod, 12 g Total Carb, 0 g Sugar, 2 g Fib, 4 g Prot. SmartPoints value: 1

 Cook's Tip

These chips are better than what you can buy and so much kinder on the wallet! Crunchy, cheesy, and a touch garlicky, they make a healthful snack, or try them crumbled over salads, soups, or casseroles. They'll stay crisp in an airtight container up to 3 days.

BAKED BEEF ZITI

SERVES 8

12   ounces ziti

2   teaspoons olive oil

2   garlic cloves, minced

⅓   pound ground lean beef
     (7% fat or less)

1   teaspoon dried oregano

1   teaspoon dried thyme

1   teaspoon dried rosemary

½   teaspoon salt

½   teaspoon black pepper

1   (28-ounce) can crushed tomatoes

1   cup shredded part-skim
     mozzarella cheese

1. Preheat oven to 350°F.

2. Cook ziti according to package directions. Drain and set aside.

3. Meanwhile, heat oil in medium saucepan over medium heat. Add garlic and cook, stirring, until fragrant, about 30 seconds. Add beef and cook, breaking it up with wooden spoon, until browned, about 5 minutes; drain off any fat and return pan to heat. Stir in oregano, thyme, rosemary, salt, and pepper; cook until fragrant, about 2 minutes. Add tomatoes and bring to boil; reduce heat and simmer 5 minutes longer.

4. Spread small amount of tomato-beef mixture in 4-quart casserole dish (just enough to cover bottom of dish); top with half of ziti. Layer with half of remaining tomato-beef mixture, ½ cup of mozzarella, and remaining ziti. Top with remaining tomato-beef mixture and sprinkle with remaining ½ cup cheese. Bake until heated through and cheese is melted and golden, about 30 minutes.

Per serving (⅛ of casserole): 250 Cal, 5 g Total Fat, 2 g Sat Fat, 389 mg Sod, 37 g Total Carb, 4 g Sugar, 2 g Fib, 14 g Prot. SmartPoints value: 7

SWEET 'N' SPICY DRUMETTES

SERVES 4

2 tablespoons ketchup

1½ tablespoons reduced-sodium soy sauce

1 tablespoon honey

2 teaspoons hot sauce, such as Frank's

12 chicken drumettes (about 1 pound), skinned

1. Stir together ketchup, soy sauce, honey, and hot sauce in large shallow bowl. Add drumettes, turning to coat. Refrigerate, covered, at least 1 hour or up to overnight.

2. Preheat broiler. Spray broiler rack with nonstick spray.

3. Remove chicken from marinade; discard marinade. Arrange chicken on prepared broiler rack and spray with nonstick spray. Broil 5 inches from heat, turning, until lightly charred in spots and cooked through, about 12 minutes.

Per serving (**3 drumettes**): 158 Cal, 4 g Total Fat, 1 g Sat Fat, 488 mg Sod, 7 g Total Carb, 6 g Sugar, 0 g Fib, 22 g Prot. SmartPoints value: 4

 Cook's Tip

The perfect balance of sweet and hot will keep 'em coming back for more of these eat-out-of-hand drumettes. Serve them with additional hot sauce, if you like.

BISON SLIDERS WITH
BALSAMIC-BRAISED ONIONS

BISON SLIDERS WITH BALSAMIC-BRAISED ONIONS

SERVES 8

3   teaspoons olive oil

1   large onion, thinly sliced (2 cups)

¼   cup balsamic vinegar

3   tablespoons orange juice

1   pound ground grass-fed bison

1   tablespoon + 2 teaspoons Dijon mustard

2½ teaspoons Worcestershire sauce

½   teaspoon salt

4   (½-ounce) slices reduced-fat Cheddar cheese, quartered

8   mini potato rolls, split and toasted, if desired

1. Heat 2 teaspoons of oil in large nonstick skillet over medium-low heat. Add onion and cook, stirring frequently, until golden, about 8 minutes. Add vinegar and orange juice; cook until evaporated, about 3 minutes. Transfer onion to bowl and keep warm. Wipe skillet clean.

2. Meanwhile, mix together bison, mustard, Worcestershire sauce, and salt in medium bowl until mixed well. With damp hands, shape into 8 (¾-inch-thick) mini patties.

3. Heat remaining 1 teaspoon oil in same skillet over medium heat. Add patties and cook until instant-read thermometer inserted into side of burger registers 160°F, about 3 minutes per side. Top each burger with 2 pieces of Cheddar; cook, covered, just until cheese is melted, about 1 minute.

4. Place burgers on bottoms of rolls; top each with about 2 tablespoons onion. Cover with tops of rolls.

Per serving (1 slider): 225 Cal, 8 g Total Fat, 3 g Sat Fat, 405 mg Sod, 20 g Total Carb, 7 g Sugar, 2 g Fib, 18 g Prot. SmartPoints value: 6

 Cook's Tip

Lean and flavorful, bison makes tasty, satisfying burgers. Also known as buffalo, bison is available in 1-pound packages in the meat department of supermarkets. Add a bit of traditional flavor by spooning 1 teaspoon of ketchup onto each slider for no additional SmartPoints value.

SPANISH-STYLE SMOKY ROASTED POTATOES

SERVES 4
Gluten Free, Vegetarian

1½	pounds small fingerling potatoes, halved lengthwise
1	tablespoon olive oil
1	teaspoon kosher salt
1	small garlic clove, minced
½– 1	teaspoon smoked paprika

1. Preheat oven to 450°F degrees. Line large rimmed baking sheet with parchment paper or spray with nonstick spray.

2. Toss together potatoes, oil, and salt in medium bowl; spread on prepared baking sheet in single layer. Roast, stirring half-way through roasting time, until tender on inside and crispy on outside, about 35 minutes. Transfer potatoes to serving platter; sprinkle with garlic and paprika. Toss until coated.

Per serving (1 cup): 150 Cal, 4 g Total Fat, 0 g Sat Fat, 510 mg Sod, 27 g Total Carb, 2 g Sugar, 4 g Fib, 3 g Prot. SmartPoints value: 5

ULTIMATE ONION RINGS

SERVES 4
Vegetarian

⅓ cup all-purpose flour

1 cup low-fat buttermilk

½ teaspoon salt

½ teaspoon black pepper

½ cup plain dried bread crumbs

½ teaspoon Old Bay Seasoning

2 large sweet onions, cut into ½-inch rounds and separated into 32 rings

1. Preheat oven to 450°F. Spray two large baking sheets with nonstick spray.

2. Put flour in large zip-close plastic bag. Whisk together buttermilk, salt, and pepper in shallow bowl. Combine bread crumbs and Old Bay Seasoning in large shallow bowl.

3. Add onion rings, a few at a time, to flour; shake until coated. Dip rings, one at a time, into buttermilk mixture, then lightly coat with bread crumbs, transferring rings as they are coated to prepared baking sheets. Spray onion rings with nonstick spray. Bake, turning once, until golden and crispy, about 20 minutes.

Per serving (8 onion rings): 145 Cal, 1 g Total Fat, 1 g Sat Fat, 543 mg Sod, 28 g Total Carb, 7 g Sugar, 2 g Fib, 6 g Prot. SmartPoints value: 4

FROZEN PB-BANANA COOKIE BITES

MAKES 12
Vegetarian

½ cup prepared chocolate pudding, made with fat-free milk

2 tablespoons creamy peanut butter

24 reduced-fat vanilla wafer cookies

12 (¼-inch) slices ripe banana

1. Stir together pudding and peanut butter in small bowl until blended well.

2. Spoon 1 teaspoon of pudding mixture onto flat side of each of 12 cookies. Top each with 1 banana slice and 1 teaspoon pudding mixture; top with remaining cookies, flat side down.

3. Arrange cookies on small baking sheet and freeze until firm, about 2 hours. Can be stored in airtight container in freezer up to 2 weeks.

Per serving (1 cookie): 90 Cal, 3 g Total Fat, 1 g Sat Fat, 72 mg Sod, 14 g Total Carb, 8 g Sugar, 1 g Fib, 1 g Prot. SmartPoints value: 3

CRANBERRY-GINGER
OATMEAL COOKIES

CRANBERRY-GINGER OATMEAL COOKIES

MAKES 28
Vegetarian

1 cup all-purpose flour

¾ teaspoon ground ginger

½ teaspoon baking soda

¼ teaspoon cinnamon

¼ teaspoon baking powder

¼ teaspoon salt

4 tablespoons unsalted butter, softened

¾ cup packed light brown sugar

1 large egg

¼ cup prune puree or prune baby food

1 teaspoon vanilla extract

1 cup old-fashioned (rolled) or quick-cooking oats

¾ cup dried cranberries, chopped

½ cup crystallized ginger, chopped

1. Preheat oven to 375°F. Line two large baking sheets with parchment paper.

2. Whisk together flour, ginger, baking soda, cinnamon, baking powder, and salt in small bowl.

3. With electric mixer on medium-high speed, beat butter and brown sugar in large bowl until light and fluffy; beat in egg, prune puree, and vanilla until mixed. Reduce mixer speed to low. Add flour mixture in two additions, beating just until combined. Stir in oats, cranberries, and crystallized ginger.

4. Drop dough by level tablespoonfuls, about 2 inches apart, onto prepared baking sheets, making total of 28 cookies. Bake until lightly browned, about 8 minutes. Let cool on baking sheets on wire racks 5 minutes. Transfer to racks and let cool completely.

Per serving (1 cookie): 87 Cal, 2 g Total Fat, 1 g Sat Fat, 49 mg Sod, 16 g Total Carb, 10 g Sugar, 1 g Fib, 1 g Prot. SmartPoints value: 4

 Cook's Tip

If you don't have dried cranberries on hand, substitute golden or dark raisins, dried blueberries, or dried sweet or tart cherries.

SWEET ONION, BACON, AND CHEESE TARTS

MAKES 24

1 teaspoon olive oil

1 sweet onion, quartered and thinly sliced

¼ teaspoon salt

⅛ teaspoon black pepper

3 slices Canadian bacon, finely chopped

¼ cup fat-free egg substitute

2 tablespoons fat-free half-and-half

1 teaspoon Dijon mustard

   Pinch cayenne

24 frozen mini phyllo tart shells

⅓ cup shredded reduced-fat Swiss cheese

1. Heat oil in medium nonstick skillet over medium heat. Add onion, salt, and pepper; cook, stirring, until onion is golden brown, about 12 minutes. Transfer to small bowl.

2. Add bacon to skillet and cook, stirring, until lightly browned, about 2 minutes. Add to onion and mix well.

3. Preheat oven to 350°F.

4. Meanwhile, whisk together egg substitute, half-and-half, mustard, and cayenne in small bowl. Arrange tart shells on baking sheet. Spoon onion-bacon mixture evenly into shells. Top each with about ¾ teaspoon egg mixture. Sprinkle evenly with Swiss cheese; bake until filling is set, about 15 minutes. Serve warm.

Per serving (1 tart): 27 Cal, 1 g Total Fat, 0 g Sat Fat, 74 mg Sod, 3 g Total Carb, 0 g Sugar, 0 g Fib, 2 g Prot. SmartPoints value: 1

SPICY ROASTED BROCCOLI AND CAULIFLOWER BITES

SERVES 12
Gluten Free, Vegetarian

1   small bunch broccoli, cut into small florets

1   small head cauliflower, cut into small florets

1   tablespoon olive oil

1   tablespoon water

1   teaspoon Dijon mustard

1   teaspoon curry powder

1   teaspoon chili powder

1   teaspoon ground cumin

1   teaspoon kosher salt

¼   teaspoon cayenne

1. Preheat oven to 400°F. Spray large rimmed baking sheet with nonstick spray.

2. Combine broccoli and cauliflower in large bowl. Whisk together oil, water, mustard, curry powder, chili powder, cumin, salt, and cayenne in cup. Drizzle over broccoli and cauliflower; toss until coated evenly.

3. Spread vegetables on prepared baking sheet to form single layer; roast 15 minutes. Toss vegetables; continue to roast until tender and beginning to brown, about 5 minutes longer. Serve warm.

Per serving (about ½ cup): 35 Cal, 1 g Total Fat, 0 g Sat Fat, 196 mg Sod, 5 g Total Carb, 1 g Sugar, 2 g Fib, 2 g Prot. SmartPoints value: 0

VIETNAMESE BANH MI CHICKEN BURGERS

SERVES 4
20 Minutes or Less

1 pound ground skinless chicken breast

2 large shallots, finely chopped

1¾ teaspoons Sriracha

¾ teaspoon kosher salt

⅓ cup fat-free mayonnaise

4 light whole wheat hamburger rolls, split

¼ cup very thin matchstick strips or shredded carrot

¼ cup lightly packed fresh cilantro leaves

1. Mix together chicken, shallots, 1 teaspoon of Sriracha, and the salt in medium bowl until combined well. With damp hands, shape mixture into 4 (½-inch-thick) patties.

2. Spray grill pan with nonstick spray and set over medium heat. Place patties in pan and grill until instant-read thermometer inserted into side of burger registers 165°F, about 5 minutes per side.

3. Meanwhile, stir together mayonnaise and remaining ¾ teaspoon Sriracha in cup. Spread bottoms of buns with Sriracha mayonnaise. Place burgers in buns and top evenly with carrot and cilantro.

Per serving (1 garnished burger): 250 Cal, 3 g Total Fat, 1 g Sat Fat, 835 mg Sod, 27 g Total Carb, 5 g Sugar, 4 g Fib, 31 g Prot. SmartPoints value: 5

 Cook's Tip

The more ingredients the better in this classic Vietnamese sandwich. Add thinly sliced English (seedless) cucumber, matchstick-cut daikon radish, and/or thinly sliced sweet onion.

VIETNAMESE BANH MI
CHICKEN BURGERS

TERIYAKI TURKEY
AND PINEAPPLE KEBABS

TERIYAKI TURKEY AND PINEAPPLE KEBABS

SERVES 4

¼ cup teriyaki sauce

1 jalapeño pepper, seeded and minced

3 garlic cloves, crushed through a press

1 pound skinless boneless turkey breast, cut into 1-inch chunks

1 red bell pepper, cut into chunks

1½ cups fresh pineapple chunks

2 tablespoons chopped fresh cilantro

1. Combine teriyaki sauce, jalapeño, and garlic in large zip-close plastic bag; add turkey. Squeeze out air and seal bag; turn to coat turkey. Refrigerate, turning bag occasionally, at least 20 minutes or up to 1 day.

2. Preheat broiler. Line broiler pan with foil and spray broiler rack with nonstick spray.

3. Remove turkey from marinade; discard marinade. Thread turkey, bell pepper, and pineapple alternately onto 4 (12-inch) metal skewers. Broil kebabs 5 inches from heat, turning frequently, until turkey is cooked through, 5–7 minutes. Sprinkle with cilantro.

Per serving (1 kebab): 183 Cal, 1 g Total Fat, 0 g Sat Fat, 748 Sod, 14 g Total Carb, 8 g Sugar, 2 g Fib, 30 g Prot. SmartPoints value: 2

Cook's Tip

If you'd prefer to use bamboo skewers for the kebabs, soak them in water for 30 minutes before using so they don't char. Consider double-skewering the kebabs to hold them securely in place when they are turned.

PARMESAN-AND-HERB-CRUSTED LAMB CHOPS

SERVES 8

2 tablespoons chopped fresh rosemary

1½ tablespoons chopped fresh flat-leaf parsley + whole leaves

⅓ cup grated Parmesan cheese

¼ cup dried whole wheat bread crumbs

¼ cup fat-free egg substitute

1 (8-rib) trimmed and frenched rack of lamb (1¾ pounds)

½ teaspoon salt

¼ teaspoon black pepper

2 teaspoons olive oil

1. Preheat oven to 450°F. Spray large heavy rimmed baking sheet with nonstick spray.

2. Mix together rosemary, chopped parsley, Parmesan, and bread crumbs on sheet of wax paper. Pour egg substitute into small bowl.

3. With sharp knife, cut lamb between bones into 8 chops; sprinkle with salt and pepper.

4. Dip meaty end of chops into egg substitute, then coat with Parmesan mixture, pressing firmly so it adheres.

5. Heat oil in large heavy nonstick skillet over medium-high heat until very hot, swirling pan to spread oil. Add 4 chops to skillet; cook until crusty and golden brown on bottom, 1½–2 minutes. With tongs, grip bone of each chop and turn. Cook on second side until crusty and golden brown, about 1½ minutes, browning any unseared edges of meat. Transfer chops to prepared baking sheet. Repeat with remaining 4 chops.

6. Transfer chops to oven and roast until instant-read thermometer inserted into side of chop registers 145°F, about 4 minutes. Transfer chops to platter. Sprinkle with parsley leaves.

Per serving (1 chop): 185 Cal, 8 g Total Fat, 3 g Sat Fat, 294 mg Sod, 2 g Total Carb, 0 g Sugar, 0 g Fib, 24 g Prot. SmartPoints value: 4

Cook's Tip

These delectable chops are perfect for picking up and eating out of hand.

MUSTARD-ROASTED POTATOES AND ONION

SERVES 4
Gluten Free, Vegetarian

3   (5-ounce) Yukon Gold potatoes, scrubbed

1   red onion

⅓   cup coarse-grain Dijon mustard or a combination of smooth Dijon and coarse-grain Dijon

2   teaspoons extra-virgin olive oil

2   teaspoons chopped fresh rosemary + 2 teaspoons rosemary needles

¼   teaspoon black pepper

1. Preheat oven to 400°F. Spray medium rimmed baking sheet with olive oil nonstick spray.

2. Cut potatoes lengthwise in half; cut each half into 4 wedges. Cut onion in half through stem end and cut each half into 6 wedges.

3. Toss together potatoes, onion, mustard, oil, chopped rosemary, and pepper in medium bowl. Spread potato-onion mixture on prepared baking sheet to form single layer, placing potatoes cut side down. Roast until potatoes are deep golden and crisp on bottom, about 30 minutes. Turn potatoes over and roast until crisp on outside and tender inside, about 20 minutes longer. Sprinkle with rosemary needles.

Per serving (6 potato wedges and 3 onion wedges): 125 Cal, 2 g Total Fat, 0 g Sat Fat, 478 mg Sod, 19 g Total Carb, 2 g Sugar, 3 g Fib, 2 g Prot. SmartPoints value: 4

GREEN BEANS WITH MUSHROOMS AND CRISP ONION CRUMBS

SERVES 8
20 Minutes or Less,
Vegetarian

2   tablespoons unsalted butter

¾   cup panko bread crumbs

2   tablespoons dried onion flakes

¾   teaspoon salt

1   teaspoon olive oil

1½   pounds green beans, trimmed and halved crosswise

1   pound small white mushrooms, thinly sliced

1. To make crumb topping, melt 1 tablespoon of butter in large heavy nonstick skillet over medium-low heat; add panko, onion flakes, and ¼ teaspoon of salt. Increase heat to medium and cook, stirring often, until crumbs are lightly toasted, about 3 minutes. Transfer crumb mixture to plate and set aside. Wipe skillet clean.

2. Heat oil and remaining 1 tablespoon butter in skillet over medium-high heat until butter is melted. Add green beans, mushrooms, and remaining ½ teaspoon salt; cook, stirring, until mushrooms are lightly browned and green beans are crisp-tender, about 5 minutes. Sprinkle with reserved crumb topping.

Per serving (1 cup): 110 Cal, 4 g Total Fat, 2 g Sat Fat, 291 mg Sod, 15 g Total Carb, 3 g Sugar, 4 g Fib, 4 g Prot. SmartPoints value: 3

Cook's Tip

Turn this side dish into a tempting main dish by tossing the green bean mixture with cooked whole wheat penne and sprinkling each serving with the crumb mixture. One cup of cooked whole wheat penne for each serving will up the SmartPoints value by 5.

KEY LIME DESSERT SHOTS

MAKES 8
Vegetarian

½ cup fat-free sweetened condensed milk

2 large egg yolks

⅓ cup lime juice, preferably key lime

2 teaspoons butter

½ cup plain low-fat Greek yogurt

½ cup graham cracker crumbs

1 pinch salt

½ cup aerosol whipped cream

1 tablespoon grated lime zest

1. Combine condensed milk and egg yolks in small heavy saucepan; cook over medium-low heat, whisking constantly, until mixture begins to boil. Stir in lime juice and 1 teaspoon of butter; pour into shallow bowl and refrigerate until cool, about 30 minutes.

2. Fold yogurt into cooled lime mixture just until combined; set aside.

3. Melt remaining 1 teaspoon butter in microwave in small microwavable bowl. Add graham cracker crumbs and salt, stirring until crumbs are evenly moistened.

4. Line up 8 (2-ounce) shot glasses. Spoon 1 tablespoon crumb mixture into each glass, pressing to form crust. Top each crust with 2 heaping tablespoons lime filling and 1 tablespoon whipped cream; sprinkle evenly with lime zest.

Per serving (1 dessert): 127 Cal, 4 g Total Fat, 2 g Sat Fat, 119 mg Sod, 19 g Total Carb, 15 g Sugar, 0 g Fib, 4 g Prot. SmartPoints value: 6

 Cook's Tip

Small and elegant, these dessert shots make the perfect ending to a fun evening.

RED VELVET MERINGUE SANDWICH COOKIES

MAKES 18
Gluten Free, Vegetarian

1¾ cups confectioners' sugar

½ cup light cream cheese (Neufchâtel), softened

¼ teaspoon vanilla extract

½ cup pecans

3 tablespoons unsweetened cocoa

3 large egg whites, at room temperature

¼ teaspoon salt

1 teaspoon red food coloring

1. Preheat oven to 275°F. Line two baking sheets with parchment paper.

2. To make filling, stir together ¼ cup of confectioners' sugar, the cream cheese, and vanilla in small bowl until smooth. Cover and refrigerate.

3. Pulse pecans in food processor until coarsely ground. Add 1 cup confectioners' sugar and the cocoa; process until nuts are finely ground.

4. With electric mixer on medium speed, beat egg whites and salt in medium bowl until foamy. Gradually beat in remaining ½ cup confectioners' sugar, 2 tablespoons at a time, until stiff, glossy peaks form when beaters are lifted. Beat in food coloring just until mixed well. With rubber spatula, gently fold in pecan mixture in three additions just until combined.

5. Transfer meringue batter to large pastry bag fitted with ½-inch plain tip. Pipe 1½-inch mounds, 1 inch apart, onto prepared baking sheets, making total of 36 cookies. Gently tap baking sheets 3 or 4 times against work surface to remove air bubbles.

6. Bake until cookies are crisp, about 30 minutes, rotating baking sheets halfway through baking time. Slide parchment onto wire racks and let meringues cool 10 minutes. Gently peel meringues off parchment and transfer to racks to cool completely.

7. Spread about 1 teaspoon filling on flat side of 18 cookies. Top with remaining 18 cookies, flat side down, pressing gently to form sandwiches. Cookies can be stacked between layers of wax paper in airtight container and refrigerated up to 2 days.

Per serving (1 cookie): 86 Cal, 3 g Total Fat, 1 g Sat Fat, 73 mg Sod, 13 g Total Carb, 12 g Sugar, 1 g Fib, 2 g Prot. SmartPoints value: 4

RED VELVET MERINGUE
SANDWICH COOKIES

MINI CHOCOLATE-BANANA CUPCAKES WITH PEANUT BUTTER FROSTING

MAKES 24

Vegetarian

¾ cup all-purpose flour

⅓ cup unsweetened cocoa

1 teaspoon baking powder

1 teaspoon baking soda

¼ teaspoon salt

3 very ripe small bananas, mashed (1½ cups)

¼ cup plain low-fat Greek yogurt

⅓ cup sugar

1 large egg

1 teaspoon vanilla extract

½ cup + 2 tablespoons mini semisweet chocolate chips

1 cup thawed frozen light whipped topping

3 tablespoons creamy peanut butter

1. Preheat oven to 350°F. Line 24-cup mini muffin pan with paper liners or spray with nonstick spray.

2. Whisk together flour, cocoa, baking powder, baking soda, and salt in small bowl. Stir together bananas, yogurt, sugar, egg, and vanilla in large bowl. With rubber spatula, fold flour mixture into yogurt mixture just until combined; gently stir in chocolate chips.

3. Fill each prepared muffin cup with heaping 1 tablespoon batter. Bake until toothpick inserted into center of cupcake comes out clean, about 12 minutes. Let cool in pan on wire rack 10 minutes; transfer cupcakes to rack to cool completely.

4. Meanwhile, to make frosting, whisk together whipped topping and peanut butter until light and fluffy. Frost each cupcake with generous 1 teaspoon frosting. (Can be refrigerated up to several hours.)

Per serving (1 mini cupcake): 92 Cal, 4 g Total Fat, 2 g Sat Fat, 112 mg Sod, 13 g Total Carb, 7 g Sugar, 1 g Fib, 2 g Prot. SmartPoints value: 3

 Cook's Tip

The addition of Greek yogurt and ripe bananas makes these cupcakes super moist. Did you know that unpeeled bananas can be stored in the refrigerator up to 3 days? The skins will darken, but the flesh will remain in the same state of ripeness as when first refrigerated.

CHUNKY PORK CHILI

SERVES 6
Gluten Free

1 pound lean pork tenderloin, trimmed and cut into 1-inch chunks

½ teaspoon kosher salt

2 teaspoons canola oil

1 onion, chopped

3 garlic cloves, minced

1½ teaspoons ancho chile powder

1 teaspoon ground cumin

1 (14½-ounce) can diced fire-roasted tomatoes

1 (15½-ounce) can pinto beans, rinsed and drained

1 (15½-ounce) can red kidney beans, rinsed and drained

1 (10-ounce) package frozen succotash

1 (14½-ounce) can reduced-sodium chicken broth

1. Sprinkle pork with ¼ teaspoon of salt. Heat oil in Dutch oven over medium-high heat. Cook pork, in batches, until browned, 3–4 minutes per batch, transferring pork to plate as it is browned using slotted spoon.

2. Add onion to Dutch oven; reduce heat to medium and cook, stirring, until softened, about 5 minutes. Stir in garlic, chile powder, cumin, and remaining ¼ teaspoon salt. Cook, stirring, until fragrant, about 30 seconds. Add tomatoes and bring to boil. Stir in pinto beans, kidney beans, succotash, and broth; return to boil.

3. Reduce heat and simmer until chili is slightly thickened, about 10 minutes. Stir in pork and any accumulated juices; simmer until pork is cooked through, 3–4 minutes longer. Divide chili evenly among 6 bowls.

Per serving (about 1 cup): 288 Cal, 5 g Total Fat, 1 g Sat Fat, 853 mg Sod, 36 g Total Carb, 5 g Sugar, 10 g Fib, 26 g Prot. SmartPoints value: 6

Cook's Tip

Top each serving of chili with 2 tablespoons plain reduced-fat Greek yogurt to tame the heat for no additional SmartPoints value.

TURKEY, BLACK BEAN,
AND MUSHROOM CHILI

TURKEY, BLACK BEAN, AND MUSHROOM CHILI

SERVES 4
Gluten Free

2   teaspoons olive oil

1   red bell pepper, chopped

1   onion, chopped

4   garlic cloves, minced

¾   pound ground skinless
     turkey breast

1   (28-ounce) can diced tomatoes

1   (15½-ounce) can black beans,
     rinsed and drained

2   cups thickly sliced white or
     cremini mushrooms

1   tablespoon chili powder

2   teaspoons ground cumin

1   teaspoon dried oregano

½   teaspoon salt

1. Heat oil in Dutch oven over medium heat. Add bell pepper, onion, and garlic; cook, stirring, until onion is softened, about 5 minutes. Add turkey and cook, breaking it apart with wooden spoon, until no longer pink, about 5 minutes.

2. Add tomatoes, beans, mushrooms, chili powder, cumin, oregano, and salt to Dutch oven; bring to boil. Reduce heat and simmer, covered, until vegetables are tender, about 30 minutes.

Per serving (about 1¼ cups): 301 Cal, 7 g Total Fat, 1 g Sat Fat, 1,060 mg Sod, 34 g Total Carb, 8 g Sugar, 12 g Fib, 29 g Prot. SmartPoints value: 5

 Cook's Tip

Spooning each serving of chili over ½ cup cooked brown rice will up the SmartPoints value by 3.

CHICKEN, SAUSAGE, AND BEAN CHILI

SERVES 8
Gluten Free

½ pound sweet or hot Italian-style turkey sausages, casings removed

1 pound skinless boneless chicken thighs, cut into 1-inch chunks

1 large onion, chopped

2 any-color bell peppers, cut into ½-inch dice

3 large garlic cloves, minced

2 tablespoons chili powder

1 tablespoon ground cumin

½ teaspoon salt

1 (28-ounce) can diced tomatoes

1 (15½-ounce) can pinto beans, rinsed and drained

1 (¾-pound) sweet potato, peeled and cut into ¾-inch chunks

1 cup spicy vegetable juice

1 cup water

1. Spray large Dutch oven with nonstick spray and set over medium-high heat. Add sausage and cook, breaking it up with wooden spoon, until browned, about 5 minutes. Transfer to medium bowl. Add half of chicken to Dutch oven and cook, stirring, until browned, about 8 minutes, transferring chicken to Dutch oven as it is browned. Repeat with remaining chicken.

2. Add onion to Dutch oven and cook, stirring, until softened, about 5 minutes. Stir in bell peppers, garlic, chili powder, cumin, and salt. Cook, stirring, until fragrant, about 30 seconds. Add tomatoes, beans, sweet potato, vegetable juice, and water; bring to boil. Add chicken and sausage and stir in.

3. Reduce heat and simmer, covered, 30 minutes, stirring occasionally. Uncover and simmer until potato is tender and chili is slightly thickened, about 15 minutes longer.

Per serving (about 1¼ cups): 236 Cal, 6 g Total Fat, 1 g Sat Fat, 756 mg Sod, 27 g Total Carb, 7 g Sugar, 7 g Fib, 21 g Prot. SmartPoints value: 5

Cook's Tip

Top each serving of chili with 2 tablespoons each shredded reduced-fat Cheddar cheese, sliced scallion, diced tomato, and chopped fresh cilantro for 1 additional SmartPoints value per serving.

TENDER BUTTERMILK CORN BREAD

SERVES 12
Vegetarian

2 teaspoons canola oil

1¾ cups yellow cornmeal, preferably stone ground

½ cup all-purpose flour

1 tablespoon sugar

2 teaspoons baking powder

¾ teaspoon salt

½ teaspoon baking soda

½ cup boiling water

1⅓ cups low-fat buttermilk

½ cup fat-free egg substitute

1 large jalapeño pepper, seeded and minced

2½ tablespoons butter, melted

1. Preheat oven to 425°F. Brush bottom and side of 10-inch cast-iron skillet with the oil. Place pan in oven to preheat 15 minutes.

2. Meanwhile, whisk together 1¼ cups of cornmeal, the flour, sugar, baking powder, salt, and baking soda in medium bowl.

3. Whisk together remaining ½ cup cornmeal and the boiling water in large bowl until smooth. Whisk in buttermilk, egg substitute, jalapeño, and butter. With rubber spatula, fold flour mixture into buttermilk mixture just until blended (do not overmix).

4. Using oven mitts, transfer hot skillet to stovetop. Scrape batter into hot pan. Return pan to oven and bake until corn bread is golden and toothpick inserted into center comes out clean, 18–20 minutes. Let cool in pan on wire rack 5 minutes. Cut into 12 wedges.

Per serving (1 wedge): 142 Cal, 4 g Total Fat, 2 g Sat Fat, 349 mg Sod, 23 g Total Carb, 3 g Sugar, 1 g Fib, 4 g Prot. SmartPoints value: 5

 Cook's Tip

Stone-ground cornmeal is a whole grain, which means it contains three parts: the outer layer (bran), the large middle portion (endosperm), and germ (the heart). To turn dried corn into meal, it is slowly ground between two stones, which creates a coarser texture and lends more corn flavor than regular cornmeal.

CAESAR SALAD WITH POBLANO DRESSING

SERVES 6
Vegetarian

1 small poblano pepper

¼ cup low-fat buttermilk

2 tablespoons reduced-calorie mayonnaise

2 tablespoons chopped fresh cilantro

Grated zest of ½ large lime

1 tablespoon lime juice

1 garlic clove, crushed through a press

½ teaspoon kosher salt

1 (12-ounce) package romaine lettuce hearts, thickly sliced

1 cup fat-free croutons

⅓ cup coarsely grated pecorino-Romano cheese

1. Preheat broiler.

2. To roast poblano, put pepper on broiler rack and broil 5 inches from heat, turning, until charred on all sides, 8–9 minutes. Transfer to small zip-close plastic bag and seal; let steam 10 minutes. Peel off charred skin, remove stems and seeds, and mince flesh.

3. To make dressing, transfer poblano to salad bowl. Add buttermilk, mayonnaise, cilantro, lime zest and juice, garlic, and salt, whisking until blended well. Add romaine, croutons, and Romano; toss until coated evenly with dressing.

Per serving (2½ cups): 93 Cal, 3 g Total Fat, 1 g Sat Fat, 374 mg Sod, 11 g Total Carb, 2 g Sugar, 1 g Fib, 4 g Prot. SmartPoints value: 2

 Cook's Tip

Some poblano peppers are milder than others. Roast the pepper, then taste a little piece. If it's mild, add the whole pepper, and if it is hot, add only half.

CAESAR SALAD WITH
POBLANO DRESSING

FENNEL-APPLE SLAW WITH LEMON AND MINT

SERVES 8
20 Minutes or Less,
Gluten Free, Vegetarian

- 1   teaspoon grated lemon zest
- ¼   cup lemon juice
- 2½   tablespoons extra-virgin olive oil
- 1   large shallot, minced
- 2   teaspoons sugar
- ½   teaspoon salt
- ¼   teaspoon black pepper
- 1   fennel bulb, very thinly sliced, + enough chopped fronds to equal ¼ cup
- 2   celery stalks, very thinly sliced
- 1   large apple, unpeeled, cored, and cut into matchstick strips
- ½   cup chopped fresh mint

1. To make dressing, whisk together lemon zest and juice, oil, shallot, sugar, salt, and pepper in salad bowl.

2. Add fennel, fennel fronds, celery, apple, and mint to dressing in bowl; toss until coated evenly. Let stand 10 minutes to allow flavors to blend.

Per serving (¾ cup): 76 Cal, 4 g Total Fat, 1 g Sat Fat, 171 mg Sod, 10 g Total Carb, 4 g Sugar, 2 g Fib, 1 g Prot. SmartPoints value: 2

 Cook's Tip

A mandoline, vegetable slicer, or the slicing disk of a food processor makes thinly slicing the fennel and celery very easy.

FAMILY HOLIDAYS AROUND THE WORLD

The desire to gather and commemorate, share special foods and drinks, and generally have a rollicking good time is universal. Customs and traditions vary from family to family and even from year to year, but the goal is always the same. Here are some of the fascinating ways that people in different parts of the world celebrate special holidays with their families and communities.

INDIA'S DIWALI

(October or November) Also known as the Festival of Lights, this multi-day celebration coincides with the Hindu New Year but is observed by people of many faiths in India and around the globe. Indians illuminate the inside and outside of their homes to symbolize inner light conquering spiritual darkness, an important Diwali theme. Fireworks, bonfires, and elaborate flower displays mark the occasion both in homes and in the streets. Families gather for huge feasts, and friends and relatives exchange gifts and good-will. The sharing of sweets is customary during Diwali, and families prepare impressive displays of colorful confections featuring traditional ingredients like coconut, almonds, pistachios, dried fruits, and rosewater.

RAMADAN

(Dates vary depending on the Islamic calendar) During the holy month of Ramadan, Egypt's streets are decorated with colored lights and the nights are illuminated with traditional lanterns known as *fawanees*. It is a time of introspection and devotion for Muslims across the globe. Each evening brings *Iftar*, the end of the day's fast, marked with the gathering of friends and family and lively socializing inside and outside the home. Ramadan culminates in the three-day Eid El-Fitr, "festival of the breaking of the fast." Families celebrate with joy and blessings, and visits to amusement parks or neighborhood carnivals are traditional. Relatives come together for feasts, and quantities of *kahk* (cookies stuffed with nuts and dusted with confectioners' sugar) are shared with neighbors and visitors.

SOUTH KOREA'S CH'USOK

(September or October) Also known as the Harvest Moon Festival, Ch'usok is Korea's most popular holiday, drawing families back to the homes of their ancestors for the most joyous celebration of the year. The day marks the rising of the harvest moon and begins in the morning with special foods set out at a shrine to honor ancestors and give thanks for the harvest. Following time-honored observances, the family sits down to a lavish meal of traditional dishes, most famously *songpyeon*, half-moon-shaped sweet rice cakes stuffed with sesame, red bean paste, and chestnuts. Families then set off to visit ancestral graves. Afterwards, merriment is the order of the day: Time-honored games, sports, and cultural activities are welcomed by young and old alike. Come evening, gazing at the harvest moon and dancing in its light are the activities of choice.

SWEDEN'S MIDSUMMER

(Late June) Sweden's most important holiday apart from Christmas, Midsummer is centered around the summer solstice, when in much of the country the sun barely dips below the horizon. The highlight of the celebration is large gatherings planned for Midsummer's Eve. Most are held in the countryside, and city dwellers head out en masse, clogging the roadways. Traditionally, flowers are picked to make wreaths and crowns and to decorate a maypole, the site of traditional ring dances for which many Swedes don folk costume. A typical Midsummer menu might feature pickled herring, boiled new potatoes with dill, and salmon, plus beer or spirits for numerous toasts. After dinner, the entertainment usually consists of live music and dancing, which often becomes raucous and lasts into the wee hours.

CHEDDAR-SCALLION BISCUITS

MAKES 19
Vegetarian

1   cup self-rising flour
    Pinch cayenne

2   tablespoons cold unsalted butter,
    cut into pieces

⅓   cup finely shredded reduced-fat
    sharp Cheddar cheese

2   tablespoons finely chopped
    scallion

1   tablespoon grated pecorino-
    Romano cheese

¾   cup + 2 tablespoons light
    sour cream

1. Preheat oven to 425°F. Line large baking sheet with parchment paper.

2. Whisk together flour and cayenne in medium bowl. With pastry blender or two knives used scissors-fashion, cut in butter until mixture resembles coarse crumbs. Add Cheddar, scallion, and Romano, tossing just until mixed. Add sour cream, stirring with fork just until very soft dough forms.

3. On lightly floured work surface, with floured hands, pat dough to ¾-inch thickness. With floured 1½-inch round cutter, cut out biscuits, pressing scraps together, making total of 19 biscuits.

4. Place biscuits, 2 inches apart, on prepared baking sheet. Bake until lightly browned, 13–15 minutes. Transfer to wire rack and let cool slightly before serving.

Per serving (1 biscuit): 101 Cal, 5 g Total Fat, 3 g Sat Fat, 207 mg Sod, 11 g Total Carb, 0 g Sugar, 0 g Fib, 3 g Prot. SmartPoints value: 4

Cook's Tip

No self-rising flour in your pantry? Substitute 1 cup all-purpose flour mixed with 1½ teaspoons baking powder and ¼ teaspoon salt.

CHEDDAR-SCALLION BISCUITS

CHOCOLATE-PECAN THINS

MAKES 18
Vegetarian

18 pecan halves

⅓ cup all-purpose flour

¼ cup unsweetened cocoa

½ teaspoon baking powder

½ cup sugar

2 tablespoons butter

2 tablespoons apple butter

1 large egg white

1 teaspoon vanilla extract

1. Preheat oven to 350°F.

2. Spread pecans on small baking sheet; bake until nuts begin to brown and are fragrant, about 5 minutes. Remove from oven; set aside to cool.

3. Meanwhile, whisk together flour, cocoa, and baking powder in medium bowl. With electric mixer on medium-high speed, beat sugar, butter, and apple butter in another medium bowl until light and fluffy. Add egg white and vanilla; beat until combined. Reduce mixer speed to low; stir in flour mixture just until mixed.

4. Drop dough by ½ tablespoonfuls onto one or two ungreased baking sheets, 1 inch apart, making total of 18 cookies. Place pecan half on top of each cookie. Bake 12 minutes; let cookies cool on baking sheet on wire rack 5 minutes. With spatula, transfer cookies to rack and let cool completely.

Per serving (1 cookie): 59 Cal, 3 g Total Fat, 1 g Sat Fat, 28 mg Sod, 9 g Total Carb, 6 g Sugar, 1 g Fib, 1 g Prot. SmartPoints value: 3

MINI CHOCOLATE CHIP COOKIES

MAKES 48
Vegetarian

¾ cup all-purpose flour

¼ teaspoon baking soda

⅛ teaspoon salt

½ cup packed dark brown sugar

2 tablespoons butter, softened

2 teaspoons canola oil

1 large egg white

1 teaspoon vanilla extract

½ cup semisweet chocolate chips

1. Preheat oven to 375°F. Line two baking sheets with parchment paper.

2. Whisk together flour, baking soda, and salt in small bowl. With electric mixer on medium-high speed, beat brown sugar, butter, and oil in medium bowl until creamy. Beat in egg white and vanilla until combined well. Reduce mixer speed to low. Stir in flour mixture just until mixed. Stir in chocolate chips.

3. Drop dough by ½ teaspoonfuls onto prepared baking sheets, about 1 inch apart, making total of 48 cookies. Bake until cookies are golden along edges, 4–6 minutes; let cool on baking sheets on wire racks 5 minutes. Transfer cookies to racks and let cool completely.

Per serving (1 cookie): 31 Cal, 1 g Total Fat, 1 g Sat Fat, 19 mg Sod, 5 g Total Carb, 3 g Sugar, 0 g Fib, 0 g Prot. SmartPoints value: 1

 Cook's Tip

Both light brown sugar and dark brown sugar are made of granulated sugar with molasses added back in. Dark brown sugar contains more molasses than light brown, giving it a slightly richer flavor and deeper color. They are usually interchangeable in recipes.

BUFFALO-STYLE STUFFED CELERY

SERVES 10
20 Minutes or Less,
Gluten Free, Vegetarian

½   cup light cream cheese
     (Neufchâtel), softened

2   tablespoons blue cheese, softened

1   small garlic clove, minced

¼   teaspoon salt

5   celery stalks, each cut into
     4 pieces

2½ teaspoons hot pepper sauce,
     or to taste

1   tablespoon chopped fresh chives

1. Stir together cream cheese, blue cheese, garlic, and salt in small bowl until smooth. Spoon or pipe about ½ tablespoon cheese mixture into each piece of celery.

2. Arrange stuffed celery on serving plate; drizzle each with about ¼ teaspoon hot sauce and sprinkle with chives.

Per serving (2 pieces stuffed celery): 38 Cal, 3 g Total Fat, 2 g Sat Fat, 177 mg Sod, 1 g Total Carb, 1 g Sugar, 0 g Fib, 1 g Prot. SmartPoints value: 2

SILKEN RANCH DIP

SERVES 4
20 Minutes or Less,
Gluten Free, Vegetarian

½   (1-pound) package light silken tofu, drained

⅓   cup low-fat buttermilk

¼   cup fat-free mayonnaise

2   tablespoons chopped fresh chives

2   tablespoons chopped fresh dill

2   tablespoons chopped fresh
     flat-leaf parsley

1½ tablespoons cider vinegar

1   garlic clove, finely chopped

¼   teaspoon black pepper

⅛   teaspoon salt

1. Place tofu on paper towel–lined plate. Set another plate on top to weigh it down. Let stand 10 minutes to remove excess liquid. Drain off liquid and discard.

2. Combine tofu, buttermilk, mayonnaise, chives, dill, parsley, vinegar, garlic, pepper, and salt in food processor; process until smooth. (Can be refrigerated in airtight container up to 3 days.)

Per serving (generous ¼ cup): 45 Cal, 1 g Total Fat, 1 g Sat Fat, 265 mg Sod, 5 g Total Carb, 3 g Sugar, 0 g Fib, 5 g Prot. SmartPoints value: 1

NEW ENGLAND BACON AND CLAM CHOWDER

SERVES 6
Gluten Free

¾ cup water

30 littleneck clams, scrubbed

2 ounces diced pancetta
   (about ¼ cup)

1 small onion, chopped

2 shallots, finely chopped

1 pound Yukon Gold potatoes,
   peeled and cut into ¾-inch dice

1 (8-ounce) bottle clam juice

1 teaspoon chopped fresh thyme

¼ teaspoon black pepper

½ cup fat-free half-and-half

2 tablespoons chopped fresh
   flat-leaf parsley

1. Bring water to boil in large Dutch oven. Add clams and cook, covered, until they open, 8–10 minutes, transferring clams to bowl as they open. Discard any clams that do not open. Strain clam liquid through sieve lined with cheesecloth or paper towels into 2-cup glass measuring cup. Add enough water to equal 2 cups; set aside. When cool enough to handle, remove clams from shells and coarsely chop. Discard shells. Wipe Dutch oven clean.

2. Add pancetta to Dutch oven and cook over medium heat, stirring occasionally, until crisp, about 4 minutes. With slotted spoon, transfer to paper towel–lined plate to drain. Add onion and shallots to pot; cook, covered, stirring occasionally, until tender, about 3 minutes. Add potatoes, reserved clam liquid, bottled clam juice, thyme, and pepper; bring to boil. Reduce heat and simmer, covered, until potatoes are fork-tender, about 20 minutes.

3. With potato masher or large spoon, crush potatoes. Stir in half-and-half and chopped clams; cook just until heated through, about 2 minutes (do not boil). Stir in pancetta and parsley. Ladle chowder evenly into 6 bowls.

Per serving (1 cup): 202 Cal, 5 g Total Fat, 2 g Sat Fat, 521 mg Sod, 18 g Total Carb, 2 g Sugar, 2 g Fib, 12 g Prot. SmartPoints value: 5

 Cook's Tip

Break four multi-seed brown rice gluten-free crackers over each serving of chowder for a bit of welcome crunch. Four multi-seed brown rice gluten-free crackers per serving will up the SmartPoints value by 1.

CAPE COD CLAMBAKE

CAPE COD CLAMBAKE

SERVES 8
Gluten Free

8 small red potatoes, scrubbed and halved

4 ears of corn, husks and silk removed, halved crosswise

1 large onion, thickly sliced

3 large garlic cloves, chopped

1 cup reduced-sodium chicken broth

3 tablespoons lemon juice

2 tablespoons unsalted butter, cut into pieces

4 fresh oregano sprigs

½ teaspoon salt

¼ teaspoon black pepper

⅛ teaspoon cayenne

16 littleneck clams, scrubbed

16 mussels, scrubbed and debearded

2 (1¼-pound) live lobsters

1. Preheat grill to medium-high or prepare medium-high fire.

2. Toss together potatoes, corn, onion, garlic, broth, lemon juice, butter, oregano sprigs, salt, black pepper, and cayenne in large deep disposable foil pan. Cover pan tightly with heavy foil and place on grill rack. Grill, covered, until corn and onion are almost tender, about 20 minutes.

3. Remove pan from grill; carefully open foil to avoid steam. Arrange clams and mussels on top of vegetables in even layer. Set lobsters on top and cover pan tightly with foil. Return pan to grill rack. Grill, covered, until potatoes are tender, lobsters are cooked through, and clams and mussels are opened, 20–25 minutes. Carefully open foil. Discard any clams and mussels that do not open.

Per serving (¼ lobster, 2 clams, 2 mussels, 1 potato, 1 piece corn, and about 2 tablespoons broth): 358 Cal, 6 g Total Fat, 2 g Sat Fat, 1,021 mg Sod, 43 g Total Carb, 6 g Sugar, 4 g Fib, 35 g Prot. SmartPoints value: 9

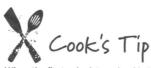 Cook's Tip

When the first colonists arrived in New England, they saw Native Americans baking clams and other shellfish over hot stones that were covered with seaweed. Preparing an old-fashioned clambake on a backyard grill is reminiscent of those early years.

HEIRLOOM TOMATO AND BASIL PLATTER

SERVES 6
20 Minutes or Less,
Gluten Free, Vegetarian

2   tablespoons extra-virgin olive oil

1   tablespoon red wine vinegar

1   tablespoon water

1   small garlic clove, minced

½   teaspoon salt

¼   teaspoon dried oregano, crumbled

¼   teaspoon black pepper

3   large assorted heirloom tomatoes, sliced

½   small red onion, very thinly sliced

½   cup torn fresh basil

1. To make dressing, whisk together oil, vinegar, water, garlic, salt, oregano, and pepper in small bowl.

2. Arrange tomatoes on platter in decorative overlapping pattern. Scatter onion and basil on top; drizzle with dressing.

Per serving (½ tomato, a few onion slices, and about 2 teaspoons dressing): 60 Cal, 5 g Total Fat, 1 g Sat Fat, 199 mg Sod, 4 g Total Carb, 3 g Sugar, 1 g Fib, 1 g Prot. SmartPoints value: 1

 Cook's Tip

For a heartier salad, top it with coarsely crumbled ricotta salata and serve on a bed of baby arugula or another dark salad green. Ricotta salata is ricotta cheese that has been pressed and salted. It can be crumbled or sliced. Topping this salad with ¾ cup coarsely crumbled ricotta salata will up the per-serving SmartPoints value by 3.

HEIRLOOM TOMATO
AND BASIL PLATTER

LEMONY COLESLAW WITH APPLES

SERVES 12
Gluten Free, Vegetarian

½   cup reduced-calorie mayonnaise

¼   cup plain fat-free Greek yogurt

1   teaspoon grated lemon zest

3   tablespoons lemon juice

1   teaspoon sugar

½   teaspoon salt

½   teaspoon black pepper

1   (14-ounce) package coleslaw mix

2   Gala apples, peeled, cored, and
      cut into ¼-inch-thick matchstick
      strips

2   scallions, thinly sliced

¼   cup chopped fresh flat-leaf
      parsley

To make dressing, whisk together mayonnaise, yogurt, lemon zest and juice, sugar, salt, and pepper in large bowl. Add coleslaw mix, apples, scallions, and parsley; toss until mixed well and coated evenly with dressing. Cover and refrigerate about 30 minutes to allow flavors to blend.

Per serving (about ⅔ cup): 65 Cal, 3 g Total Fat, 0 g Sat Fat, 181 mg Sod, 8 g Total Carb, 5 g Sugar, 2 g Fib, 1 g Prot. SmartPoints value: 1

 Cook's Tip

This flavorful coleslaw can be made up to 6 hours ahead, but keep it refrigerated until about 30 minutes before serving time. Bear in mind that the longer it sits, the softer the slaw will be. Taste it before serving so you can adjust the seasonings, if needed.

MARCONA ALMOND AND ORANGE THUMBPRINT COOKIES

MAKES 48
Vegetarian

⅔ cup marcona almonds

1¼ cups all-purpose flour

½ teaspoon ground ginger

½ teaspoon baking soda

½ teaspoon salt

⅓ cup granulated sugar

¼ cup packed light brown sugar

6 tablespoons unsalted butter, softened

1 large egg

½ teaspoon almond extract

¼ cup sweet orange marmalade or preserves

1. Pulse almonds in food processor until finely chopped. Whisk together ¼ cup of almonds, the flour, ginger, baking soda, and salt in medium bowl; reserve remaining almonds in shallow bowl.

2. With electric mixer on medium-high speed, beat granulated sugar, brown sugar, and butter in large bowl until light and fluffy. Add egg and almond extract; beat until mixed well. Reduce mixer speed to low. Stir in flour mixture until just combined. Cover and refrigerate until dough is firm, at least 3 hours or up to overnight.

3. Preheat oven to 350°F. Line two large baking sheets with parchment paper.

4. Scoop dough by teaspoonfuls and roll into 48 balls; gently roll in reserved chopped almonds until coated. Place about 2 inches apart on prepared baking sheets.

5. Bake 5 minutes. Remove pans from oven and, using end of wooden spoon, make small indentation in center of each cookie. Return cookies to oven and bake until lightly browned and set, about 4 minutes longer. Remove from oven and fill each cookie with ¼ teaspoon marmalade. Transfer to wire racks and let cool completely.

Per serving (1 cookie): 54 Cal, 3 g Total Fat, 1 g Sat Fat, 50 mg Sod, 7 g Total Carb, 4 g Sugar, 0 g Fib, 1 g Prot. SmartPoints value: 2

 Cook's Tip

Marcona almonds are shorter and plumper than regular almonds. They are also sweeter, softer, and more expensive. You can substitute regular almonds or hazelnuts for the marcona almonds in this recipe. If you're not a fan of orange marmalade, use your favorite jam.

MINI PEANUT BUTTER
ICE-CREAM SANDWICHES

MINI PEANUT BUTTER ICE-CREAM SANDWICHES

MAKES 12
Vegetarian

2   ounces light cream cheese (Neufchâtel), softened

¼   cup confectioners' sugar

¼   cup creamy peanut butter
    Pinch salt

1½ cups thawed frozen light whipped topping

24 chocolate wafer cookies

1. With electric mixer on medium speed, beat cream cheese, confectioners' sugar, peanut butter, and salt in medium bowl until smooth. Beat in whipped topping until just combined.

2. Place 1½ tablespoons of peanut-butter filling on flat side of each wafer cookie; place second cookie, flat side down, on top to form sandwiches, lightly pressing down. Arrange cookies on small baking sheet and freeze until firm, about 1 hour.

Per serving (1 ice-cream sandwich): 124 Cal, 6 g Total Fat, 2 g Sat Fat, 153 mg Sod, 14 g Total Carb, 7 g Sugar, 1 g Fib, 2 g Prot. SmartPoints value: 5

CHAPTER 4
SPECIAL GUEST DINNERS
Made Super Simple

We love inviting family and friends over for a home-cooked meal as a way to express how important they are and how much they mean to us. But when it comes to the actual menu, not everyone enjoys eating the same food. So as good hosts, we know the thoughtful, caring thing to do is to prepare dishes that are geared to our guests and their food preferences. To that end, in this chapter you'll find gluten-free recipes that will satisfy everyone, extra-hearty dishes for the "meat-and-potatoes" crowd, the perfect recipes for people who love something out of the ordinary, and dishes meant for those times when you feel like dressing up the table with a crisply ironed linen tablecloth and your best wineglasses. And just in case you're in the mood to serve up some fun cocktails, savory nibbles, and tasty sweet bites, we have that covered too. Simply mix and match the recipes within each section to create a special menu.

FOR THE "MEAT-AND-POTATOES" CROWD
Super-Hearty Mains and Sides

FOR YOUR NO-GLUTEN FRIENDS
Mains, Sides, and Desserts That Are Delectable

FOR THE FOODIES
Elegant and Sophisticated Apps, Mains, Sides, and Desserts

FOR THE ADVENTUROUS EATERS
Try Something Different Mains, Sides, and Sweets

FOR THOSE WHO LOVE A COCKTAIL PARTY
Small Bites and Sweets to Entice

SUNDAY POT ROAST

SUNDAY POT ROAST

SERVES 8
Gluten Free

2 teaspoons herbes de Provence

1½ teaspoons kosher salt

¼ teaspoon black pepper

1 (2½-pound) lean beef round roast, trimmed

1 tablespoon canola oil

¾ pound shallots (about 10), peeled

6 large garlic cloves, peeled

1 cup dry red wine

2 cups water

3 tablespoons tomato paste

1 bay leaf

¾ pound carrots, cut into ½-inch slices

1. Preheat oven to 350°F.

2. Mix together herbes de Provence, 1 teaspoon of salt, and the pepper in cup; rub all over roast.

3. Heat oil in Dutch oven over medium-high heat. Add beef and cook until browned on all sides, about 7 minutes. Transfer to plate.

4. Add shallots and garlic to Dutch oven; cook, stirring occasionally, until beginning to brown, about 2 minutes. Add wine and cook until slightly reduced, about 2 minutes. Stir in water, tomato paste, remaining ½ teaspoon salt, and the bay leaf; bring to boil. Return meat to pot. Cover and transfer to oven; bake 2 hours.

5. Remove roast from oven. Stir in carrots. Cover and bake until meat is fork-tender, about 1 hour, turning meat over after 30 minutes. Transfer roast to cutting board; cut into ¼-inch slices. Return sliced meat to sauce in Dutch oven; keep warm until ready to serve. Discard bay leaf.

Per serving (2 slices meat and about ⅓ cup sauce with vegetables): 292 Cal, 9 g Total Fat, 2 g Sat Fat, 533 mg Sod, 14 g Total Carb, 3 g Sugar, 2 g Fib, 33 g Prot. SmartPoints value: 5

 Cook's Tip

If you've got the time, make this dish a day or two ahead—it will taste even better. At serving time, gently reheat it over low heat.

MEAT LOAF WITH CHIVE MASHED POTATOES

SERVES 6
Gluten Free

½ pound ground lean beef (7% fat or less)

¾ pound ground skinless turkey breast

1 onion, chopped

½ cup old-fashioned (rolled) oats

1 (8-ounce) can tomato sauce

1 large egg, lightly beaten

2 tablespoons Worcestershire sauce

1 tablespoon hot pepper sauce

¼ + ⅛ teaspoon salt

¼ + ⅛ teaspoon black pepper

4 large all-purpose potatoes, such as Yukon Gold

¼ cup fat-free milk

¼ cup plain fat-free yogurt

¼ cup light sour cream

1 tablespoon chopped fresh chives

1. Preheat oven to 350°F. Spray 5 x 9-inch loaf pan with nonstick spray.

2. Combine beef, turkey, onion, and oats in large bowl. Stir together tomato sauce, egg, Worcestershire sauce, hot sauce, ¼ teaspoon of salt, and ¼ teaspoon of black pepper in small bowl. Add to beef mixture and stir until combined but not overmixed. Press meat-loaf mixture into prepared pan. Bake until instant-read thermometer inserted into center of meat loaf registers 165°F, about 1 hour.

3. Meanwhile, peel potatoes and cut into large chunks. Combine potatoes with enough salted water to cover in large saucepan; bring to boil. Reduce heat and cook, partially covered, until fork-tender about 12 minutes; drain and return to saucepan. With potato masher, mash potatoes until smooth. Stir in milk, yogurt, sour cream, chives, and remaining ⅛ teaspoon salt and ⅛ teaspoon black pepper. Rewarm over low heat.

4. Cut meat loaf into 12 slices. Serve with potatoes.

Per serving (2 slices meat loaf and ⅙ of potatoes): 378 Cal, 7 g Total Fat, 2 g Sat Fat, 534 mg Sod, 50 g Total Carb, 7 g Sugar, 8 g Fib, 29 g Prot. SmartPoints value: 9

 Cook's Tip

Food is fork-tender when a knife can be inserted with little or no resistance. This term is most often used to describe braised meats and root vegetables, such as beets, carrots, parsnips, and potatoes.

MIXED GRILL WITH SPICY PIRI-PIRI SAUCE

SERVES 6
Gluten Free

2 red bell peppers, chopped

½– 1 jalapeño pepper, seeded and coarsely chopped

2 tablespoons lime juice

2 teaspoons olive oil

2 teaspoons sugar

¾ teaspoon salt

2 garlic cloves, minced

1 teaspoon ground cumin

¾ pound lean flank steak, trimmed

¾ pound lean pork tenderloin, trimmed and cut into 18 chunks

¾ pound fully cooked Italian-style chicken sausages

1. To make sauce, combine bell peppers, jalapeño, lime juice, oil, sugar, and ¼ teaspoon of salt in blender; process until smooth. Measure out 1 cup of sauce and refrigerate. Transfer remaining sauce to large zip-close plastic bag; stir in garlic and cumin. Add flank steak and pork. Squeeze out air and seal bag; turn to coat meat. Refrigerate 2 hours or overnight.

2. Spray grill rack with nonstick spray. Preheat grill to medium or prepare medium fire.

3. Remove steak and pork from marinade; discard marinade. Thread pork onto 6 skewers. Sprinkle pork and flank steak with remaining ½ teaspoon salt. Place skewers, steak, and sausages on grill rack. Grill steak until instant-read thermometer registers 145°F, 5–6 minutes per side. Grill pork, turning skewers, until cooked through, about 8 minutes. Grill sausages until well-marked and skin blisters slightly, about 8 minutes. Transfer steak, pork, and sausages to cutting board; let steak stand about 10 minutes.

4. Cut steak against grain into 12 thin slices; transfer to platter. Remove pork from skewers and arrange alongside steak. Slice sausages into 18 pieces and add to platter. Transfer reserved 1 cup sauce to serving bowl and place on platter.

Per serving (2 slices steak, 3 pieces pork, 3 pieces sausage, and 2½ tablespoons sauce): 250 Cal, 10 g Total Fat, 3 g Sat Fat, 731 mg Sod, 5 g Total Carb, 3 g Sugar, 1 g Fib, 34 g Prot. SmartPoints value: 5

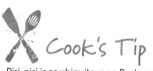

Cook's Tip

Piri-piri is as ubiquitous on Portuguese tables as ketchup is in the United States. Serving grilled meat without it is practically unheard of. A classic recipe would be much heavier on the olive oil than ours, and it would be considerably hotter.

BEER-BRAISED BRATWURST AND SAUERKRAUT

SERVES 4

4 (3-ounce) fully cooked low-fat smoked bratwursts or other low-fat wursts, each cut diagonally into thirds

1 onion, thinly sliced

½ teaspoon caraway seeds

⅛ teaspoon coarse black pepper

1 sweet apple, halved, cored, and cut into ¼-inch-thick pieces

1 (16-ounce) bag sauerkraut, rinsed and drained well

1 cup amber or dark beer

1 bay leaf

1. Spray bratwursts with nonstick spray. Place in large cast iron or heavy nonstick skillet and cook over medium heat until browned on all sides, about 10 minutes. Transfer to plate.

2. Add onion, caraway seeds, and pepper to skillet; cook, stirring occasionally, until onion is golden, 6–8 minutes. Add apple and cook, stirring, until softened, 3–4 minutes longer.

3. Stir sauerkraut, beer, and bay leaf into onion mixture; bring to boil. Reduce heat and simmer, stirring occasionally, until most of liquid is evaporated, 10–15 minutes. Return bratwursts to skillet and cook, stirring once or twice, until heated through, about 5 minutes longer. Discard bay leaf.

Per serving (3 pieces bratwurst and 1 cup sauerkraut mixture): 188 Cal, 3 g Total Fat, 1 g Sat Fat, 1,464 mg Sod, 23 g Total Carb, 11 g Sugar, 5 g Fib, 15 g Prot. SmartPoints value: 3

 Cook's Tip

Steamed baby potatoes would be the ideal accompaniment for this hearty dish. One pound of steamed baby potatoes will up the per-serving SmartPoints value by 3.

BEER-BRAISED BRATWURST
AND SAUERKRAUT

POTATO GRATIN WITH PARMESAN AND ROSEMARY

SERVES 8
Vegetarian

3   tablespoons all-purpose flour

2¼ cups reduced-fat (2%) milk

2   large garlic cloves, minced

½   teaspoon dried rosemary, crumbled

¼   teaspoon dried thyme

½   teaspoon salt

¼   teaspoon black pepper

2   tablespoons light cream cheese (Neufchâtel)

½   cup grated Parmesan cheese

2½ pounds russet (baking) potatoes, peeled and cut into ⅛-inch slices

1. Preheat oven to 400°F. Spray 9-inch sqaure or round shallow baking dish with nonstick spray.

2. Put flour in medium saucepan and gradually whisk in milk until smooth. Add garlic, rosemary, thyme, salt, and pepper; bring to simmer over medium heat. Cook, stirring, until sauce is consistency of heavy cream and no floury taste remains, about 5 minutes. Stir in cream cheese and cook, stirring, until melted, about 2 minutes; stir in Parmesan.

3. Put potatoes into large bowl; add cheese mixture and stir until coated evenly. Pile potatoes into prepared casserole dish, arranging top layer of potatoes.

4. Cover pan with foil; bake 1 hour. Uncover and bake until potatoes are tender and browned on top, about 35 minutes longer.

Per serving (generous 1¼ cups): 191 Cal, 4 g Total Fat, 2 g Sat Fat, 296 mg Sod, 31 g Total Carb, 5 g Sugar, 3 g Fib, 8 g Prot. SmartPoints value: 6

Cook's Tip

If the gratin doesn't get as browned on top as you would like, place it under the broiler for a couple of minutes.

POTATO GRATIN WITH
PARMESAN AND ROSEMARY

BLUE CHEESE-DRESSED
ICEBERG LETTUCE "STEAKS"

BLUE CHEESE—DRESSED ICEBERG LETTUCE "STEAKS"

SERVES 4
Vegetarian

2   very thin slices firm sandwich bread, cut into ½-inch cubes

½   cup low-fat buttermilk

1   tablespoon reduced-calorie mayonnaise

¼   teaspoon salt

¼   teaspoon hot pepper sauce, such as Frank's

1   firm head iceberg lettuce, cored, ends trimmed, and cut into 4 thick slices

2   plum tomatoes, cut into ½-inch pieces (about ¾ cup)

½   cup chopped sweet onion

½   cup coarsely crumbled blue cheese

1. Preheat oven to 350°F.

2. To make croutons, spread bread cubes on small baking sheet and bake, turning once or twice, until golden and crisp, about 5 minutes.

3. To make dressing, whisk together buttermilk, mayonnaise, salt, and hot sauce in small bowl.

4. Place 1 lettuce "steak" on each of 4 plates. Drizzle evenly with dressing and top with tomatoes, onion, blue cheese, and croutons.

Per serving (1 lettuce "steak," ¼ of tomato, ¼ of onion, 2 tablespoons cheese, and 2½ tablespoons dressing): 185 Cal, 7 g Total Fat, 4 g Sat Fat, 581 mg Sod, 24 g Total Carb, 10 g Sugar, 6 g Fib, 10 g Prot. SmartPoints value: 5

 Cook's Tip

This unique way of serving this classic salad combo is a great conversation starter. Be sure to choose a lettuce that is very firm when pressed for the best "steaks." A serrated bread knife makes neatly slicing the lettuce easy to do.

ROASTED FINGERLINGS WITH GARLIC AND HERBS

SERVES 4
Gluten Free, Vegetarian

1 pound fingerling potatoes, scrubbed and halved lengthwise

1 tablespoon olive oil

2 garlic cloves, minced

1 teaspoon chopped fresh oregano or ¼ teaspoon dried

½ teaspoon salt

¼ teaspoon black pepper

1 tablespoon chopped fresh flat-leaf parsley

1 tablespoon chopped fresh chives

1. Preheat oven to 375°F. Spray small roasting pan with nonstick spray.

2. Combine potatoes, oil, garlic, oregano, salt, and pepper in prepared pan; toss until coated evenly. Roast, stirring occasionally, until potatoes are browned on outside and tender on inside, 35–40 minutes. Spoon into serving bowl and sprinkle with parsley and chives.

Per serving (¾ cup): 112 Cal, 4 g Total Fat, 0 g Sat Fat, 310 mg Sod, 19 g Total Carb, 1 g Sugar, 3 g Fib, 2 g Prot. SmartPoints value: 3

 Cook's Tip

Here's how to turn this side dish into a hearty salad: Transfer the roasted potatoes to a large bowl and let cool until just warm. Add 2 cups baby arugula, 1 cup halved cherry tomatoes, and 2 teaspoons red wine vinegar and toss until mixed well. The SmartPoints value will remain the same.

BEEF AND "ZUCCHINI NOODLE" LASAGNA

SERVES 6

Gluten Free

3   large zucchini
    (about ½ pound each), cut into
    ¼-inch lengthwise slices

¾   pound ground lean beef
    (7% fat or less)

1   (14½-ounce) can crushed
    tomatoes, preferably fire roasted

½   teaspoon salt

¼   teaspoon black pepper

¾   cup part-skim ricotta cheese

1   large egg

3   tablespoons grated Parmesan
    cheese

1   cup shredded part-skim
    mozzarella cheese

1. Preheat oven to 400°F. Spray 9-inch square baking dish or casserole dish with nonstick spray. Spray large rimmed baking sheet with nonstick spray.

2. Place zucchini on prepared baking sheet and spray with nonstick spray; bake 10 minutes. With tongs, carefully turn zucchini over; bake just until tender, about 10 minutes longer. Let cool slightly.

3. Reduce oven temperature to 350°F.

4. Meanwhile, cook beef in large nonstick skillet over medium heat, breaking it apart with wooden spoon, until browned, about 5 minutes. Add tomatoes, ¼ teaspoon of salt, and ⅛ teaspoon of pepper; cook until slightly thickened, about 7 minutes longer.

5. Stir together ricotta, egg, 1 tablespoon of Parmesan, and remaining ¼ teaspoon salt and ⅛ teaspoon pepper in small bowl until blended well.

6. Spread ⅓ cup of tomato-meat sauce in prepared baking dish. Arrange half of zucchini on top of sauce, filling in any spaces with extra pieces of zucchini. Spoon half of remaining tomato-meat sauce over zucchini and dollop with half of ricotta mixture, spacing dollops evenly. Sprinkle with ½ cup of mozzarella. Repeat with remaining zucchini, tomato-meat sauce, ricotta mixture, ½ cup mozzarella, and 2 tablespoons Parmesan.

7. Bake until bubbly, 30–35 minutes. Let stand 10 minutes before cutting into 6 portions.

Per serving (generous 1 cup): 233 Cal, 11 g Total Fat, 6 g Sat Fat, 557 mg Sod, 10 g Total Carb, 6 g Sugar, 2 g Fib, 25 g Prot. SmartPoints value: 5

LONDON BROIL WITH SWEET ONIONS AND PEPPERS

SERVES 4
Gluten Free

1   (1-pound) lean boneless sirloin steak, trimmed

4   teaspoons taco seasoning

2   large assorted-color bell peppers, each cut into 4 slabs

2   sweet or red onions, thickly sliced

½   lemon

¼   cup chopped fresh flat-leaf parsley

1. Spray grill rack with nonstick spray. Preheat grill to medium or prepare medium fire.

2. Sprinkle steak with 2 teaspoons of taco seasoning. Sprinkle bell peppers and onions with remaining 2 teaspoons seasoning. Lightly spray bell peppers, onions, and cut side of lemon with nonstick spray. Place steak, vegetables, and lemon (cut side down) on grill rack and grill until vegetables and lemon are browned and instant-read thermometer inserted into side of steak registers 145°F, about 5 minutes per side.

3. Transfer steak to cutting board and let stand 10 minutes. Cut against grain into 16 slices. Sprinkle vegetables with parsley and squeeze lemon juice over; serve with steak.

Per serving (4 slices steak and ⅔ cup vegetables): 197 Cal, 4 g Total Fat, 2 g Sat Fat, 276 mg Sod, 12 g Total Carb, 5 g Sugar, 3 g Fib, 27 g Prot. SmartPoints value: 3

 Cook's Tip

For an extra 4 SmartPoints per serving, round out this hearty steak dinner with ½ medium-size baked potato topped with 2 tablespoons light sour cream and sprinkled with chopped fresh chives.

LONDON BROIL WITH
SWEET ONIONS AND PEPPERS

TURKEY-AND-QUINOA MEAT LOAF

SERVES 6
Gluten Free

1   cup water

½   cup quinoa, rinsed

1   zucchini, shredded

¾   cup chili sauce or ketchup

2   large egg whites

1   small red onion, finely chopped

1   tablespoon chopped fresh
    flat-leaf parsley

1½   teaspoons dried Italian seasoning

½   teaspoon salt

½   teaspoon black pepper

1   pound ground skinless
    turkey breast

1. Bring water to boil in small saucepan; add quinoa. Reduce heat and simmer, covered, until quinoa is tender and water is absorbed, about 15 minutes. Remove saucepan from heat; fluff quinoa with fork and let cool slightly.

2. Meanwhile, preheat oven to 375°F. Line bottom of 9 x 13-inch baking dish or baking pan with parchment paper.

3. Squeeze zucchini dry and put in large bowl. Stir in ¼ cup of chili sauce, the egg whites, onion, parsley, Italian seasoning, salt, and pepper. Add turkey and quinoa; stir until combined well but not overmixed.

4. Transfer turkey mixture to prepared baking dish and shape into 5 x 11-inch loaf. Spread remaining ½ cup chili sauce on top of loaf.

5. Bake until instant-read thermometer inserted into center of loaf registers 165°F. Let stand 5 minutes. Cut into 6 slices.

Per serving (1 slice): 198 Cal, 4 g Total Fat, 1 g Sat Fat, 660 mg Sod, 19 g Total Carb, 5 g Sugar, 3 g Fib, 21 g Prot. SmartPoints value: 4

 Cook's Tip

Quinoa grains are covered with a protective bitter coating called saponin, so giving it a good rinse in a fine sieve is essential before cooking it.

VEGGIE BOLOGNESE WITH SOY CRUMBLES AND MUSHROOMS

SERVES 4

Vegetarian, Gluten Free

8   ounces brown rice penne

½   ounce dried porcini mushrooms

¾   cup boiling water

1   teaspoon olive oil

¼   pound fresh cremini mushrooms, thinly sliced

6   ounces frozen soy crumbles, thawed

2   garlic cloves, finely chopped

1½   cups fat-free marinara sauce

¼   cup thinly sliced fresh basil

1. Cook penne according to package directions. Drain and keep warm.

2. Meanwhile, put porcini mushrooms in glass measuring cup and pour boiling water over. Let stand until softened, about 5 minutes. Lift mushrooms from liquid and coarsely chop. Pour mushroom liquid through paper towel–lined sieve; reserve liquid.

3. Heat oil in large nonstick saucepan over medium heat. Add cremini mushrooms and cook, stirring frequently, until softened and browned, about 6 minutes. Stir in porcini mushrooms, soy crumbles, and garlic; cook, stirring frequently, about 2 minutes. Stir in marinara sauce and reserved mushroom liquid; bring to boil. Reduce heat and simmer 5 minutes. Remove skillet from heat; stir in penne until mixed well. Sprinkle with basil.

Per serving (about 1⅔ cups): 341 Cal, 4 g Total Fat, 1 g Sat Fat, 446 mg Sod, 57 g Total Carb, 5 g Sugar, 7 g Fib, 16 g Prot. SmartPoints value: 9

Cook's Tip

When buying fresh mushrooms, look for firm, fresh-smelling mushrooms without any signs of drying or shriveling. Wipe them clean with a damp paper towel or mushroom brush before slicing.

GRILLED SWORDFISH WITH MEYER LEMONS

SERVES 4
20 Minutes or Less,
Gluten Free

4   (5-ounce) swordfish steaks

¼   teaspoon salt

¼   teaspoon black pepper

2   Meyer lemons, halved crosswise

8   tablespoons fat-free balsamic vinaigrette

1   (5-ounce) container baby kale

1   (10-ounce) container cherry tomatoes, halved

½   small red onion, thinly sliced

1. **Sprinkle swordfish with salt and pepper. Brush swordfish and cut sides of lemons with 3 tablespoons of vinaigrette. Set grill pan over medium-high heat. When pan is very hot, place swordfish and lemons, cut side down, in pan. Grill until fish is just opaque in center, 2–3 minutes per side, and lemons are deeply browned on cut side, about 5 minutes.**

2. **Meanwhile, toss together kale, tomatoes, onion, and remaining 5 tablespoons vinaigrette in large bowl. Divide salad evenly among 4 plates. Top with swordfish steaks and place 1 grilled lemon half on each plate.**

Per serving (1 swordfish steak, 2½ cups salad, and ½ lemon): 263 Cal, 10 g Total Fat, 2 g Sat Fat, 596 mg Sod, 14 g Total Carb, 6 g Sugar, 3 g Fib, 30 g Prot. SmartPoints value: 5

 Cook's Tip

Meyer lemons are a cross between a regular lemon and a mandarin orange. They have a distinctive orange-lemon flavor, making them less acidic than Eureka (regular) lemons. Look for them in larger supermarkets and specialty food stores from November through January, or substitute regular lemons in this recipe.

GRILLED SWORDFISH
WITH MEYER LEMONS

SPAGHETTI SQUASH WITH CHERRY TOMATOES, PARSLEY, AND PARMESAN

SPAGHETTI SQUASH WITH CHERRY TOMATOES, PARSLEY, AND PARMESAN

SERVES 4
Gluten Free, Vegetarian

1   (2-pound) spaghetti squash

1½ tablespoons olive oil

3   large garlic cloves, thinly sliced

1   pint cherry or grape tomatoes, halved

½   teaspoon salt

¼   teaspoon black pepper

¼   cup grated Parmesan cheese

¼   cup coarsely chopped fresh flat-leaf parsley

1. Preheat oven to 375°F. Line small rimmed baking sheet with parchment paper.

2. With fork or small knife, pierce squash in several places. Put on prepared baking sheet and bake until squash gives when gently pressed, 50–60 minutes. Let cool.

3. Meanwhile, heat oil in large skillet over medium-low heat. Add garlic and cook, stirring, until almost softened, about 2 minutes. Add tomatoes and cook, stirring occasionally, until softened and they release some juice, about 5 minutes longer. Remove skillet from heat.

4. When squash is cool enough to handle, cut lengthwise in half; scrape out seeds and discard. With fork, scrape out spaghetti-like strands and add to tomato mixture; sprinkle with salt and pepper. Cook over medium heat, tossing, until squash is heated through, about 5 minutes. Add Parmesan and parsley; gently toss.

Per serving (generous 1¼ cups): 166 Cal, 9 g Total Fat, 2 g Sat Fat, 432 mg Sod, 21 g Total Carb, 4 g Sugar, 1 g Fib, 5 g Prot. SmartPoints value: 3

Cook's Tip

Spaghetti squash is gluten free and a tasty and light alternative to regular spaghetti. It is available year-round.

PAN-FRIED GREEN TOMATOES WITH CAYENNE RÉMOULADE

SERVES 4
20 Minutes or Less,
Gluten Free, Vegetarian

2 tablespoons fat-free mayonnaise

2 tablespoons plain fat-free Greek yogurt

½ teaspoon Dijon mustard

½ teaspoon Creole seasoning

4 green tomatoes, cut into ½-inch slices

¼ teaspoon salt

⅛ teaspoon black pepper

4 teaspoons canola oil

1. To make rémoulade, stir together mayonnaise, yogurt, mustard, and Creole seasoning in small bowl. Set aside.

2. Sprinkle tomatoes with salt and pepper.

3. Heat 2 teaspoons of oil in large heavy nonstick skillet over medium-high heat. Add half of tomatoes and cook, turning once, until lightly browned, about 4 minutes. Transfer to platter and keep warm. Repeat with remaining oil and tomatoes. Serve tomatoes topped with rémoulade.

Per serving (3 tomato slices and 1 tablespoon rémoulade): 79 Cal, 5 g Total Fat, 0 g Sat Fat, 333 mg Sod, 8 g Total Carb, 6 g Sugar, 2 g Fib, 2 g Prot. SmartPoints value: 2

 Cook's Tip

Rémoulade is a classic French mayonnaise sauce that typically contains mustard, capers, gherkins, fresh herbs, and anchovies. Our version gets its Cajun flair from the addition of Creole seasoning. You can substitute hot pepper sauce, if you like.

WHITE CHOCOLATE–DRIZZLED COCONUT MACAROONS

MAKES 24

Gluten Free, Vegetarian

2 large egg whites

½ cup sugar

⅛ teaspoon salt

1 (7-ounce) package sweetened flaked coconut

½ teaspoon vanilla extract

¼ teaspoon almond extract

1 ounce white chocolate, coarsely chopped

1. Preheat oven to 325°F. Line two large baking sheets with parchment paper.

2. Whisk together egg whites, sugar, and salt in large bowl until frothy. Add coconut, vanilla, and almond extract, stirring until combined well.

3. With small ice-cream scoop, scoop batter by scant 2 tablespoonfuls and place, 1 inch apart, on prepared baking sheets. (Or using dampened hands, form coconut mixture into 24 [1-inch] balls.) With dampened fingers, slightly flatten each mound.

4. Bake until macaroons are set and golden brown on bottom, 22–25 minutes. Lightly spray wire rack with nonstick spray; transfer cookies to rack and let cool completely.

5. Place cookies with rack over sheet of wax paper. Put chocolate in small bowl and set over small saucepan of simmering water until melted. With small spoon, drizzle chocolate over macaroons. Let stand until chocolate is set, 15–20 minutes. (Can be stored in single layer in airtight container at room temperature up to 1 week.)

Per serving (1 macaroon): 62 Cal, 3 g Total Fat, 2 g Sat Fat, 40 mg Sod, 9 g Total Carb, 8 g Sugar, 1 g Fib, 1 g Prot. SmartPoints value: 3

Cook's Tip

Spraying the wire rack with nonstick spray ensures that the macaroons will not stick.

CHOCOLATE GINGERBREAD

SERVES 12
Gluten Free, Vegetarian

¾ cup buckwheat flour

½ cup tapioca starch

¼ cup unsweetened cocoa

2 teaspoons ground ginger

1½ teaspoons baking powder

1 teaspoon cinnamon

½ teaspoon baking soda

¼ teaspoon cloves

¼ teaspoon salt

⅔ cup packed dark brown sugar

⅔ cup low-fat buttermilk

½ cup unsweetened applesauce

¼ cup canola oil

¼ cup light (mild) molasses

1 large egg

1. Preheat oven to 375°F. Spray 8-inch square baking pan with nonstick spray. Line pan with foil or parchment paper allowing foil to overhang rim by 2 inches on two opposite sides. Spray with nonstick spray.

2. Whisk together buckwheat flour, tapioca starch, cocoa, ginger, baking powder, cinnamon, baking soda, cloves, and salt in medium bowl. Stir together brown sugar, buttermilk, applesauce, oil, molasses, and egg in large bowl. Stir buckwheat-flour mixture into applesauce mixture until combined well.

3. Pour batter into prepared pan and smooth top. Bake until toothpick inserted into center comes out with few moist crumbs clinging, about 30 minutes. Let cool completely in pan on wire rack. Using foil as handles, lift cake from pan. Cut gingerbread into 4 strips then cut each strip crosswise into thirds, making total of 12 pieces.

Per serving (1 piece): 188 Cal, 6 g Total Fat, 1 g Sat Fat, 237 mg Sod, 35 g Total Carb, 24 g Sugar, 2 g Fib, 2 g Prot. SmartPoints value: 8

 Cook's Tip

Despite its name, earthy buckwheat flour does not contain wheat. In fact, this gluten-free whole grain is in the rhubarb family. Look for it in health food stores or in supermarkets. If you like, cut the bars, wrap them individually, and freeze—they'll keep up to 3 months.

COFFEE FLAN WITH ORANGE CARAMEL

SERVES 10
Gluten Free, Vegetarian

Caramel and Sauce

¾ cup sugar

¼ cup + ⅓ cup water

6 (3-inch) orange zest strips, removed with vegetable peeler

1 tablespoon orange liqueur (such as Gran Marnier or Cointreau) or orange juice

Custard

2 cups reduced-fat (2%) milk

1 cup fat-free half-and-half

3 tablespoons instant coffee powder (not espresso)

1 (3-inch) cinnamon stick, broken in half

6 (3-inch) orange zest strips, removed with vegetable peeler

4 large eggs

1 large egg white

½ cup sugar

2 teaspoons vanilla extract

1. Put 8-inch round cake pan with 2-inch-high side into 9 x 13-inch baking pan.

2. To make caramel, combine sugar and ¼ cup of water in saucepan and set over medium-high heat, swirling pan to evenly moisten sugar. Cook until caramel turns deep amber. Remove pan from heat; pour enough caramel into cake pan to coat bottom thinly (about ¼ cup). Set aside.

3. To make sauce, add remaining ⅓ cup water to caramel in saucepan; bring to boil over medium heat, stirring to melt caramel. Pour into cup and add orange strips, twisting strips to release oils. Let cool. Discard strips; stir in liqueur. Cover and refrigerate until ready to serve.

4. To make custard, combine milk, half-and-half, coffee powder, cinnamon stick, and orange strips in medium saucepan and bring to simmer over medium heat; remove pan from heat and let steep 20 minutes.

5. Meanwhile, preheat oven to 325°F.

6. Whisk eggs, egg white, sugar, and vanilla in bowl. Discard cinnamon stick and orange strips; stir milk mixture into egg mixture. Strain through sieve into caramel-lined pan. Pour enough very hot tap water into pan to come halfway up sides of cake pan.

7. Bake until custard is set but jiggly in center, 45 minutes. Let cool in water bath 10 minutes. Transfer to rack and cool. Cover and refrigerate at least 6 hours or up to 1 day.

8. To serve, run knife around edge of flan to loosen. Place plate on top of pan and invert. Lift off pan. Cut flan into wedges and drizzle with sauce.

Per serving (¹⁄₁₀ of flan and 1 tablespoon sauce): 184 Cal, 3 g Total Fat, 1 g Sat Fat, 89 mg Sod, 33 g Total Carb, 30 g Sugar, 1 g Fib, 5 g Prot. SmartPoints value: 9

GRAVLAX WITH MUSTARD-DILL SAUCE

SERVES 12
Gluten Free

1 tablespoon + 2 teaspoons kosher salt

3 teaspoons sugar

⅛ teaspoon hickory liquid smoke

1 (¾-pound) center-cut salmon fillet, skinned

1 cup lightly packed fresh dill sprigs

⅓ cup spicy brown mustard

1 teaspoon cider vinegar

1. Stir together salt, 1½ teaspoons of sugar, and the liquid smoke in small bowl; rub all over salmon. Place salmon, skinned side down, on piece of plastic wrap large enough to wrap salmon in. Place ½ cup of dill sprigs on top of fish; wrap tightly in plastic wrap and place in shallow baking dish to catch any drips. Refrigerate 2 days, turning salmon over once a day.

2. Remove salmon from plastic wrap; discard plastic wrap, dill, and any accumulated juices. Place fillet, skinned side down, on large piece of plastic wrap. Place remaining ½ cup dill sprigs on top; wrap tightly in plastic, then in sheet of foil. Place on small rimmed baking sheet or in shallow baking dish. Top with another small baking sheet or pan and place heavy weight (such as a large can or two) on top. Refrigerate 1 day.

3. To make sauce, stir together mustard, remaining 1½ teaspoons sugar, and the vinegar in medium bowl. (Can be prepared up to 1 day ahead and refrigerated.)

4. To serve, with long, thin knife, thinly slice salmon against the grain. Arrange slices on platter and serve with mustard sauce.

Per serving (about 3 slices gravlax and 1½ teaspoons sauce): 60 Cal, 3 g Total Fat, 1 g Sat Fat, 1,378 mg Sod, 2 g Total Carb, 1 g Sugar, 0 g Fib, 6 g Prot. SmartPoints value: 2

 Cook's Tip

Adding liquid smoke to the salt mixture gives the gravlax a slightly smoky, woodsy flavor that makes it special. If you like, serve the gravlax with thin rice and sesame seed gluten-free crackers. Three gluten-free crackers per serving will up the SmartPoints value by 1.

GRAVLAX WITH MUSTARD-DILL SAUCE

ASPARAGUS VICHYSSOISE
WITH CHIVE FLOWERS

ASPARAGUS VICHYSSOISE WITH CHIVE FLOWERS

SERVES 6
Gluten Free, Vegetarian

1   pound asparagus

2   teaspoons olive oil

2   leeks (white and pale green parts only), halved lengthwise and thinly sliced

3   cups reduced-sodium vegetable broth

1   (½-pound) russet (baking) potato, peeled and cut into ½-inch pieces

2   fresh thyme sprigs

1   teaspoon salt

⅛   teaspoon pepper, preferably white

½   cup fat-free half-and-half

2   teaspoons fruity extra-virgin olive oil

4   fresh chive flowers, crumbled, for garnish (optional)

1. Trim asparagus and cut into 2-inch lengths.

2. Heat olive oil in large saucepan over medium heat. Add leeks and cook, stirring, until softened, about 5 minutes. Add broth, asparagus, potato, thyme sprigs, salt, and pepper. Cover and bring to boil. Reduce heat and simmer, covered, until vegetables are fork-tender, about 20 minutes. Discard thyme sprigs. Let soup cool about 5 minutes.

3. Puree soup, in batches, in blender. Transfer to large bowl and let cool to room temperature. Stir in half-and-half; cover and refrigerate until well chilled, at least 4 hours or up to 2 days.

4. Ladle soup evenly into 6 bowls. Drizzle with extra-virgin olive oil and sprinkle with chive flowers (if using).

Per serving (1 cup): 107 Cal, 4 g Total Fat, 1 g Sat Fat, 527 mg Sod, 17 g Total Carb, 5 g Sugar, 3 g Fib, 3 g Prot. SmartPoints value: 3

 Cook's Tip

For an additional garnish, trim 18 pencil (thin) asparagus and cut into 4- to 5-inch lengths (reserve bottoms of stalks for another use). Bring ½ inch of water to a boil in a large skillet. Add the asparagus and cook, covered, just until tender, about 2 minutes. Drain and rinse under cold water. Place 3 asparagus in each bowl of soup, then garnish with oil and chive flowers as directed.

SWEET CARROT SOUP WITH FAVA BEANS

SERVES 6
Gluten Free

2   cups thawed frozen shelled fava beans

6   cups chicken broth

1   pound carrots, thinly sliced

2   sweet-tart apples, such as Fuji or Gala, peeled, cored, and diced

½   onion, chopped

2   garlic cloves, minced

½   teaspoon ground coriander

½   teaspoon salt

¼   teaspoon black pepper

1. Cook fava beans according to package directions. Drain in colander; rinse under cold water to stop cooking. Remove tough outer skins by splitting beans open and squeezing out beans; discard skins. Set beans aside.

2. Meanwhile, combine broth, carrots, apples, onion, garlic, coriander, and salt in large saucepan; bring to boil. Reduce heat and simmer until carrots are very tender, about 25 minutes.

3. Remove saucepan from heat and let soup cool 5 minutes. Puree soup, in batches, in blender. Return soup to saucepan and add fava beans; simmer until heated through, about 5 minutes. Ladle soup evenly into 6 bowls; sprinkle with pepper.

Per serving (1⅓ cups): 142 Cal, 2 g Total Fat, 0 g Sat Fat, 1,020 mg Sod, 25 g Total Carb, 14 g Sugar, 7 g Fib, 9 g Prot. SmartPoints value: 2

Cook's Tip

Make this dish vegetarian by using vegetable broth instead of chicken broth.

CRANBERRY-STUFFED PORK LOIN

SERVES 6

⅓ cup dried cranberries, chopped

½ cup cranberry-blueberry all-fruit spread

3 tablespoons plain dried bread crumbs

2 teaspoons chopped fresh thyme

2 teaspoons chopped fresh rosemary

1 (1½-pound) lean boneless center-cut pork loin roast, trimmed

¾ teaspoon salt

¼ teaspoon black pepper

1. Preheat oven to 400°F. Place rack in roasting pan and spray rack and pan with nonstick spray.

2. To make stuffing, put cranberries in small bowl. Add enough boiling water to cover; let steep 10 minutes, then pour off water. Stir in ¼ cup of fruit spread, the bread crumbs, thyme, and rosemary.

3. To butterfly pork, holding knife parallel to work surface, cut pork lengthwise in half, cutting about three-quarters of way through, being careful not to cut all the way through. Open up pork and spread flat like book. Place pork, cut side down, between two pieces of plastic wrap; gently pound with meat mallet or rolling pin until ½ inch thick. Remove top piece of plastic wrap; sprinkle pork with salt and pepper. Turn pork over; spoon stuffing down center. Fold pork over filling and roll up, jelly-roll fashion, to enclose. With kitchen string, tie securely in 3 or 4 places.

4. Place pork on prepared rack and roast 35 minutes. Brush with 1 tablespoon of remaining fruit spread; roast 5 minutes. Continue roasting, brushing pork with remaining 3 tablespoons fruit spread, until instant-read thermometer inserted into center of pork registers 145°F, about 5 minutes longer. Transfer pork to cutting board and let stand 10 minutes. Cut into 12 slices.

Per serving (2 slices pork): 255 Cal, 5 g Total Fat, 2 g Sat Fat, 382 mg Sod, 26 g Total Carb, 17 g Sugar, 1 g Fib, 25 g Prot. SmartPoints value: 8

TILAPIA WITH WARM SHERRY
VINAIGRETTE AND WILD RICE

TILAPIA WITH WARM SHERRY VINAIGRETTE AND WILD RICE

SERVES 4
Gluten Free

¾ cup wild rice blend

½ cup finely diced red bell pepper

2 teaspoons olive oil

4 (5-ounce) tilapia fillets

½ teaspoon salt

¼ teaspoon black pepper

1 shallot, minced

1 tablespoon sherry vinegar

¾ cup vegetable broth

2 tablespoons chopped fresh chives

1. Cook rice according to package directions, adding bell pepper during last 5 minutes of cooking time. Remove saucepan from heat and keep warm.

2. Heat oil in large heavy nonstick skillet over medium heat. Sprinkle fillets with salt and black pepper. Add fillets to skillet and cook, shaking skillet constantly for first 30 seconds to prevent sticking, until browned and crispy on bottom, about 5 minutes. Turn fillets over and cook just until opaque in center, about 2 minutes longer. Transfer to platter.

3. To make vinaigrette, set same skillet over medium-high heat. Add shallot and cook, stirring frequently, until softened, about 1 minute. Add vinegar and bring to boil. Add broth and bring to simmer, stirring to scrape up any browned bits from bottom of skillet. Simmer until sauce is reduced by half, about 5 minutes. Stir in chives.

4. Pour sauce over fillets and serve with rice.

Per serving (1 tilapia fillet, 1½ tablespoons sauce, and about ½ cup rice): 255 Cal, 4 g Total Fat, 1 g Sat Fat, 520 mg Sod, 25 g Total Carb, 1 g Sugar, 2 g Fib, 31 g Prot. SmartPoints value: 5

 Cook's Tip

Serve this elegant fish dish with a side of steamed baby bok choy or slender green beans.

ROASTED BEETS WITH ORANGE AND MINT

SERVES 4
Gluten Free, Vegetarian

1½ pounds small beets

1 small shallot, thinly sliced

2 tablespoons thinly sliced fresh mint

2 teaspoons olive oil

2 teaspoons white balsamic vinegar

1 teaspoon grated orange zest

¼ teaspoon salt

⅛ teaspoon black pepper

1. Preheat oven to 400°F.

2. Trim beets, leaving root and 1 inch of stem intact; scrub skins. Wrap beets tightly in foil and place directly on oven rack; roast until beets are fork-tender, 45–60 minutes. Unwrap beets and let cool.

3. When beets are cool enough to handle, with paper towel, rub off skins. Cut each beet in half or into quarters, depending on size. Transfer beets to medium bowl; stir in shallot, mint, oil, vinegar, orange zest, salt, and pepper.

Per serving (¾ cup): 98 Cal, 3 g Total Fat, 0 g Sat Fat, 278 mg Sod, 18 g Total Carb, 12 g Sugar, 5 g Fib, 3 g Prot. SmartPoints value: 1

Cook's Tip

Use a variety of beets to dress up this dish: Try golden or yellow beets and chioggia (striped) beets.

ROASTED BEETS WITH
ORANGE AND MINT

THYME-ROASTED SUNCHOKES

SERVES 4
Gluten Free, Vegetarian

1   pound sunchokes, scrubbed
    and cut into 1-inch chunks

3   large garlic cloves, unpeeled

2   teaspoons chopped fresh thyme
    or ½ teaspoon dried

½   teaspoon kosher salt

¼   teaspoon black pepper

1   tablespoon olive oil

1. Preheat oven to 450°F. Spray small rimmed baking sheet with nonstick spray.

2. Toss together sunchokes, garlic, thyme, salt, and pepper in large bowl. Add oil and toss until coated evenly.

3. Spoon sunchoke mixture onto prepared baking sheet; spread to form single layer. Bake until sunchokes are golden and crisp on outside and tender on inside, 20–25 minutes. Squeeze out pulp from garlic cloves; add to sunchokes and toss until mixed.

Per serving (scant 1 cup): 116 Cal, 3 g Total Fat, 0 g Sat Fat, 247 mg Sod, 21 g Total Carb, 11 g Sugar, 2 g Fib, 2 g Prot. SmartPoints value: 1

 Cook's Tip

Sunchokes, also called Jerusalem artichokes and earth apples, are a tuberous root of a North American plant that is in the sunflower family. They are a great source of fiber, iron, potassium, and thiamin and are low in calories. Their sweet, nutty flavor is reminiscent of artichokes.

TOMATO, WATERMELON, AND BASIL SALAD

SERVES 4
20 Minutes or Less,
Gluten Free, Vegetarian

- 2 tablespoons balsamic vinegar
- 2 teaspoons olive oil
- ½ teaspoon minced seeded jalapeño pepper
- ¼ teaspoon salt
- 3 cups diced seedless watermelon
- 3 cups diced yellow or orange tomatoes
- ⅓ cup torn fresh basil leaves

To make dressing, whisk together vinegar, oil, jalapeño, and salt in serving bowl. Add watermelon, tomatoes, and basil; gently toss until coated evenly.

Per serving (1⅓ cups): 77 Cal, 3 g Total Fat, 0 g Sat Fat, 173 mg Sod, 13 g Total Carb, 8 g Sugar, 1 g Fib, 2 g Prot. SmartPoints value: 1

 Cook's Tip

Add 1 peeled, seeded, and diced cucumber to this refreshing salad for extra crunch and no additional SmartPoints value.

APPLE SHARLOTKA

SERVES 12

Vegetarian

1 cup all-purpose flour

½ teaspoon cinnamon

¼ teaspoon nutmeg

¼ teaspoon baking soda

¼ teaspoon salt

2½ pounds apples, such as Fuji, Braeburn, or Granny Smith, peeled, cored, and thinly sliced

1½ teaspoons grated lemon zest

2 tablespoons lemon juice

3 large eggs

⅔ cup granulated sugar

⅓ cup packed light brown sugar

⅓ cup plain fat-free Greek yogurt

1 teaspoon vanilla extract

1 tablespoon confectioners' sugar

1. Preheat oven to 350°F. Line bottom of 9-inch springform pan with round of parchment paper. Spray parchment and side of pan with nonstick spray.

2. Whisk together flour, cinnamon, nutmeg, baking soda, and salt in small bowl; set aside.

3. Put apples in large bowl. Add lemon zest and juice; toss until coated. Transfer apple mixture to prepared springform pan, pressing down to form compact layer.

4. With electric mixer on medium-high speed, beat eggs, granulated sugar, and brown sugar in large bowl until thickened. Reduce speed to low; beat in yogurt and vanilla. With rubber spatula, fold in flour mixture just until no longer visible.

5. Pour batter over apples, spreading to completely cover apples. Bake until toothpick inserted into center comes out clean and apples are tender, about 1 hour. Let cool in pan on wire rack 10 minutes. Run thin knife around edge of pan to loosen pie. Carefully remove side of pan and let cool completely on rack. Dust with confectioners' sugar just before serving.

Per serving (¹⁄₁₂ of pie): 177 Cal, 1 g Total Fat, 0 g Sat Fat, 97 mg Sod, 39 g Total Carb, 27 g Sugar, 3 g Fib, 4 g Prot. SmartPoints value: 6

Cook's Tip

Apple sharlotka is a traditional Russian-style apple pie, where the filling is on the bottom and batter-type crust is on the top. Some sharlotkas are made with one type of apple, such as Golden Delicious, while others use a variety. Sometimes the apples are chopped and sometimes they are thinly sliced—it simply depends on the baker.

APPLE SHARLOTKA

POACHED PEARS WITH RED WINE AND STAR ANISE

SERVES 8
Gluten Free, Vegetarian

2   cups boiling water

3   Red Zinger or Raspberry Zinger tea bags

2   cups dry red wine

½   cup sugar

3   (3-inch) orange zest strips, removed with vegetable peeler

2   cardamom pods

1   star anise

4   (½-pound) firm-ripe Bosc pears, peeled, halved, and cored

½   cup plain fat-free Greek yogurt

2   tablespoons coarsely chopped pistachios

1. Pour boiling water into glass measuring cup or bowl; add tea bags and let steep 4 minutes. Remove tea bags and discard; pour tea into large saucepan. Add wine, sugar, orange zest, cardamom pods, and star anise; bring to boil over medium heat, stirring until sugar is dissolved.

2. Reduce heat to simmer and add pears; place sheet of wax paper on top of pears to keep them submerged. Cook, covered, until pears are just tender when pierced with small knife, 30–35 minutes. Remove saucepan from heat; uncover and let pears cool in wine mixture.

3. When pears are cool, with slotted spoon, transfer to large bowl; set aside.

4. Bring wine mixture to boil over high heat. Boil until reduced to about ⅔ cup, 10–15 minutes. Remove saucepan from heat and let syrup cool to room temperature. Discard orange zest, cardamom, and star anise.

5. To serve, place 1 pear half, cut side up, in each of 8 serving dishes or dessert plates. Spoon syrup evenly over pears. Spoon yogurt evenly on top of or alongside pears and sprinkle with pistachios.

Per serving (1 pear half, about 1½ tablespoons syrup, 1 tablespoon yogurt, and scant 1 teaspoon pistachios): 179 Cal, 1 g Total Fat, 0 g Sat Fat, 10 mg Sod, 30 g Total Carb, 23 g Sugar, 3 g Fib, 2 g Prot. SmartPoints value: 5

Cook's Tip

To neatly remove the core from each pear, use a melon baller. The pears can be prepared ahead and refrigerated in the wine mixture—before it is reduced—up to 3 days. Remove the pears from the wine mixture and reduce it as directed in step 4.

OXTAIL AND ROOT VEGETABLE STEW

SERVES 8
Gluten Free

1 pound meaty oxtails, trimmed

1 pound lean boneless beef chuck, trimmed and cut into 1½-inch chunks

1¼ teaspoons kosher salt

3 carrots, finely chopped

½ fennel bulb, chopped

1 onion, chopped

1 large garlic clove, minced

1½ teaspoons chopped fresh thyme or ¾ teaspoon dried

1 (14½-ounce) can whole tomatoes in juice, broken up, juice reserved

1 (14½-ounce) can reduced-sodium chicken broth

⅔ cup dry red wine

½ teaspoon black pepper

½ pound parsnips, halved lengthwise and cut into 1-inch chunks

1 (½-pound) sweet potato, peeled and cut into 1-inch chunks

1. Spray large Dutch oven with olive oil nonstick spray and set over medium-high heat. Sprinkle oxtails and beef with ½ teaspoon of salt. Cook oxtails and beef, in batches, until browned on all sides, about 8 minutes per batch, transferring meat to plate as it is browned.

2. Spray Dutch oven with nonstick spray and reduce heat to medium. Add carrots, fennel, and onion; cook, covered, stirring occasionally, until carrots are tender, 8–10 minutes. Add garlic and thyme; cook, stirring, until fragrant, about 30 seconds.

3. Stir tomatoes with their juice, broth, wine, oxtails, beef, remaining ¾ teaspoon salt, and the pepper into vegetable mixture; bring to boil. Reduce heat and simmer, covered, until oxtails and beef are fork-tender, 1½–2 hours. With slotted spoon, transfer oxtails to plate and let cool slightly (leave beef in pot).

4. Stir parsnips and sweet potato into stew; simmer, covered, until potato is fork-tender, about 20 minutes.

5. Meanwhile, remove meat from oxtail bones; discard bones. Stir oxtail meat into stew and cook until heated through, about 5 minutes longer. Skim off and discard any surface fat from stew before serving.

Per serving (about 1 cup): 316 Cal, 13 g Total Fat, 5 g Sat Fat, 663 mg Sod, 18 g Total Carb, 6 g Sugar, 4 g Fib, 28 g Prot. SmartPoints value: 8

 Cook's Tip

To simmer the stew with superior results, cover the Dutch oven with foil, then add the lid to form an airtight seal in step 3. To completely remove the surface fat from the stew, refrigerate the stew overnight, then spoon off the solidified fat and discard. Reheat the stew over gentle heat.

TENDER BEEF SHANKS
WITH POLENTA

TENDER BEEF SHANKS WITH POLENTA

SERVES 4
Gluten Free

4 (5-ounce) beef shanks, trimmed

1½ teaspoons salt

2 garlic cloves, minced

1 (14½-ounce) can diced tomatoes

¾ cup dry red wine

¾ cup reduced-sodium beef broth

¼ teaspoon black pepper

1 bay leaf

1¼ cups water

½ cup instant polenta

Coarsely chopped fresh flat-leaf parsley

1. Sprinkle beef shanks with ½ teaspoon of salt and lightly spray with nonstick spray. Add beef to Dutch oven and cook over medium heat until browned, about 5 minutes per side. Transfer to large bowl.

2. Add garlic to Dutch oven and cook, stirring constantly, until fragrant, about 30 seconds. Stir in tomatoes, wine, and broth, scraping up browned bits from bottom of pot. Bring to boil and cook 3 minutes. Return beef to pot along with ½ teaspoon salt, the pepper, and bay leaf. Reduce heat and simmer, covered, until beef is fork-tender, 2–2½ hours.

3. With slotted spoon, transfer beef to large bowl; skim off and discard any fat from surface of sauce. Discard bay leaf. Return beef to Dutch oven and keep warm.

4. Bring water and remaining ½ teaspoon salt to boil in medium saucepan over medium-high heat. Slowly whisk in polenta. Reduce heat to medium-low and cook, stirring frequently, until polenta is very thick, about 4 minutes. Spoon evenly onto 4 plates or into large shallow bowls. Place beef shanks on top, and spoon sauce over. Sprinkle with parsley.

Per serving (1 beef shank, generous ½ cup sauce, and about ½ cup polenta): 304 Cal, 6 g Total Fat, 2 g Sat Fat, 1191 mg Sod, 20 g Total Carb, 4 g Sugar, 2 g Fib, 33 g Prot. SmartPoints value: 6

 Cook's Tip

The browned bits that are scraped up from the bottom of a pot are called the *fond* (fahn), the French word for "bottom." They have a concentrated flavor that adds depth to a finished dish. The fond is incorporated by adding a liquid, such as wine, broth, or water to the pot, which helps to dislodge the tasty bits.

WHOLE ROASTED TANDOORI CAULIFLOWER

SERVES 6
Gluten Free, Vegetarian

1 large head cauliflower

⅔ cup plain fat-free Greek yogurt

2 garlic cloves, minced

1½ teaspoons tandoori seasoning

½ teaspoon salt

2 tablespoons lime juice

2 tablespoons chopped fresh cilantro

1. Preheat oven to 400°F. Spray 9-inch pie plate or small baking dish with nonstick spray.

2. Remove and discard outer leaves and core of cauliflower, keeping head intact. Place cauliflower in prepared pie plate. Whisk together yogurt, garlic, tandoori seasoning, and salt in small bowl. Spread yogurt mixture all over cauliflower.

3. Roast until small knife inserted into center of cauliflower goes in easily and yogurt topping is browned, about 1½ hours, rotating pie plate once or twice during roasting time so cauliflower cooks evenly.

4. Let cauliflower stand 10 minutes to cool slightly. Drizzle with lime juice and sprinkle with cilantro. Cut into 6 wedges.

Per serving (1 wedge): 53 Cal, 0 g Total Fat, 0 g Sat Fat, 249 mg Sod, 9 g Total Carb, 4 g Sugar, 4 g Fib, 5 g Prot. SmartPoints value: 0

 Cook's Tip

To remove the core of the cauliflower, turn it stem side up. With a small knife, cut down around the stem at an angle towards the stem, removing a "cone" of stem about 1 inch deep. Tandoori seasoning is available in specialty food stores and online.

WHOLE ROASTED
TANDOORI CAULIFLOWER

NOPALES SALAD WITH
TOMATO AND CHILES

NOPALES SALAD WITH TOMATO AND CHILES

SERVES 4
Gluten Free, Vegetarian

2 large fresh nopales (cactus paddles), cleaned and trimmed

¾ teaspoon kosher salt

¼ teaspoon black pepper

2 small ears of corn, husks and silk removed

1 tablespoon olive oil

1 tablespoon white balsamic vinegar

2 teaspoons seeded and minced jalapeño pepper

1 (12-ounce) container assorted mini tomatoes, halved

2 tablespoons finely chopped red onion

2 tablespoons fresh cilantro leaves

1. Heat large cast-iron skillet over medium-high heat until hot. Lightly spray both sides of nopales with olive oil nonstick spray; sprinkle with ¼ teaspoon of salt and the black pepper. Cook nopales, in batches, until lightly charred and tender, 2–3 minutes per side, transferring each batch to cutting board as it is cooked. Spray corn with nonstick spray. Place corn in skillet and cook, turning occasionally, until charred, 8–9 minutes. Transfer to cutting board.

2. Meanwhile, to make dressing, whisk together oil, vinegar, jalapeño, and remaining ½ teaspoon salt in salad bowl.

3. When cool enough to handle, cut nopales into 1-inch pieces and cut off kernels from ears of corn. Add nopales, corn, tomatoes, onion, and cilantro to dressing in bowl; toss until coated evenly.

Per serving (1¼ cups): 121 Cal, 4 g Total Fat, 1 g Sat Fat, 379 mg Sod, 21 g Total Carb, 6 g Sugar, 4 g Fib, 3 g Prot. SmartPoints value: 3

 Cook's Tip

To clean and trim nopales, with tongs, hold a paddle and rinse under cold water, being careful not to prick your fingers on the small thorns. With a small, sharp knife, scrape off the dark bumps and thorns (do not remove all the outer dark green skin). Rinse paddle again. Trim ¼ inch off the edge and ½ inch off the thick base; discard trimmings.

GRILLED PORK CHOPS WITH ORANGE-TAMARIND GLAZE

SERVES 4
20 Minutes or Less,
Gluten Free

⅔ cup chicken broth

¼ cup orange juice

4 teaspoons tamarind paste

1 teaspoon honey

½ teaspoon grated peeled fresh ginger

1 teaspoon butter

1 teaspoon curry powder

½ teaspoon kosher salt

¼ teaspoon black pepper

4 (4½- to 5-ounce) lean thin-sliced bone-in center-cut pork loin chops, trimmed

1. To make glaze, stir together broth, orange juice, tamarind paste, honey, and ginger in medium skillet until combined well; bring to boil over medium-high heat. Reduce heat and cook, stirring occasionally, until mixture is slightly thickened, about 8 minutes (you should have ¼ cup). Remove skillet from heat; swirl in butter until melted. Transfer 1 tablespoon glaze to cup for basting. Set aside remaining 3 tablespoons glaze.

2. Meanwhile, to make rub, stir together curry powder, salt, and pepper in another cup. Rub spice mixture on both sides of pork; lightly spray with olive oil nonstick spray.

3. Heat grill pan over medium-high heat until hot. Add pork to pan and grill 3 minutes per side. Brush pork with ½ tablespoon of glaze reserved for basting; turn pork over and grill 1 minute. Brush pork with remaining ½ tablespoon glaze; turn pork and grill until cooked through, about 1 minute longer. Serve pork drizzled with reserved 3 tablespoons glaze.

Per serving (1 pork chop and about 2 teaspoons glaze): 258 Cal, 10 g Total Fat, 4 g Sat Fat, 442 mg Sod, 9 g Total Carb, 4 g Sugar, 0 g Fib, 30 g Prot. SmartPoints value: 7

NO-COOK PEANUT BUTTERY COOKIE DOUGH BITES

MAKES 36
Vegetarian

¾ cup canned chickpeas, rinsed and drained

⅓ cup packed dark brown sugar

3 tablespoons creamy peanut butter

1 teaspoon light cream cheese (Neufchâtel)

½ teaspoon vanilla extract

¼ teaspoon salt

⅛ teaspoon baking soda

2 tablespoons all-purpose flour

2 tablespoons peanut butter chips

2 tablespoons confectioners' sugar

2 tablespoons unsweetened cocoa

1. Combine chickpeas, brown sugar, peanut butter, cream cheese, vanilla, salt, and baking soda in food processor; process until very smooth. Add flour and peanut butter chips; pulse just until combined. Refrigerate until dough is chilled, at least 1 hour or up to 4 hours.

2. Using melon baller, scoop out dough to make 36 small balls, gently placing them in large shallow bowl.

3. Whisk together confectioners' sugar and cocoa in small bowl. Sprinkle 2 tablespoons of sugar-cocoa mixture over dough balls and toss until coated evenly. Set aside remaining sugar-cocoa mixture. Arrange dough bites on serving plate; refrigerate up to several hours. Dust with remaining sugar-cocoa mixture just before serving.

Per serving (1 cookie): 32 Cal, 1 g Total Fat, 0 g Sat Fat, 41 mg Sod, 5 g Total Carb, 3 g Sugar, 1 g Fib, 1 g Prot. SmartPoints value: 1

 Cook's Tip

The chickpeas contribute protein and fiber, along with some tempting texture, to these cookies.

LEMON-BUTTERMILK
BUNDT CAKE

LEMON-BUTTERMILK BUNDT CAKE

SERVES 16
Vegetarian

2¼ cups all-purpose flour

1½ teaspoons baking soda

1 teaspoon + pinch salt

1 cup low-fat buttermilk

¾ cup finely grated beets

1 tablespoon grated lemon zest (about 2 large lemons)

2 tablespoons lemon juice

6 tablespoons unsalted butter, softened

1 cup + 2 tablespoons granulated sugar

2 large eggs

1 tablespoon + ½ teaspoon vanilla extract

3 ounces light cream cheese (Neufchâtel), softened

⅓ cup confectioners' sugar

1½ tablespoons low-fat (1%) milk

1. Preheat oven to 350°F. Spray 10-cup Bundt pan with nonstick spray.

2. Whisk together flour, baking soda, and 1 teaspoon of salt in medium bowl. Stir together buttermilk, beets, and lemon zest and juice in another medium bowl.

3. With electric mixer on medium-high speed, beat butter and granulated sugar in large bowl until light and fluffy. Add eggs and 1 tablespoon of vanilla, beating until mixed well. Reduce mixer speed to low. Add flour mixture alternately with beet mixture, beginning and ending with flour mixture and beating just until mixed (batter will be thick).

4. Spoon batter into prepared pan and spread evenly. Bake until toothpick inserted into center comes out clean, about 45 minutes. Let cake cool completely in pan on wire rack. Place cake plate on top of pan. Turn plate and pan over. Lift off pan to unmold cake.

5. To make glaze, with electric mixer on medium speed, beat cream cheese, confectioners' sugar, milk, and remaining ½ teaspoon vanilla and pinch salt in medium bowl until smooth. Drizzle over top of cake. Cut into 16 slices.

Per serving (¹⁄₁₆ of cake): 200 Cal, 6 g Total Fat, 4 g Sat Fat, 333 mg Sod, 32 g Total Carb, 18 g Sugar, 1 g Fib, 4 g Prot. SmartPoints value: 9

Cook's Tip

This delectably lemony cake is very moist thanks to the addition of red beets. The bright pink batter magically turns yellow when baked.

DOUBLE GERMAN CHOCOLATE MINI CUPCAKES

MAKES 24
Vegetarian

⅔ cup all-purpose flour

½ teaspoon baking powder

½ teaspoon baking soda

½ teaspoon salt

3 tablespoons hot brewed coffee

3 tablespoons unsweetened cocoa

⅓ cup low-fat buttermilk

3 tablespoons unsalted butter, softened

½ cup granulated sugar

1 large egg

1 teaspoon vanilla extract

½ cup canned low-sodium sauerkraut, rinsed, drained, and finely chopped

¼ cup chopped pecans

¼ cup sweetened coconut flakes

Frosting

⅓ cup fat-free evaporated milk

¼ cup packed light brown sugar

2 teaspoons cornstarch

⅛ teaspoon salt

½ teaspoon vanilla extract

1. Preheat oven to 350°F. Spray 24-cup mini-muffin pan with nonstick spray.

2. Whisk together flour, baking powder, baking soda, and salt in small bowl. Stir together coffee and cocoa in medium bowl until cocoa is dissolved; whisk in buttermilk until blended.

3. With electric mixer on medium-high speed, beat butter and granulated sugar in large bowl until light and fluffy. Beat in egg and vanilla. Reduce mixer speed to low. Add flour mixture alternately with cocoa mixture, beating just until combined; stir in sauerkraut.

4. Spoon batter evenly into prepared muffin cups. Bake until toothpick inserted into center of cupcake comes out clean, 12–15 minutes. Let cupcakes cool in pan on wire rack 5 minutes. Remove cupcakes from pan and let cool completely on rack.

5. Meanwhile, reduce oven temperature to 300°F. Spread pecans and coconut on baking sheet; toast until coconut is lightly browned and pecans are toasted, 5–6 minutes. Transfer to plate and let cool completely.

6. To make frosting, whisk together evaporated milk, brown sugar, cornstarch, and salt in small saucepan. Cook over medium-high heat until mixture bubbles and thickens, about 4 minutes; stir in vanilla and ¼ cup of coconut-pecan mixture. Remove saucepan from heat and let cool to room temperature.

7. Spread cooled frosting evenly over cupcakes; sprinkle with remaining coconut-pecan mixture.

Per serving (1 cupcake): 75 Cal, 3 g Total Fat, 1 g Sat Fat, 121 mg Sod, 11 g Total Carb, 8 g Sugar, 1 g Fib, 1 g Prot. SmartPoints value: 3

BEEF AND BLUE CHEESE PICKUPS

SERVES 12

4   teaspoons olive oil

1   (1-pound) white onion, halved and thinly sliced

¾   teaspoon salt

1   teaspoon fresh thyme leaves

1   (8-ounce) whole wheat baguette, cut diagonally into 24 (¼-inch) slices

1   (1-pound) lean flank steak, trimmed

1   teaspoon fennel seeds, ground using spice grinder or mortar and pestle

½   teaspoon garlic powder

½   teaspoon paprika

¼   teaspoon black pepper

1   ounce Gorgonzola or blue cheese, crumbled

1. Heat 2 teaspoons of oil in large nonstick skillet over medium heat; add onion and ¼ teaspoon of salt. Cook, stirring occasionally, until onion is softened, about 5 minutes. Reduce heat to low and cook onion, stirring occasionally, until light golden, about 20 minutes longer. Transfer to small bowl and stir in thyme; let cool. (Can be made up to 1 day ahead and refrigerated.)

2. Preheat broiler.

3. Arrange bread on baking sheet. Lightly spray tops of bread slices with olive oil nonstick spray. Broil 5 inches from heat, without turning, until golden, about 2 minutes.

4. Rub remaining 2 teaspoons oil all over steak. Mix together fennel, garlic powder, paprika, pepper, and remaining ½ teaspoon salt in cup; rub all over steak.

5. Spray grill pan with nonstick spray and set over medium heat. Put steak in grill pan and grill until instant-read thermometer inserted into side of steak registers 145°F, about 5 minutes per side. Transfer steak to cutting board; let stand 10 minutes.

6. To serve, cut steak against grain on slight diagonal into 24 thin slices. Arrange bread, toasted side up, on platter. Top each toast with about 2 teaspoons caramelized onion, 1 slice of steak (folded to fit bread), and few crumbles Gorgonzola.

Per serving (2 pieces): 62 Cal, 2 g Total Fat, 1 g Sat Fat, 147 mg Sod, 5 g Total Carb, 1 g Sugar, 1 g Fib, 5 g Prot. SmartPoints value: 2

 Cook's Tip

To ensure that the onion gets well caramelized, don't stir it more often than about every 5 minutes.

SMOKED DUCK ON CRANBERRY CORN BREAD

SERVES 18

1 cup all-purpose flour

¾ cup yellow cornmeal

3 tablespoons sugar

1 teaspoon baking powder

½ teaspoon salt

¼ teaspoon baking soda

⅔ cup fresh or frozen cranberries, chopped

¾ cup low-fat buttermilk

¼ cup fat-free egg substitute

1½ tablespoons canola oil

1½ teaspoons grated orange zest

⅓ cup orange preserves

1 (10-ounce) smoked duck breast or chicken breast, skin removed, trimmed, and cut into 36 thin slices

36 fresh flat-leaf parsley leaves

1. Preheat oven to 400°F. Spray 9 x 13-inch baking pan with nonstick spray.

2. Whisk together flour, cornmeal, sugar, baking powder, salt, and baking soda in medium bowl. Stir in cranberries. Stir together buttermilk, egg substitute, oil, and orange zest in small bowl until blended. Add buttermilk mixture to flour mixture; stir just until flour mixture is moistened (batter will be lumpy). Spread batter in prepared pan.

3. Bake until light golden and toothpick inserted into center of corn bread comes out with few moist crumbs clinging, 12–15 minutes. Let cool in pan on wire rack 5 minutes, then invert onto another rack; lift off pan and turn corn bread right side up. Let cool completely.

4. To serve, cut corn bread into 6 long strips; cut each strip crosswise into 6 pieces. Arrange pieces of corn bread on platter; top each with about ½ teaspoonful of preserves. Fold each slice of duck in half and place on piece of corn bread. Top each with parsley leaf.

Per serving (2 pieces): 63 Cal, 2 g Total Fat, 0 g Sat Fat, 141 mg Sod, 9 g Total Carb, 3 g Sugar, 0 g Fib, 3 g Prot. SmartPoints value: 2

SMOKED DUCK ON
CRANBERRY CORN BREAD

BLOODY MARY
SHRIMP COCKTAIL

BLOODY MARY SHRIMP COCKTAIL

SERVES 8
20 Minutes or Less,
Gluten Free

⅔ cup tomato juice

5 tablespoons vodka

2 tablespoons lemon juice

1¾ teaspoons Old Bay Seasoning

24 peeled and deveined medium shrimp (about 12 ounces), tails left on

⅓ cup ketchup

2 teaspoons prepared drained horseradish

1 teaspoon Worcestershire sauce

1 tablespoon chopped fresh flat-leaf parsley

8 celery sticks

8 lemon wedges

1. To poach shrimp, combine tomato juice, 4 tablespoons of vodka, the lemon juice, and Old Bay Seasoning in medium saucepan. Bring to boil over medium-high heat; boil 2 minutes. Reduce heat to medium; add shrimp and cook, stirring occasionally, until almost opaque in center, about 1½ minutes. Remove pan from heat and cover. Let stand until shrimp are opaque throughout, about 3 minutes longer. With slotted spoon, transfer shrimp to medium bowl and let cool. Reserve poaching liquid.

2. To make sauce, stir together ketchup, horseradish, Worcestershire sauce, and remaining 1 tablespoon vodka into reserved poaching liquid; pour over shrimp and toss until coated evenly.

3. To serve, put 8 small glass cups, wineglasses, or champagne flutes on platter. Place 3 shrimp in each cup and evenly spoon sauce over. Sprinkle with parsley. Garnish each cocktail with celery stick and lemon wedge.

Per serving (3 shrimp, 1 celery stick, and 2 tablespoons sauce): 61 Cal, 0 g Total Fat, 0 g Sat Fat, 248 mg Sod, 6 g Total Carb, 4 g Sugar, 1 g Fib, 4 g Prot. SmartPoints value: 2

 Cook's Tip

This riff on a bloody Mary is flavorful and fun to eat. Be sure to use a gluten-free vodka if you are following a gluten-free diet. Make it nonalcoholic by substituting 5 tablespoons water for the vodka.

PROVENÇAL BAKED MUSSELS

SERVES 8

¼ cup plain dried whole wheat bread crumbs

¼ cup grated pecorino-Romano cheese

2 tablespoons sun-dried tomatoes (not oil packed), finely chopped

1 tablespoon chopped fresh flat-leaf parsley

2 large garlic cloves, minced

1 tablespoon extra-virgin olive oil

1½ teaspoons herbes de Provence

¼ teaspoon black pepper

16 mussels, scrubbed and debearded

1. Preheat oven to 425°F.

2. Stir together bread crumbs, Romano, sun-dried tomatoes, parsley, garlic, oil, herbes de Provence, and pepper in small bowl until bread crumbs are moistened, adding a little water if needed.

3. Fill large saucepan with ½ inch of water and bring to boil over high heat; add mussels. Cook, covered, until mussels open, about 5 minutes; drain. Discard any mussels that do not open. Remove saucepan from heat and let mussels cool.

4. When mussels are cool enough to handle, remove and discard top half of each shell. Spoon heaping teaspoonful of bread-crumb mixture onto each mussel; lightly spray with olive oil nonstick spray. Arrange mussels on small rimmed baking sheet or shallow baking pan. Bake until topping is golden and crispy, about 5 minutes. Serve warm.

Per serving (2 stuffed mussels): 67 Cal, 3 g Total Fat, 1 g Sat Fat, 163 mg Sod, 4 g Total Carb, 0 g Sugar, 1 g Fib, 5 g Prot. SmartPoints value: 2

 Cook's Tip

Herbes de Provence is a blend of dried herbs native to southern France that usually consists of basil, fennel, lavender, marjoram, rosemary, sage, and thyme. It is often added to stews, braises, soups, and vegetables, and usually comes packed in a small red clay crock with decorative black writing.

5 TEMPTING DRINKS THAT SET THE SCENE

Drinks—including glitzy cocktails, long and lean summertime sippers, and nonalcoholic libations—put everyone in just the right mood for having a good time. To that end, we've created a list of favorite drinks to appeal to every palate and suit every occasion. Serve them without garnishes or all gussied up; we've included instructions on how to do that, too. Offer these drinks on your kitchen counter or on a pretty tray and hand them out as soon as your guests settle. There are no rules . . . except to have fun!

Raspberry-Lemonade Vodka Slushies

SERVES 8

Prepare **6 cups low-calorie raspberry-flavored lemonade mix** according to package directions. Pour 4 cups of lemonade into two standard ice-cube trays (16 cubes each). Freeze until solid. Reserve remaining 2 cups lemonade in refrigerator. To make slushies, puree 1 tray lemonade ice cubes, 1 cup reserved lemonade, ½ **cup diet lemon-lime soda**, ½ **cup raspberry-flavored vodka**, and ¼ **cup lemon juice** in blender. Pour into 4 glasses. Repeat to make 4 more drinks.

Per serving (1 cup): SmartPoints value: 1

Dress Them Up: Garnish each drink with a small skewer of raspberries and a fresh mint sprig or lemon twist.

White Wine–Peach Sangria

SERVES 12

Combine **1 (750-ml) bottle dry Riesling wine, 1½ cups diet peach-flavored iced tea, ¼ cup peach liqueur, 3 pitted and thinly sliced ripe peaches, 1 cored and thinly sliced large Granny Smith apple,** and **1 thinly sliced lemon** in large pitcher. Refrigerate until chilled, 3 hours or overnight. To serve, add **1½ cups diet lemon-lime soda** to wine mixture. Fill 12 glasses with **ice cubes;** add sangria and fruit.

Per serving (about 1 cup): SmartPoints value: 3

Dress Them Up: Garnish each drink with a few small fresh strawberries and blueberries.

Frozen Peach-and-Prosecco Bellinis

SERVES 8

Stir together **1 tablespoon lemon juice** and **1 tablespoon superfine sugar** in cup until sugar is dissolved. Combine **1 (16-ounce) bag frozen unsweetened peaches, 2½ cups prosecco, sparkling white wine, or champagne** (let bubbles settle before measuring), **⅓ cup peach liqueur,** and lemon-juice mixture in blender (in batches if needed); process until smooth. Pour into 8 glasses.

Per serving (about ½ cup): SmartPoints value: 4

Dress Them Up: Garnish each drink by placing a fresh peach wedge on the rim of each glass.

Pomegranate Cooler

SERVES 8

Stir together **3 cups pomegranate juice, ½ cup lime juice,** and **¼ cup grenadine** in large pitcher. Gently stir in **2 cups sugar-free raspberry-flavored seltzer.** Fill 8 tall glasses with ice cubes and add pomegranate-juice mixture.

Per serving (¾ cup): SmartPoints value: 5

Dress Them Up: Garnish each drink with a decorative straw, fresh mint sprig, and lime twist.

Raspberry-Lime "Rickey"

SERVES 4

Combine **2 cups frozen unsweetened raspberries, 2 cups seltzer, ¼ cup sugar,** and **2 tablespoons lime juice** in blender; process until smooth. Stir mixture. Process again until smooth. Fill 4 old-fashioned glasses or wineglasses with ice cubes; top with raspberry mixture.

Per serving (1 cup): SmartPoints value: 3

Dress Them Up: Garnish each drink with a thin lime slice and a few fresh or frozen raspberries.

SAVORY PARMESAN–BLACK PEPPER BISCOTTI

MAKES 44

Vegetarian

1   cup + 3 tablespoons all-purpose flour

¾   cup grated Parmesan cheese

1½   teaspoons chopped fresh thyme (optional)

1   teaspoon baking powder

½   teaspoon salt

½– ¾ teaspoon black pepper

1   large egg

1   large egg yolk

¼   cup reduced-fat (2%) milk

3   tablespoons light olive oil

1. Preheat oven to 350°F. Line large baking sheet with parchment paper.

2. Whisk together flour, Parmesan, thyme (if using), baking powder, salt, and pepper in medium bowl. Whisk together egg, egg yolk, milk, and oil in small bowl until blended well. Stir egg mixture into flour mixture until sticky dough forms.

3. On lightly floured work surface, with floured hands, knead dough until blended thoroughly. Divide dough into 2 equal pieces. Form each piece of dough into 10-inch log. Place logs on prepared baking sheet. Bake until biscotti are golden on bottom, about 20 minutes. Let logs cool on baking sheets on wire racks about 15 minutes.

4. With serrated knife, cut each log on diagonal into scant ½-inch slices, making total of 44 biscotti. Place, cut side down, on baking sheet; bake until dry to touch, about 10 minutes. Turn biscotti over and bake until just until dry to touch, about 5 minutes longer (biscotti will not be hard). Transfer to racks and let cool completely.

Per serving (2 biscotti): 31 Cal, 2 g Total Fat, 0 g Sat Fat, 64 mg Sod, 3 g Total Carb, 0 g Sugar, 0 g Fib, 1 g Prot. SmartPoints value: 1

 **Cook's Tip**

To keep some biscotti on hand to serve later, wrap them in packets of four in plastic wrap, pack them into a zip-close plastic freezer bag, and pop into the freezer. This way you won't be tempted to eat too many at a time, and they will stay fresh up to several months.

SAVORY PARMESAN—
BLACK PEPPER BISCOTTI

CHERRY TOMATOES STUFFED WITH BLUE CHEESE AND BACON

SERVES 12
20 Minutes or Less,
Gluten Free

24   cherry tomatoes

½   cup crumbled blue cheese

4   slices bacon, crisp-cooked
    and crumbled

1   tablespoon chopped fresh chives

Cut off tops of tomatoes. With melon baller or tip of teaspoon, remove seeds and discard. Fill each tomato with about 1 teaspoon blue cheese, mounding it slightly. Top evenly with bacon and sprinkle with chives. Arrange on platter.

Per serving (2 stuffed tomatoes): 44 Cal, 3 g Total Fat, 2 g Sat Fat, 160 mg Sod, 2 g Total Carb, 1 g Sugar, 0 g Fib, 3 g Prot. SmartPoints value: 1

 Cook's Tip

If blue cheese isn't your favorite, substitute mild goat cheese, feta cheese, or Cheddar cheese.

COCONUT—ICE CREAM BONBONS

MAKES 24
Gluten Free, Vegetarian

1 cup sweetened flaked coconut, toasted

1½ pints vanilla light ice cream

3 ounces semisweet chocolate, chopped

1. Line small baking sheet with sheet of wax paper or parchment paper; freeze 1 hour.

2. Spread coconut on separate sheet of wax paper or parchment paper.

3. Using mini ice-cream scoop or teaspoon, scoop ice cream by scant 1 tablespoonful to form ball; quickly roll in coconut, lightly pressing coconut into ice cream so it adheres. Transfer bonbon to baking sheet in freezer. Repeat with remaining ice cream and coconut, making total of 24 bonbons. Freeze at least 6 hours or up to overnight (if freezing overnight, cover with foil).

4. Up to 4 hours before serving, put chocolate in microwavable cup or small bowl and microwave on Medium 1 minute; stir. If chocolate is not melted, return to microwave and repeat, stirring every 30 seconds to avoid scorching. Let cool slightly. Scrape melted chocolate into small zip-close plastic bag; squeeze out air and seal bag.

5. Remove bonbons from freezer. Press chocolate into one corner of bag. Snip off tip of bag and drizzle chocolate over bonbons in zigzag pattern. Return bonbons to freezer until chocolate is set. Arrange bonbons on platter or place in mini baking cups. Serve at once.

Per serving (2 bonbons): 75 Cal, 3 g Total Fat, 3 g Sat Fat, 28 mg Sod, 10 g Total Carb, 8 g Sugar, 1 g Fib, 1 g Prot. SmartPoints value: 4

CHOCOLATE STOUT
BROWNIE BITES

CHOCOLATE STOUT BROWNIE BITES

SERVES 24
Vegetarian

¾ cup all-purpose flour

⅓ cup unsweetened cocoa

¾ teaspoon baking powder

¼ teaspoon salt

½ cup malty beer, preferably chocolate stout or porter

½ cup fat-free egg substitute

1½ teaspoons instant coffee powder (not espresso)

2 teaspoons vanilla extract

4 tablespoons light stick butter

4 ounces bittersweet chocolate, chopped

1 cup granulated sugar

1 tablespoon confectioners' sugar

1. Preheat oven to 350°F. Line 8-inch square baking pan with nonstick foil, allowing foil to overhang rim by 2 inches on two opposite sides.

2. Whisk together flour, cocoa, baking powder, and salt in medium bowl. Stir together stout, egg substitute, coffee powder, and vanilla in another medium bowl.

3. Combine butter and chocolate in medium saucepan over low heat. Cook, stirring, until melted and smooth. Remove saucepan from heat and whisk in granulated sugar until combined. Stir chocolate mixture into stout mixture until blended. Whisk in flour mixture until batter is smooth.

4. Pour batter into prepared pan. Bake until toothpick inserted into center of brownies comes out with moist crumbs clinging, about 25 minutes. Let cool completely in pan on wire rack.

5. Remove brownies from pan using foil handles; place on cutting board. Cut into 4 long strips; cut each strip crosswise into 6 pieces, making total of 24 bites. Dust with confectioners' sugar just before serving.

Per serving (1 brownie): 92 Cal, 2 g Total Fat, 3 g Sat Fat, 61 mg Sod, 14 g Total Carb, 9 g Sugar, 1 g Fib, 2 g Prot. SmartPoints value: 4

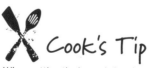 Cook's Tip

When cutting the brownie into bars, the best way to get clean edges is to dip the knife into warm water between each cut. Chocolate stout and porter are available in some supermarkets and in specialty food stores. These specialty beers are worth seeking out for the unique flavor they contribute.

BONUS CHAPTER

LET'S ALL GET DINNER ON THE TABLE

Kid- and Family-Friendly Recipe

Family mealtimes are a great opportunity to come together to share good food and encourage everyone to talk about their day. Helping your kids learn to eat right is important, but part of the joy of gathering at the table comes from being adventurous and experiencing new foods and new tastes together. Talk to your kids about what they do and don't like. You don't need to be a short-order cook, but you might try serving a problematic food with a familiar sauce or dip to make it more palatable. Or you might serve a meal, such as grilled fish and quinoa, but include one side dish that each child will eat. Encourage everyone to help with meal planning, shopping, cooking, and cleanup. And remember to praise your kids when they make good food choices and when they try something new and expand their culinary world. From tacos to "porcupine" meat loaves, from muffins to kebabs, you'll find something here that's good for you and your family—and fun to eat together.

HONEY-MUSTARD CHICKEN STRIPS

SERVES 6

¼ cup Dijon or yellow mustard

2 tablespoons honey

2 teaspoons reduced-sodium soy sauce

1 pound skinless boneless chicken breasts, cut lengthwise into ¾-inch strips

¾ cup plain dried whole wheat bread crumbs

1. Preheat oven to 400°F. Line rimmed baking sheet with nonstick foil.

2. Whisk together mustard, honey, and soy sauce in medium bowl until smooth. Add chicken and stir until coated evenly. Spread bread crumbs on plate. Coat chicken strips, one at a time, with bread crumbs.

3. Arrange chicken strips on prepared baking sheet; spray with nonstick spray. Bake until cooked through, about 15 minutes.

Per serving (about 4 strips): 160 Cal, 2 g Total Fat, 0 g Sat Fat, 391 mg Sod, 14 g Total Carb, 6 g Sugar, 1 g Fib, 18 g Prot. SmartPoints value: 4

 Kids Can Help

Let them make the honey-mustard mixture and arrange the chicken strips on the baking sheet.

CHINESE CHICKEN SALAD

SERVES 4

20 Minutes or Less

1 (14-ounce) bag coleslaw mix

1 cup shredded skinless cooked chicken breast

1 cup frozen shelled edamame, thawed

1 (8-ounce) can sliced water chestnuts, drained

3 scallions, sliced

¼ cup chopped fresh cilantro

⅓ cup seasoned rice vinegar

2 tablespoons reduced-sodium soy sauce

2 teaspoons Asian (dark) sesame oil

1 large garlic clove, crushed through a press

1 teaspoon grated peeled fresh ginger

1. Mix together coleslaw mix, chicken, edamame, water chestnuts, scallions, and cilantro in serving bowl.

2. To make dressing, combine vinegar, soy sauce, sesame oil, garlic, and ginger in small jar with tight-fitting lid; shake until blended well. Pour over chicken mixture and toss until coated evenly. (Can be refrigerated up to 4 hours.)

Per serving (about 2 cups): 203 Cal, 6 g Total Fat, 1 g Sat Fat, 332 mg Sod, 20 g Total Carb, 7 g Sugar, 5 g Fib, 18 g Prot. SmartPoints value: 3

 Kids Can Help

Let them toss the ingredients in step 1 and shake the dressing.

CHICKEN IN COCONUT CURRY SAUCE

SERVES 4
Gluten Free

2 teaspoons olive oil

1 onion, chopped

2 teaspoons curry powder

1 cup light (reduced-fat) coconut milk

1 (14½-ounce) can diced tomatoes

2 tablespoons tomato paste

½ teaspoon salt

1 pound skinless boneless chicken breasts, cut into 1-inch chunks

1 (5-ounce) bag baby spinach

1 cup frozen peas

1. Heat oil in large nonstick skillet over medium heat. Add onion and cook, stirring, until softened, about 5 minutes. Add curry powder and cook, stirring, until fragrant, about 1 minute. Stir in coconut milk, tomatoes, tomato paste, and salt; bring to boil. Reduce heat and simmer, stirring occasionally, until sauce is slightly thickened, 6–8 minutes longer.

2. Add chicken to skillet; cook, stirring occasionally, until chicken is cooked through, about 4 minutes. Add spinach and peas; cook, stirring, until spinach is wilted and peas are tender, about 3 minutes longer.

Per serving (1½ cups): 262 Cal, 9 g Total Fat, 3 g Sat Fat, 710 mg Sod, 17 g Total Carb, 7 g Sugar, 5 g Fib, 29 g Prot. SmartPoints value: 6

 Let's All Do It

Kids Can—open the bag of spinach and add it to the skillet.

Pre-Teens and Guests Can—cook up brown rice to serve alongside the curry.

MOJO-MARINATED CHICKEN AND VEGETABLE KEBABS WITH MIXED GREENS

SERVES 4
Gluten Free

1   cup orange juice
    (from about 4 oranges)

⅔   cup lime juice
    (from about 5 limes)

⅓   cup lightly packed fresh
    oregano leaves

3   tablespoons canola oil

6   garlic cloves, peeled

½   teaspoon salt

1   pound skinless boneless chicken
    breasts, cut into 1-inch chunks

1   zucchini, thickly sliced

1   red onion, cut into 1- to
    1½-inch chunks

1   red bell pepper, cut into 1- to
    1½-inch pieces

4   cups lightly packed mixed salad
    greens

1. Combine orange juice, lime juice, oregano, oil, garlic, and salt in blender; process until smooth. Reserve ¼ cup of orange-juice mixture; pour remaining juice mixture into large bowl. Add chicken, zucchini, onion, and bell pepper, tossing until coated; marinate 30 minutes in refrigerator.

2. Meanwhile, spray grill rack with nonstick spray. Preheat grill to medium or prepare medium fire.

3. Thread chicken and vegetables onto 4 (10-inch) metal skewers, dividing evenly; brush with marinade remaining in bowl. Discard any remaining marinade. Place skewers on grill rack and grill until chicken and vegetables are lightly charred and cooked through, about 6 minutes per side.

4. To serve, toss mixed greens with 2 tablespoons of reserved orange-juice mixture in salad bowl until coated evenly. Drizzle skewers with remaining 2 tablespoons orange-juice mixture.

Per serving (1 skewer and about 1 cup salad): 317Cal, 14 g Total fat, 2 g Sat Fat, 482 mg Sod, 21 g Total Carb, 11 g Sugar, 4 g Fib, 29 g Prot. SmartPoints value: 7

 Let's All Do It

Kids Can—add the ingredients to the blender.

Pre-Teens and Guests Can—assemble the kebabs.

MOJO-MARINATED CHICKEN AND VEGETABLE KEBABS (PAGE 359) WITH MIXED GREENS, SAFFRON RICE, AND MANGO AVOCADO SALSA

MANGO-AVOCADO SALSA

SERVES 12

Gluten Free, Vegetarian

1   large Hass avocado, pitted, peeled, and cut into ¼-inch dice

1   large mango, pitted, peeled, and cut into ¼-inch dice

1   large beefsteak tomato, cut into ¼-inch dice

2   tablespoons finely chopped red onion

2   tablespoons lime juice

2   teaspoons chopped fresh cilantro

    Pinch salt

Gently toss together all ingredients in serving bowl; let stand 15 minutes to allow flavors to blend.

Per serving (¼ cup): 67 Cal, 4 g Total Fat, 1 g Sat Fat, 28 mg Sod, 9 g Total Carb, 6 g Sugar, 3 g Fib, 1 g Prot. SmartPoints value: 1

 Kids Can Help

Let them stir together the salsa ingredients.

SAFFRON RICE

SERVES 8

Gluten Free, Vegetarian

½   teaspoon saffron, crumbled

2   tablespoons boiling water

1   tablespoon canola oil

1   small onion, finely chopped

1   cup long-grain white rice, rinsed and drained

2   cups reduced-sodium vegetable broth, warmed

¾   teaspoon salt

¼   cup chopped fresh cilantro

1. Stir saffron into boiling water in cup; set aside to steep.

2. Heat oil in large saucepan over medium-high heat. Add onion and cook, stirring, until softened, 2–3 minutes. Add rice and cook, stirring, until translucent, about 3 minutes.

3. Stir broth, saffron water, and salt into rice; reduce heat and simmer, covered, until rice is tender, 18–20 minutes. Remove pan from heat and let stand, covered, 5 minutes; fluff with fork. Stir in cilantro.

Per serving (½ cup): 106 Cal, 2 g Total Fat, 0 g Sat Fat, 270 mg Sod, 20 g Total Carb, 1 g Sugar, 1 g Fib, 2 g Prot. SmartPoints value: 3

 Kids Can Help

Let them fluff the rice and stir in the cilantro.

LUNCHEONETTE-STYLE CLUB SANDWICHES WITH LEMON-BASIL MAYO

SERVES 4
20 Minutes or Less

3   tablespoons fat-free mayonnaise

2   tablespoons chopped fresh basil

½   teaspoon grated lemon zest

6   slices light oatmeal bread, toasted

¼   pound thinly sliced skinless cooked chicken breast

2   tomatoes, sliced

4   slices crisp-cooked turkey bacon, broken in half

2   romaine lettuce leaves

1. Stir together mayonnaise, basil, and lemon zest in small bowl until blended.

2. Lay slices of bread on work surface; spread evenly with mayonnaise mixture. Top 2 slices of bread with chicken and tomatoes, dividing evenly. Top each with another slice of bread, mayonnaise side up, bacon, and lettuce leaf. Cover with remaining slices of bread, mayonnaise side down.

3. With serrated knife, cut each sandwich into quarters and secure with decorative wooden picks.

Per serving (2 sandwich quarters): 170 Cal, 5 g Total Fat, 2 g Sat Fat, 403 mg Sod, 20 g Total Carb, 3 g Sugar, 6 g Fib, 14 g Prot. SmartPoints value: 5

Let's All Do It

Kids Can—stir together the ingredients for the basil mayonnaise and toast the bread.

Pre-Teens and Guests Can—Cook the bacon and assemble the sandwiches.

LUNCHEONETTE-STYLE
CLUB SANDWICHES WITH
LEMON-BASIL MAYO

SAUSAGE, PEPPER, AND MUSHROOM PAELLA

SERVES 8
Gluten Free

3   teaspoons olive oil

1   (13-ounce) package turkey kielbasa, cut into ½-inch slices

1   large onion, chopped

1   (10-ounce) package sliced white mushrooms

2   red bell peppers, chopped

3   garlic cloves, minced

1   (8-ounce) package yellow rice mix

2   cups water

1   (14½-ounce) can diced fire-roasted tomatoes

1   cup frozen peas, thawed

1. Heat 1 teaspoon of oil in large Dutch oven over medium-high heat. Add kielbasa and cook, stirring, until browned, about 8 minutes. With slotted spoon, transfer to plate.

2. Reduce heat to medium. Heat remaining 2 teaspoons oil in Dutch oven. Add onion and cook, stirring, until softened, about 5 minutes. Add mushrooms, bell peppers, and garlic; cook, covered, stirring occasionally, until vegetables are softened, about 3 minutes.

3. Add rice to mushroom mixture, stirring until coated well. Stir in water, tomatoes, and kielbasa; bring to boil. Reduce heat and simmer, covered, until rice is tender and liquid is absorbed, about 25 minutes. Stir in peas. Remove Dutch oven from heat; let stand, covered, until peas are heated through, about 5 minutes.

Per serving (generous 1 cup): 170 Cal, 7 g Total Fat, 2 g Sat Fat, 611 mg Sod, 17 g Total Carb, 5 g Sugar, 4 g Fib, 11 g Prot. SmartPoints value: 4

 **Kids Can Help**

Let them open the package of rice and add it to the Dutch oven along with the tomatoes and water.

TURKEY TABBOULEH

SERVES 6

1   cup bulgur

1½ cups boiling water

¾   pound skinless roasted turkey breast, diced

1   English (seedless) cucumber, cut into ½-inch dice

1   pint grape tomatoes, halved

1   cup thinly sliced scallions (about 1 bunch)

1   cup chopped fresh flat-leaf parsley (about 1 bunch)

½   cup chopped fresh mint

⅓   cup lemon juice

1   tablespoon extra-virgin olive oil

1   teaspoon salt

¼   teaspoon black pepper

1. Put bulgur in medium bowl and pour boiling water over. Cover bowl with piece of plastic wrap; let bulgur stand until liquid is absorbed and bulgur is tender, about 15 minutes. Transfer bulgur to sieve and set over same bowl; with back of wooden spoon, press out excess water and discard.

2. Transfer bulgur to serving bowl. Add turkey, cucumber, tomatoes, scallions, parsley, and mint; toss until mixed.

3. To make dressing, combine lemon juice, oil, salt, and pepper in small jar with tight-fitting lid; shake until blended well. Drizzle dressing over bulgur mixture and toss until coated evenly.

Per serving (about 1⅔ cups): 199 Cal, 3 g Total Fat, 1 g Sat Fat, 435 mg Sod, 26 g Total Carb, 4 g Sugar, 6 g Fib, 19 g Prot. SmartPoints value: 4

 Kids Can Help

Let them cut the grape tomatoes in half, squeeze the lemon, make the dressing, and pour it over the tabbouleh.

GRILLED CHICKEN SAUSAGE
WITH SPANISH CHICKPEA SALSA

GRILLED CHICKEN SAUSAGE WITH SPANISH CHICKPEA SALSA

SERVES 4

3   ounces chopped pimientos, drained

⅓   cup canned chickpeas, rinsed, drained, and chopped

1   tablespoon minced red onion

2   teaspoons sherry vinegar

½   teaspoon smoked paprika

½   teaspoon dried oregano

4   (3-ounce) fully cooked spicy chicken sausages or chorizo

4   reduced-calorie whole-grain or whole wheat hotdog buns, split

1.   **Spray grill rack with nonstick spray. Preheat grill to medium-high or prepare medium-high fire.**

2.   **To make salsa, stir together pimientos, chickpeas, onion, vinegar, paprika, and oregano in small bowl.**

3.   **Place sausages on grill rack and grill, turning, until nicely marked and heated through, about 5 minutes. Place buns, cut side down, on grill rack and grill until lightly toasted, about 1 minute.**

4.   **Place sausages in buns; top each with 2½ tablespoons salsa.**

Per serving (1 sandwich): 233 Cal, 8 g Total Fat, 2 g Sat Fat, 787 mg Sod, 25 g Total Carb, 5 g Sugar, 5 g Fib, 19 g Prot. SmartPoints value: 6

 Let's All Do It

Kids Can—stir together the salsa ingredients and split open the hotdog buns.

Pre-Teens and Guests Can—grill the sausages and fill the buns.

TURKEY TACOS

TURKEY TACOS

SERVES 4
Gluten Free

1½ tablespoons chili powder

2 teaspoons ground cumin

1 teaspoon paprika

1 teaspoon salt

½ teaspoon garlic powder

½ teaspoon onion powder

½ teaspoon dried oregano

¼ teaspoon cayenne

¾ pound ground skinless turkey breast

½ cup water

1 tablespoon cider vinegar

1½ teaspoons brown sugar

4 taco shells or (6-inch) tortillas

Pickled Onions (page 370)

Easy Pico de Gallo (page 370)

Taco Fixin's (page 370)

1. Stir together chili powder, cumin, paprika, salt, garlic powder, onion powder, oregano, and cayenne in cup. Set aside.

2. Cook turkey in large nonstick skillet over medium heat, breaking it up with wooden spoon, until no longer pink, 3–5 minutes. Add spice mixture and the water, stirring until mixed well. Reduce heat to low and simmer, stirring occasionally, until most of liquid is evaporated, 10–15 minutes. Stir in vinegar and brown sugar; simmer 3 minutes longer.

3. To assemble tacos, spoon ½ cup turkey mixture into each taco shell. Top each with 2 tablespoons pickled onion, ¼ cup pico de gallo, and Taco Fixin's of choice.

Per serving (1 taco without Taco Fixin's): 191 Cal, 7 g Total Fat, 1 g Sat Fat, 708 mg Sod, 12 g Total Carb, 2 g Sugar, 2 g Fib, 20 g Prot. SmartPoints value: 4

 Let's All Do It

Kids Can—stir together the chili powder mixture.

Pre-Teens and Guests Can—assemble the tacos.

PICKLED ONIONS

SERVES 8
Gluten Free, Vegetarian

½   cup cider vinegar

¼   cup hot water

2   teaspoons honey

½   teaspoon salt

1   red onion, thinly sliced

Stir together vinegar, hot water, honey, and salt in medium bowl. Add onion and stir until mixed well. Let stand at room temperature, stirring occasionally, about 30 minutes. Drain. Spoon into serving bowl.

Per serving (2 tablespoons): 13 Cal, 0 g Total Fat, 0 g Sat Fat, 146 mg Sod, 3 g Total Carb, 2 g Sugar, 0 g Fib, 0 g Prot. SmartPoints value: 1

 Kids Can Help

Let them stir together the vinegar mixture.

EASY PICO DE GALLO

SERVES 4
20 Minutes or Less, Gluten Free, Vegetarian

2   tomatoes, seeded and diced

¼   cup finely chopped red onion

1   jalapeño pepper, seeded and minced

2   tablespoons chopped fresh cilantro
    Juice of 1 lime

¼   teaspoon salt

Stir together all ingredients in serving bowl.

Per serving (¼ cup): 19 Cal, 0 g Total Fat, 0 g Sat Fat, 150 mg Sod, 4 g Total Carb, 3 g Sugar, 1 g Fib, 1 g Prot. SmartPoints value: 0

 Kids Can Help

Let them stir together the ingredients in the serving bowl.

TACO FIXIN'S

ENJOY THESE TASTY EXTRAS FOR NO ADDITIONAL SMARTPOINTS!

- Thinly sliced radishes
- Diced fresh tomato, cucumber, jicama, or bell pepper
- Shredded cabbage, lettuce, spinach, or carrots
- Fat-free salsa
- Whole cilantro leaves
- Pickled jalapeños
- Lime wedges

CHOOSE THESE FOR JUST A FEW EXTRA SMARTPOINTS

- Refried beans (1 SmartPoint per ¼ cup)
- Guacamole (2 SmartPoints per 2 tablespoons)
- Sliced Hass avocado (2 SmartPoints per ¼ avocado)
- Shredded reduced-fat Cheddar cheese (1 SmartPoint per ¼ cup)
- Light sour cream (2 SmartPoints per 2 tablespoons)
- Sliced large black olives (1 SmartPoint per 4)

BABY "PORCUPINES"

SERVES 8

1   pound ground skinless turkey breast

1   cup cool cooked brown rice

1   cup fresh whole wheat bread crumbs

1   small onion, grated

¼   cup ketchup

¾   teaspoon salt

¼   teaspoon black pepper

16   slices pitted black olives (about 4 olives)

½   cup apple juice

1. Preheat oven to 350°F.

2. Combine turkey, rice, bread crumbs, onion, ketchup, salt, and pepper in large bowl. Stir until combined well. Form into 8 small oval-shaped loaves; press 2 olive slices into each loaf for eyes.

3. Place loaves in 9 x 13-inch baking dish. Pour apple juice around loaves. Bake until instant-read thermometer inserted into center of loaves registers 165°F, about 35 minutes.

Per serving (1 "porcupine"): 161 Cal, 3 g Total Fat, 0 g Sat Fat, 345 mg Sod, 18 g Total Carb, 4 g Sugar, 2 g Fib, 15 g Prot. SmartPoints value: 4

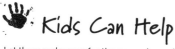 **Kids Can Help**

Let them make eyes for the porcupines with olives. After baking, spoon ketchup into a zip-close plastic bag. Cut off one corner and have helpers pipe a nose, mouth, and ears onto porcupines.

PHILLY CHEESE STEAKS

SERVES 4

1   teaspoon canola oil

1   large onion, thinly sliced

2   Italian frying peppers, sliced

2   garlic cloves, finely chopped

¾   teaspoon salt

¾   pound lean boneless sirloin steak, trimmed and thinly sliced

4   (¾-ounce) slices reduced-fat provolone cheese

4   whole wheat sandwich thins, split

1. Heat oil in large nonstick skillet over medium-high heat. Add onion and cook, stirring, until softened, 5 minutes. Add peppers, garlic, and ¼ teaspoon of salt. Cook, covered, stirring occasionally, until onion is golden, about 10 minutes. Transfer to small bowl.

2. Wipe skillet clean. Sprinkle steak with remaining ½ teaspoon salt and spray with nonstick spray, tossing to coat. Cook steak, in batches, until browned, about 2 minutes, transferring to plate as it is browned.

3. Place 1 slice of provolone on bottom of each roll. Top with about ½ cup steak and one-fourth of onion mixture. Cover with tops of rolls.

Per serving (1 sandwich): 307 Cal, 9 g Total Fat, 4 g Sat Fat, 847 mg Sod, 28 g Total Carb, 6 g Sugar, 7 g Fib, 30 g Prot. SmartPoints value: 7

 **Kids Can Help**

Let them assemble the sandwiches.

WESTERN BURGERS WITH GRILLED FENNEL AND SPICED-UP KETCHUP

SERVES 4

½   cup no-salt-added ketchup

4   teaspoons red wine vinegar

1   large garlic clove, minced

⅛– ¼ teaspoon red pepper flakes

2   tablespoons chopped fresh basil

1   pound ground grass-fed bison

1   fennel bulb, sliced

3   tablespoons grated Parmesan cheese

4   light whole wheat hamburger buns, split

8   small romaine lettuce leaves

1. Spray grill rack with nonstick spray. Preheat grill to medium-high or prepare medium-high fire.

2. Meanwhile, to make spiced-up ketchup, combine ketchup, vinegar, garlic, and pepper flakes in small saucepan; bring to boil. Reduce heat and simmer until thickened, about 5 minutes. Stir in basil.

3. Shape bison into 4 (½-inch-thick) patties.

4. Place fennel on grill rack and grill, turning occasionally, until lightly charred and tender, about 8 minutes. Transfer to plate. Place patties on grill rack and grill 4 minutes. Turn and sprinkle evenly with Parmesan. Grill burgers until instant-read thermometer inserted into side of burger registers 160°F, about 4 minutes longer. Transfer burgers to plate. Place buns, cut side down, on grill rack and grill until lightly toasted, about 1 minute.

5. Place bottoms of buns on 4 plates. Top each with one-fourth of fennel, 1 burger, one-fourth of ketchup, and 2 lettuce leaves. Cover with tops of buns.

Per serving (1 garnished burger): 324 Cal, 11 g Total Fat, 4 g Sat Fat, 366 mg Sod, 31 g Total Carb, 9 g Sugar, 5 g Fib, 30 g Prot. SmartPoints value: 9

 Let's All Do It

Kids Can—stir together the ingredients for the ketchup.

Pre-Teens and Guests Can—shape the bison into patties. Grill the fennel and burgers.

GRILLED LAMB
BURGERS IN PITAS

GRILLED LAMB BURGERS IN PITAS

SERVES 4

20 Minutes or Less

¾ pound ground lean lamb, trimmed

2 tablespoons finely chopped onion

3 tablespoons chopped fresh mint

½ teaspoon ground coriander

¼ teaspoon salt

¼ teaspoon black pepper

4 (6-inch) whole wheat pita breads, top third cut off and discarded, warmed

1⅓ cups lightly packed chopped romaine lettuce

1 small red bell pepper, thinly sliced

½ kirby cucumber, halved lengthwise and thinly sliced

⅓ cup plain fat-free yogurt

1. Stir together lamb, onion, mint, coriander, salt, and black pepper in medium bowl just until mixed well. Shape into 4 (½-inch-thick) patties.

2. Spray grill pan with nonstick spray and set over medium-high heat. Place patties in grill pan and grill until instant-read thermometer inserted into side of burger registers 160°F, about 4 minutes per side.

3. Stuff each pita with ⅓ cup lettuce, one-fourth of bell pepper, one-fourth of cucumber, 1 burger, and about 1 tablespoon yogurt.

Per serving (1 stuffed pita): 336 Cal, 21 g Total Fat, 9 g Sat Fat, 362 mg Sod, 19 g Total Carb, 3 g Sugar, 3 g Fib, 18 g Prot. SmartPoints value: 11

 **Kids Can Help**

Let them stir together the ingredients for the lamb burgers.

CONFETTI ORZO WITH HAM AND VEGETABLES

SERVES 4

2   teaspoons canola oil

1   red bell pepper, chopped

1   (16-ounce) bag frozen mixed vegetables, thawed

3   cups reduced-sodium chicken broth

½   teaspoon dried thyme

¼   teaspoon salt

1   cup orzo, preferably tri-color

1   (6-ounce) piece low-sodium baked ham, diced

3   tablespoons grated Parmesan cheese

2   scallions, thinly sliced

1. Heat oil in large heavy nonstick skillet over medium-high heat. Add bell pepper and cook, stirring, until softened, about 3 minutes. Add mixed vegetables, broth, thyme, and salt; bring to boil.

2. Add orzo to vegetable mixture and return to boil. Reduce heat and cook, covered, stirring occasionally, until orzo is tender and liquid is absorbed, about 10 minutes. Stir in ham, Parmesan, and scallions; cook until heated through, about 2 minutes longer.

Per serving (1¼ cups): 355 Cal, 8 g Total Fat, 2 g Sat Fat, 1118 mg Sod, 50 g Carb, 4 g Sugar, 6 g Fib, 22 g Prot. SmartPoints value: 10

 Let's All Do It

Kids Can—measure out the chicken broth.

Pre-Teens and Guests Can—grate and measure the Parmesan and add the ham, cheese, and scallions to the orzo.

POTLUCK PARTY RULES OF THE ROAD

Potluck parties are a fun and easy way to entertain friends and family. The host provides the location, everyone brings a dish, and the result is a tasty feast. As the host, you can assign guests the type of dish to bring to make sure all your bases are covered. Here are useful strategies:

Bring everything you need to serve your dish, such as a trivet, a knife for cutting, or serving utensil(s).

Foods that can be eaten on a plate that don't require a knife or spoon are preferable. Finger- and fork-friendly foods are winners.

Avoid overly fragrant, garlicky, or heavily spiced dishes—your offering should complement the other choices, not overwhelm them.

Try to bring food that's ready to serve. Even though your dish may only need 20 minutes to reheat in the oven, you're probably not the only one vying for oven time.

Consider bringing something light. Potlucks are often heavy on chilies, lasagnas, and casseroles. Grain dishes, rice dishes, and crunchy salads are always appreciated.

Here are 35 tempting recipes in this book that are ideal for your next potluck party. Most can easily be doubled or tripled.

Apple and Carrot Salad

Asian Beef and Scallion Bites

Bacon and Cheddar Strata

Baked Beef Ziti

Baked Shrimp with Tomato and Feta

Beef and "Zucchini Noodle" Lasagna

Celery-Parmesan Salad with Lemon-Anchovy Dressing

Cheddar-Scallion Biscuits

Cherry Tomatoes Stuffed with Blue Cheese and Bacon

Chicken and Tomatillo Enchilada Casserole

Chicken, Mushroom, and Pasta Casserole

Chocolate Stout Brownie Bites

Crunchy Oven-Fried Drumsticks with Thyme and Parmesan

Crunchy Parmesan Kale Chips

Curry-Spiced Sweet Potato–Quinoa Cakes

Deep Chocolate Chiffon Cake

Farmers' Market Tomato, Eggplant, and Zucchini Casserole

Gooey Rocky Road Bars

Grilled Asparagus, Orange, Red Onion and Feta Salad

Indian-Style Quinoa with Cranberries, Pistachios, and Mint

Lamb and Vegetable Kebabs

Lemon-Buttermilk Bundt Cake

Mini Chocolate-Banana Cupcakes with Peanut Butter Frosting

Minted Green Bean Salad

Plum-Apricot Buckle

Pork, Orange, and Fennel Salad

Red and White Quinoa Salad with Corn and Peppers

Roasted Beet and Wheat Berry Salad

Roasted Beets with Orange and Mint

Roasted Vegetable and Orzo Salad

Rosemary and Potato Flatbread

Seafood Salad with Tomatoes and Orzo

Sweet 'n' Spicy Drumettes

Turkey-and-Quinoa Meat Loaf

Vegetable Dumplings with Soy Dipping Sauce

MINI FISHWICHES

SERVES 4
20 Minutes or Less

1   (¾-pound) cod fillet

¼   cup all-purpose flour

½   cup low-fat buttermilk

¾   cup whole wheat cracker crumbs

1   tablespoon finely chopped fresh
    flat-leaf parsley

¾   teaspoon salt

¼   teaspoon garlic powder

2   teaspoons olive oil

4   mini whole wheat hamburger
    rolls, split

¼   cup prepared tartar sauce

4   lemon wedges

1. Cut fish into 4 equal pieces. Put flour on sheet of wax paper and pour buttermilk into large shallow bowl. Mix together cracker crumbs, parsley, salt, and garlic powder on another sheet of wax paper. Coat each piece of fish with flour, shaking off excess, then dip both sides into buttermilk and then into crumb mixture until coated, pressing lightly so it adheres.

2. Heat oil in medium nonstick skillet over medium heat. Add fish and cook until crust is golden and fish is just opaque in center, about 4 minutes per side. Put piece of fish in each roll. Serve with tartar sauce and lemon wedges.

Per serving (1 sandwich and 1 tablespoon tartar sauce): 274 Cal, 7 g Total Fat, 1 g Sat Fat, 949 mg Sod, 33 g Total Carb, 5 g Sugar, 4 g Fib, 20 g Prot. SmartPoints value: 7

 Kids Can Help

Let them make these delicious sandwiches even tastier by topping each with a green leaf lettuce leaf and 2 thick, juicy slices of tomato.

FISH TACOS WITH MANGO SALSA

SERVES 4
20 Minutes or Less,
Gluten Free

1   teaspoon ground cumin

¾   teaspoon salt

¼   teaspoon chipotle chile powder
or regular chili powder

1   pound tilapia or catfish fillets

2   teaspoons canola oil

½   cup plain low-fat yogurt

2   tablespoons chopped fresh
cilantro

1   tablespoon reduced-fat
mayonnaise

1   tablespoon lime juice

2   cups lightly packed coleslaw mix
or shredded cabbage

8   (6-inch) corn tortillas, warmed

8   tablespoons mango or other salsa

1. **Mix together cumin, ½ teaspoon of salt, and the chile powder in cup; sprinkle over fish.**

2. **Heat oil in large heavy nonstick skillet over medium-high heat. Add fish and cook until just opaque in center, about 3 minutes per side. Transfer fish to plate and let cool slightly. With fork, flake fish into big chunks.**

3. **To make slaw, stir together yogurt, cilantro, mayonnaise, lime juice, and remaining ¼ teaspoon salt in medium bowl. Add cabbage and toss until mixed well.**

4. **Place about ¼ cup slaw on one half of each tortilla. Top with fish and 1 tablespoon salsa. Fold tortillas over to enclose filling.**

Per serving (2 tacos): 303 Cal, 7 g Total Fat, 1 g Sat Fat, 698 mg Sod, 35 g Total Carb, 8 g Sugar, 5 g Fib, 27 g Prot. SmartPoints value: 8

 Kids Can Help

Let them stir together the spices in step 1. Kids can also help assemble the tacos.

TUNA-NOODLE CASSEROLE

SERVES 8

1 (16-ounce) container fat-free sour cream

½ cup fat-free mayonnaise

2 teaspoons Dijon mustard

2 teaspoons chopped fresh flat-leaf parsley

½ teaspoon salt

¼ teaspoon black pepper

12 ounces egg noodles, cooked according to package directions and drained

2 cups sliced white mushrooms

1 cup frozen peas, thawed

1 (12-ounce) can solid white tuna in water, drained and flaked

½ cup shredded reduced-fat Monterey Jack or Swiss cheese

1. Preheat oven to 350°F. Spray 4-quart casserole dish with nonstick spray.

2. Whisk together sour cream, mayonnaise, mustard, parsley, salt, and pepper in large bowl. Add noodles, mushrooms, peas, and tuna. Gently stir until combined well.

3. Transfer tuna mixture to prepared casserole dish or baking dish. Sprinkle with Monterey Jack. Bake until top is golden and filling is bubbly, about 30 minutes.

Per serving (1 cup): 207 Cal, 4 g Total Fat, 2 g Sat Fat, 601 mg Sod, 25 g Total Carb, 3 g Sugar, 2 g Fib, 17 g Prot. SmartPoints value: 5

 Kids Can Help

Let them make the sour cream mixture and sprinkle the casserole with the cheese.

TUNA-NOODLE CASSEROLE

TUNA AND SHELLS SALAD

SERVES 6

8   ounces medium pasta shells

1   cup plain low-fat yogurt

¼   cup reduced-calorie mayonnaise

¼   cup chopped fresh dill

¾   teaspoon salt

¼   teaspoon black pepper

2   (5-ounce) cans solid white tuna in water, drained

1   cup frozen peas, thawed

4   celery stalks, thinly sliced (about 1 cup)

4   scallions, thinly sliced

½   red bell pepper, cut into ¼-inch dice

1. Cook pasta shells according to package directions. Drain shells in colander and rinse under cold water to stop cooking. Drain again.

2. To make dressing, stir together yogurt, mayonnaise, dill, salt, and black pepper in serving bowl. Add shells, tuna, peas, celery, scallions, and bell pepper; stir until combined.

Per serving (1⅓ cups): 287 Cal, 6 g Total Fat, 1 g Sat Fat, 619 mg Sod, 37 g Total Carb, 7 g Sugar, 3 g Fib, 20 g Prot. SmartPoints value: 8

 Kids Can Help

Let them open the can of tuna, drain off the water, and snip the dill using small kitchen scissors.

FUSILLI WITH BROCCOLI, BEANS, AND WALNUTS

SERVES 4
Vegetarian

2   cups whole wheat fusilli or rotini

1   head broccoli, cut into small florets, stems peeled and thinly sliced

2   teaspoons olive oil

6   garlic cloves, thinly sliced

1   (15½-ounce) can cannellini (white kidney) beans, rinsed and drained

⅓   cup chopped walnuts

¼   cup grated Parmesan cheese

½   teaspoon salt

¼   teaspoon black pepper

    Pinch red pepper flakes

1. Cook fusilli according to package directions, adding broccoli about 4 minutes before end of cooking time. Drain, reserving ½ cup pasta cooking water. Wipe pot dry.

2. Heat oil in same pot over medium heat. Add garlic and cook, stirring, until golden, about 2 minutes. Stir in fusilli and broccoli, reserved pasta water, beans, walnuts, Parmesan, salt, black pepper, and pepper flakes; toss until combined well.

Per serving (2 cups): 392 Cal, 12 g Total Fat, 2 g Sat Fat, 446 mg Sod, 57 g Total Carb, 3 g Sugar, 13 g Fib, 20 g Prot. SmartPoints value: 9

MINI MEXICAN FRITTATAS

SERVES 6
Gluten Free, Vegetarian

4   large eggs

¼   cup low-fat (1%) milk

¼   cup fat-free chunky mild salsa, drained

¼   cup shredded reduced-fat Cheddar cheese

¼   teaspoon cumin

1. Preheat oven to 350°F. Line 6-cup muffin pan with foil liners.

2. Whisk together eggs, milk, salsa, Cheddar, and cumin in medium bowl. Ladle about ¼ cup of egg mixture into each prepared muffin cup.

3. Bake until frittatas puff up and edges are golden, about 20 minutes.

Per serving (1 frittata): 64 Cal, 4 g Total Fat, 1 g Sat Fat, 128 mg Sod, 2 g Total Carb, 1 g Sugar, 0 g Fib, 6 g Prot. SmartPoints value: 2

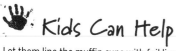 **Kids Can Help**

Let them line the muffin cups with foil liners, whisk the egg mixture, and pour it into the muffin cups.

VEGETABLE FRIED RICE

SERVES 6
20 Minutes or Less,
Vegetarian

1½   teaspoons canola oil

2   large eggs, beaten

4   scallions, sliced

2   garlic cloves, minced

¼   pound snow peas, sliced on diagonal

1   red bell pepper, chopped

4   cups leftover cold cooked brown rice

1   (10-ounce) package frozen mixed vegetables, thawed

8   ounces firm tofu, cut into ½-inch dice

3   tablespoons reduced-sodium soy sauce

2   teaspoons Asian (dark) sesame oil

1. Heat wok over medium-high heat until drop of water sizzles. Add 1 teaspoon of canola oil. Add eggs and stir-fry until set; transfer to plate.

2. Add remaining ½ teaspoon canola oil to wok; add scallions and garlic; stir-fry until fragrant. Add snow peas and bell pepper; stir-fry 2 minutes. Add rice, mixed vegetables, and tofu; stir-fry until heated through. Return eggs to wok along with soy sauce and sesame oil; stir-fry until mixed well.

Per serving (1¼ cups): 269 Cal, 7 g Total Fat, 1 g Sat Fat, 312 mg Sod, 41 g Total Carb, 3 g Sugar, 6 g Fib, 11 g Prot. SmartPoints value: 7

BAKED MACARONI AND CHEESE WITH BROCCOLI

SERVES 8
Vegetarian

1 teaspoon unsalted butter

⅓ cup fresh bread crumbs

3 tablespoons grated Parmesan cheese

2½ cups fat-free milk

⅓ cup all-purpose flour

½ cup chopped onion

1 cup shredded reduced-fat sharp Cheddar cheese

1 teaspoon Dijon mustard

1½ teaspoons salt

½ teaspoon black pepper

12 ounces gemelli or other pasta twists (about 2½ cups), cooked according to package directions and drained

2½ cups small broccoli florets, cooked

1. Preheat oven to 375°F. Spray 2-quart baking dish with nonstick spray.

2. Melt butter in large saucepan over medium heat. Add bread crumbs and cook, stirring often, until light golden, about 2 minutes. Transfer to small bowl. Stir in 1 tablespoon of Parmesan and set aside.

3. Wipe saucepan clean. Whisk together milk and flour in saucepan until blended; add onion. Bring to boil over medium-high heat, whisking frequently. Reduce heat and simmer until sauce is bubbly and thickened, about 2 minutes. Remove saucepan from heat and whisk in Cheddar, mustard, salt, pepper, and remaining 2 tablespoons Parmesan until Cheddar is melted.

4. Add pasta and broccoli to saucepan; stir until mixed well. Transfer to prepared baking dish. Sprinkle evenly with bread-crumb mixture. Bake until bubbly along edges, 20–25 minutes.

Per serving (about 1⅓ cups): 170 Cal, 3 g Total Fat, 1 g Sat Fat, 639 mg Sod, 26 g Total Carb, 3 g Sugar, 3 g Fib, 11 g Prot. SmartPoints value: 4

 Let's All Do It

Kids Can—sprinkle the casserole with the bread-crumb mixture.

Pre-Teens and Guests Can—spray the baking dish with nonstick spray, make the bread-crumb mixture, and prepare the macaroni-broccoli mixture.

FIVE-INGREDIENT TOMATO-CHEESE PIZZA

SERVES 8
Vegetarian

¾ pound refrigerated whole wheat or multigrain pizza dough, at room temperature

  Cornmeal, for the pan

½ cup tomato sauce

¼ teaspoon red pepper flakes

1 cup shredded part-skim mozzarella cheese

2 tablespoons grated Parmesan cheese

1. Place oven rack on bottom rung of oven and preheat oven to 500°F.

2. Turn dough onto lightly floured work surface. With lightly floured rolling pin, roll dough into 12-inch round. Sprinkle pizza pan or large baking sheet with cornmeal. Transfer dough to prepared pan, gently pulling dough back into 12-inch round. (If dough resists, cover lightly with clean kitchen towel and let rest about 10 minutes.)

3. Spread tomato sauce over dough; sprinkle with pepper flakes. Top evenly with mozzarella and Parmesan. Bake until crust is golden and cheeses are melted, 12–15 minutes.

Per serving (⅛ of pizza): 139 Cal, 4 g Total Fat, 2 g Sat Fat, 397 mg Sod, 19 g Total Carb, 2 g Sugar, 2 g Fib, 7 g Prot. SmartPoints value: 4

 **Kids Can Help**

Let them spread the tomato sauce over the dough and sprinkle it with the mozzarella and Parmesan.

FIVE-INGREDIENT
TOMATO-CHEESE PIZZA

PUMPKIN-SPICE MUFFINS

MAKES 12
Vegetarian

1   cup all-purpose flour

¾   cup white whole wheat flour

1   cup sugar

1¼ teaspoons baking soda

1   teaspoon cinnamon

½   teaspoon nutmeg

½   teaspoon salt

⅛   teaspoon ground cloves

½   cup raisins or currants

1   cup canned pumpkin puree

2   large eggs

⅓   cup canola oil

⅓   cup water

2   tablespoons unsalted pumpkin
    or sunflower seeds

1. Preheat oven to 350°F. Spray 12-cup muffin pan with nonstick spray.

2. Whisk together all-purpose flour, white whole wheat flour, sugar, baking soda, cinnamon, nutmeg, salt, and cloves in large bowl; stir in raisins. Stir together pumpkin puree, eggs, oil, and water in medium bowl until combined well. Add pumpkin mixture to flour mixture, stirring just until flour mixture is moistened.

3. Spoon batter into muffin cups, using about ⅓ cup batter for each muffin; sprinkle evenly with pumpkin seeds. Bake until toothpick inserted into muffin comes out clean, about 20 minutes. Let cool in pan on wire rack 10 minutes. Remove muffins from pan and serve warm or let cool completely on rack.

Per serving (1 muffin): 224 Cal, 7 g Total Fat, 1 g Sat Fat, 242 mg Sod, 37 g Total Carb, 22 g Sugar, 1 g Fib, 4 g Prot. SmartPoints value: 9

 Let's All Do It

Kids Can—mix together the flour mixture and sprinkle the muffins with the pumpkin seeds.

Pre-Teens and Guests Can—measure out the ingredients and spoon the batter into the muffin cups.

BREAKFAST BERRY SUNDAES

SERVES 2
20 Minutes or Less,
Vegetarian

8 strawberries, hulled and sliced

1 cup vanilla low-fat yogurt

2 tablespoons granola

1 banana, peeled and sliced

½ cup fresh blueberries

Divide half of strawberries between 2 parfait or other glasses; top each with ¼ cup of yogurt. Layer each with 1 tablespoon granola, ¼ cup yogurt, ½ banana, and ¼ cup blueberries.

Per serving (1 sundae): 218 Cal, 3 g Total Fat, 2 g Sat Fat, 83 mg Sod, 43 g Total Carb, 32 g Sugar, 4 g Fib, 8 g Prot. SmartPoints value: 6

 Kids Can Help

Let them peel and slice the banana and assemble the sundaes.

WATERMELON "CAKE" WITH SUMMER FRUIT AND RASPBERRY SAUCE

SERVES 16
Gluten Free, Vegetarian

½ seedless watermelon (crosswise section), rind removed

1 small cantaloupe, halved, peeled, and seeded

3 kiwifruits, peeled and sliced

1 pint fresh blueberries

1 pint fresh strawberries, hulled and halved

1 (12-ounce) bag frozen unsweetened raspberries, thawed

⅓ cup orange juice

3 tablespoons sugar

1. Cut watermelon into 1½-inch-thick rounds. Stack rounds on serving plate so they resemble a cake.

2. With melon baller, scoop out balls from cantaloupe. Decorate top of watermelon and plate with cantaloupe, kiwifruits, blueberries, and strawberries.

3. Combine raspberries, orange juice, and sugar in blender; pulse until smooth. Pour mixture through fine sieve set over small bowl. With spoon, press on solids to extract all juice; discard seeds.

4. To serve, cut watermelon "cake" into 16 wedges and serve with raspberry sauce.

Per serving (1½ cups fruit and 1½ tablespoons sauce): 105 Cal, 1 g Total Fat, 0 g Sat Fat, 7 mg Sod, 26 g Total Carb, 20 g Sugar, 3 g Fib, 2 g Prot. SmartPoints value: 1

GET THE WHOLE FAMILY IN ON THE ACT!

When everyone pitches in, dinner's on the table in a flash! You know best what your kids can handle, but these lists are a great place to start.

WITH SUPERVISION, LITTLE ONES AGES 2 TO 5 CAN

- gather ingredients
- wash vegetables
- use salad spinner
- fold napkins and place the silverware

SLIGHTLY OLDER KIDS AGES 5 TO 10 CAN ALSO

- shred cheese
- set out plates and glasses

KIDS 10 AND OLDER CAN DO ANY OF THE ABOVE, PLUS

- chop vegetables

FROZEN HOT CHOCOLATE

SERVES 4
Gluten Free, Vegetarian

½ cup sugar

¼ cup unsweetened cocoa

Pinch salt

2 cups low-fat (1%) milk

1½ teaspoons vanilla extract

1 (6-ounce) container fresh raspberries

1. Combine sugar, cocoa, and salt in medium saucepan. Slowly whisk in milk until smooth. Cook over medium-high heat stirring, until mixture simmers, about 8 minutes. Remove saucepan from heat; stir in vanilla. Pour cocoa mixture into 9 x 13-inch baking pan; let cool.

2. Place cocoa mixture in freezer 30 minutes. Remove pan from freezer; with fork, stir cocoa mixture, breaking up any ice crystals on bottom or along sides of pan. Return to freezer, stirring every 20–30 minutes, until mixture is completely frozen, about 2 hours.

3. To serve, fluff cocoa mixture with fork; spoon evenly into 4 goblets or dessert dishes and top with raspberries.

Per serving (¾ cup frozen chocolate and about ¼ cup raspberries): 185 Cal, 2 g Total Fat, 1 g Sat Fat, 126 mg Sod, 39 g Total Carb, 34 g Sugar, 5 g Fib, 6 g Prot. SmartPoints value: 9

 Kids Can Help

Let them fluff the frozen hot chocolate and garnish each serving with raspberries.

CARROT CUPCAKES WITH CREAM CHEESE FROSTING

MAKES 12
Vegetarian

Cupcakes

1¼ cups all-purpose flour

⅔ cup granulated sugar

¼ cup sweetened flaked coconut

1 teaspoon cinnamon

1 teaspoon baking soda

½ teaspoon salt

2 large eggs, lightly beaten

¼ cup canola oil

1 teaspoon grated orange zest

2 carrots, shredded

1 apple, peeled, cored, and shredded

⅓ cup golden raisins, chopped

Frosting

3 ounces whipped cream cheese, at room temperature

2 tablespoons confectioners' sugar

1½ teaspoons milk

½ teaspoon vanilla extract

1. Preheat oven to 350°F. Spray 12-cup muffin pan with nonstick spray or use paper liners.

2. Whisk together flour, granulated sugar, coconut, cinnamon, baking soda, and salt in large bowl. Stir together eggs, oil, and orange zest in medium bowl. Stir egg mixture into flour mixture just until flour mixture is moistened. Stir in carrots, apple, and raisins. Spoon batter evenly into prepared muffin cups, using about ⅓ cup batter for each cupcake.

3. Bake until toothpick inserted into center of cupcake comes out clean, about 20 minutes. Let cool in pan on wire rack 5 minutes; remove cupcakes from pan and let cool completely on rack.

4. To make frosting, with electric mixer on medium-low speed, beat cream cheese, confectioners' sugar, milk, and vanilla in small bowl until blended. Spread small amount of frosting on each cupcake.

Per serving (1 decorated cupcake): 221 Cal, 9 g Total Fat, 3 g Sat Fat, 253 mg Sod, 34 g Total Carb, 21 g Sugar, 2 g Fib, 3 g Prot. SmartPoints value: 9

 **Kids Can Help**

Let them stir together the flour mixture with the egg mixture and spoon the batter into the muffin cups, then let them spread the frosting on the cupcakes.

CARROT CUPCAKES WITH
CREAM CHEESE FROSTING

HARVEST APPLE SQUARES

MAKES 24
Vegetarian

- 1 cup + 2 tablespoons white whole wheat flour
- 1 cup all-purpose flour
- 1 cup old-fashioned (rolled) oats
- ½ cup sugar
- ½ teaspoon salt
- ½ cup (1 stick) cold unsalted butter, cut into pieces
- ½ cup apple juice
- 5 apples, such as McIntosh or Golden Delicious, peeled, cored, and diced
- 1 teaspoon cinnamon
- 1 teaspoon vanilla extract
- ¼ teaspoon nutmeg

1. Preheat oven to 350°F. Line 9 x 13-inch baking pan with nonstick foil, allowing foil to overhang rim by 2 inches on short opposite sides.

2. Combine 1 cup of white whole wheat flour, the all-purpose flour, oats, ¼ cup of sugar, and the salt in food processor; pulse until combined. Add butter and pulse until blended. Add apple juice and pulse just until dough begins to pull away from side of bowl.

3. Scrape dough into prepared pan. Using your hands or rubber spatula, press dough to form even layer. Bake until dough is set but not colored, 10–12 minutes. Let cool in pan on wire rack 10 minutes. Maintain oven temperature.

4. Meanwhile, toss together apples, remaining ¼ cup sugar and 2 tablespoons white whole wheat flour, the cinnamon, vanilla, and nutmeg in large bowl. Spoon over crust and spread evenly. Bake until apples are tender, about 45 minutes. Let cool completely in pan on rack; cut into 24 squares.

Per serving (1 square): 125 Cal, 4 g Total Fat, 2 g Sat Fat, 50 mg Sod, 20 g Total Carb, 9 g Sugar, 1 g Fib, 2 g Prot. SmartPoints value: 4

 Kids Can Help

Let them measure out the spices, core the apples, and press the dough in the pan.

SMART BARS

MAKES 32
Vegetarian

1½ cups mixed dried fruit, such as apricots, cranberries, and raisins

1 cup quick-cooking or old-fashioned (rolled) oats

½ cup unsalted sunflower seeds

½ cup toasted wheat germ

½ cup chopped pecans or walnuts

½ cup powdered nonfat dry milk

¼ cup white whole wheat flour

1 teaspoon cinnamon

½ teaspoon salt

1 ripe banana, cut into chunks

2 large eggs

⅓ cup pure maple syrup

1 teaspoon vanilla extract

1. Preheat oven to 350°F. Spray 9 x 13-inch baking pan with nonstick spray.

2. Combine dried fruit, oats, sunflower seeds, wheat germ, pecans, dry milk, flour, cinnamon, and salt in food processor; pulse until dried fruit is finely chopped but not pureed. Add banana, eggs, maple syrup, and vanilla; pulse just until combined.

3. Transfer fruit mixture to prepared pan. With wet fingertips, press down to form even layer. Bake until bars are golden and firm to touch, about 20 minutes. Let cool completely in pan on wire rack. Cut into 32 bars.

Per serving (1 bar): 83 Cal, 3 g Total Fat, 0 g Sat Fat, 48 mg Sod, 13 g Total Carb, 7 g Sugar, 2 g Fib, 3 g Prot. SmartPoints value: 3

 Kids Can Help

Let them measure out the dry ingredients, peel and cut up the banana, and press the fruit mixture in the pan.

BROWN RICE CRISPY BARS

MAKES 16

2 tablespoons almond butter or peanut butter

3 cups mini marshmallows (about half 10-ounce bag)

2 cups crisp puffed brown rice cereal

1 cup whole-grain cereal flakes

2 tablespoons mini semisweet chocolate chips

1. Spray 8-inch square baking pan with nonstick spray.

2. Put almond butter in large saucepan and cook, stirring, over medium-low heat until softened, about 30 seconds. Add marshmallows and cook, stirring, until somewhat melted but still lumpy, about 2 minutes.

3. Spray rubber spatula with nonstick spray. Remove saucepan from heat and immediately use rubber spatula to stir in rice cereal, whole-grain cereal, and chocolate chips until combined well.

4. Scrape marshmallow mixture into prepared baking pan, pressing down with rubber spatula to form even layer. Refrigerate until bars are firm, about 30 minutes. With sharp knife sprayed with nonstick spray, cut into 16 squares.

Per serving (1 square): 63 Cal, 2 g Total Fat, 0 g Sat Fat, 9 mg Sod, 12 g Total Carb, 6 g Sugar, 1 g Fib, 1 g Prot. SmartPoints value: 3

 Kids Can Help

Let them measure out the ingredients, stir the mixture together, and press it in the pan.

OATMEAL COOKIES WITH CHERRIES AND ALMONDS

MAKES 44
Vegetarian

- 1   cup all-purpose flour
- 1   teaspoon cinnamon
- 1   teaspoon baking powder
- ½   teaspoon salt
- ½   cup (1 stick) unsalted butter, softened
- 1   cup firmly packed dark brown sugar
- 1   large egg
- 1   teaspoon vanilla extract
- 1⅓ cups old-fashioned (rolled) oats
- ½   cup dried cherries, coarsely chopped
- ½   cup sliced almonds
- ¼   cup toasted wheat germ

1. Place racks in upper and lower thirds of oven. Preheat oven to 350°F. Line two large baking sheets with parchment paper.

2. Whisk together flour, cinnamon, baking powder, and salt in medium bowl. With electric mixer on medium-high speed, beat butter and brown sugar in large bowl until light and fluffy. Beat in egg and vanilla. Reduce mixer speed to low. Add flour mixture and beat just until blended. Stir in oats, cherries, almonds, and wheat germ.

3. Roll rounded tablespoonfuls of dough into balls, making total of 44 balls. Place about 2 inches apart on prepared baking sheets. Lightly flatten each ball with palm of hand.

4. Bake until cookies are golden, about 15 minutes. Transfer cookies with parchment to wire racks and let cool completely.

Per serving (1 cookie): 74 Cal, 3 g Fat, 1 g Sat Fat, 41 mg Sod, 11 g Total Carb, 7 g Sugar, 1 g Fib, 1 g Prot. SmartPoints value: 3

 Kids Can Help

Let them whisk together the dry ingredients, roll the dough into balls, and flatten them with the palms of their hands.

RECIPES BY SMARTPOINTS VALUES

0 SMARTPOINTS VALUE

Easy Pico de Gallo, 370

Endive with Chipotle Cream Cheese, 200

Grilled Vegetable Kebabs, 109

Roasted Eggplant Dip, 223

Spicy Roasted Broccoli and Cauliflower Bites, 249

Stir-Fried Asparagus and Sugar Snap Peas, 117

Whole Roasted Tandoori Cauliflower, 330

1 SMARTPOINTS VALUE

Beet Hummus on Cucumber Rounds, 201

Cherry Tomatoes Stuffed with Blue Cheese and Bacon, 348

Crunchy Parmesan Kale Chips, 238

Curried Cauliflower, 26

Fresh Figs with Boursin, 200

Gazpacho and Egg Shooters, 200

Green Beans Oreganata, 51

Grilled Stuffed Jalapeños, 214

Heirloom Tomato and Basil Platter, 278

Lemony Coleslaw with Apples, 280

Mango-Avocado Salsa, 361

Mini Chocolate Chip Cookies, 273

Minted Green Bean Salad, 229

Mixed Greens with Vinaigrette, 30

Mixed Vegetables with Orange Gremolata, 170

Mussels Vinaigrette, 200

No-Cook Peanut Buttery Cookie Dough Bites, 335

Pickled Onions, 370

Raspberry-Lemonade Vodka Slushies, 345

Ricotta and Tapenade Pita Crisps, 201

Roasted Beets with Orange and Mint, 320

Roasted Dumpling Squash and Romanesco with Sage, 143

Roasted Tri-Color Peppers and Red Onion, 50

Salmon with Tzatziki, 200

Savory Parmesan–Black Pepper Biscotti, 346

Silken Ranch Dip, 274

Spicy Scallion Salad, 205

Spinach with Parmesan Bread Crumbs, 185

Sweet Onion, Bacon, and Cheese Tarts, 245

Thyme-Roasted Sunchokes, 322

Tomato, Watermelon, and Basil Salad, 323

Watermelon "Cake" with Summer Fruit and Raspberry Sauce, 391

2 SMARTPOINTS VALUE

Apple and Carrot Salad, 21

Asian Beef and Scallion Bites, 194

Beef and Blue Cheese Pickups, 339

Bloody Mary Shrimp Cocktail, 343

Buffalo-Style Stuffed Celery, 274

Caesar Salad with Poblano Dressing, 266

Chocolate Fudge Cookie Bites, 29

Creamy Spinach-Parmesan Dip, 104

Dark Chocolate and Sea Salt Tartlets, 173

Farmers' Market Tomato, Eggplant, and Zucchini Casserole, 49

Fennel-Apple Slaw with Lemon and Mint, 268

Frisée Salad with Grilled Apricots, Spring Radishes, and Snow Peas, 120

Gravlax with Mustard-Dill Sauce, 312

Greek-Style Grilled Eggplant, 234

Grilled Asparagus, Orange, Red Onion, and Feta Salad, 98

3 SMARTPOINTS VALUE

4 SMARTPOINTS VALUE

Strawberry Meringue Mousse, 59

Sunday Pot Roast, 289

Tender Buttermilk Corn Bread, 265

Tilapia with Warm Sherry Vinaigrette and Wild Rice, 319

Tuna-Noodle Casserole, 380

Turkey, Black Bean, and Mushroom Chili, 263

Vietnamese Banh Mi Chicken Burgers, 250

6 SMARTPOINTS VALUE

Apple Sharlotka, 324

Bacon and Cheddar Strata, 95

Bison Sliders with Balsamic-Braised Onions, 243

Blue Corn Nachos, 212

Breakfast Berry Sundaes, 389

Cherry Clafoutis, 125

Chicken in Coconut Curry Sauce, 358

Chocolate-Chile Granita, 221

Chunky Pork Chili, 261

Cinnamon-Raisin Baked French Toast, 96

Crunchy Oven-Fried Drumsticks with Thyme and Parmesan, 126

Egg, Canadian Bacon, Avocado, and Tomato Sandwiches, 75

Gooey Rocky Road Bars, 136

Grilled Chicken Sausage with Spanish Chickpea Salsa, 367

Indian-Style Quinoa with Cranberries, Pistachios, and Mint, 46

Italian Pepper and Egg Sandwiches, 78

Key Lime Dessert Shots, 257

Lebanese Chicken-Pita Salad, 128

Lemony Pork Piccata, 184

Lentil and Black Bean Chili, 45

Mexican-Style Sloppy Joes, 54

Old-Fashioned Chicken Potpie, 151

Pink Grapefruit–Campari Granita, 161

Potato Gratin with Parmesan and Rosemary, 294

Potato Salad, 131

Quinoa and Apple Breakfast Cereal, 83

Rack of Lamb with Lemon-Herb Crust, 167

Rosemary and Potato Flatbread, 180

Southwestern Green Chile Cheeseburgers, 217

Spicy Slow-Cooker Vegetarian Chili, 74

Tender Beef Shanks with Polenta, 329

Turkey Salad Soft Tacos, 33

White Bean, Citrus, and Salmon Salad, 35

Winter-Spiced Pomegranate and Clementine Sangria, 211

7 SMARTPOINTS VALUE

Arugula Salad with Quince, Pomegranate, and Pecans, 146

Baked Beef Ziti, 240

Buttermilk Panna Cotta with Strawberries, 122

Chicken and Tomatillo Enchilada Casserole, 218

Cinnamon-Sugar Pineapple with Coconut Sorbet, 102

Grilled Pork Chops with Orange-Tamarind Glaze, 334

Lamb and Fennel Meatballs in Tomato Sauce, 73

Mini Blueberry Cobblers, 135

Mini Fishwiches, 378

Mojo-Marinated Chicken and Vegetable Kebabs with Mixed Greens, 359

Pan-Seared Duck with Blueberry Sauce, 166

Penne with Roasted Cauliflower, 58

Peppered Beef Tenderloin with Port Wine Sauce, 153

Philly Cheese Steaks, 371

Plum-Apricot Buckle, 112

Pork and White Bean Stew, 71

Roast Beef Sandwiches with Horseradish Mayonnaise, 129

Sage-and-Garlic-Infused Parsnip Puree, 155

Stracotto with Lemon Gremolata, 43

Turkey-and-Vegetable Stew, 63

Vegetable Fried Rice, 383

8 SMARTPOINTS VALUE

Bolognese Sauce with Spaghetti, 70

Buttermilk Sorbet with Crushed Blackberry–Mint Sauce, 175

Chocolate Gingerbread, 310

Cranberry-Stuffed Pork Loin, 317

Fish Tacos with Mango Salsa, 379

Oxtail and Root Vegetable Stew, 327

Peruvian Potato Cakes with Poached Eggs, 81

Rhubarb-Cherry Crumble, 124

Rosemary-Grilled Salmon, 107

Tuna and Shells Salad, 382

Winter Beef Stew, 44

Yogurt with Pomegranate-Orange Syrup, 235

9 SMARTPOINTS VALUE

Cape Cod Clambake, 277

Carrot Cupcakes with Cream Cheese Frosting, 392

Chocolate Chip–Peanut Butter Pie, 40

Coffee-Almond Flans, 158

Coffee Flan with Orange Caramel, 311

Curry-Spiced Sweet Potato–Quinoa Cakes, 154

Frozen Hot Chocolate, 391

Fusilli with Broccoli, Beans, and Walnuts, 382

Grilled T-Bone with Barbecue Sauce, 106

Lemon-Buttermilk Bundt Cake, 337

Meat Loaf with Chive Mashed Potatoes, 290

Pumpkin-Spice Muffins, 388

Veggie Bolognese with Soy Crumbles and Mushrooms, 303

Western Burgers with Grilled Fennel and Spiced-Up Ketchup, 372

10 SMARTPOINTS VALUE

Asian-Spiced Salmon with Baby Bok Choy and Shiitakes, 116

Burritos with Turkey and Pinto Beans, 18

Chicken Sausage, Mushroom, and Pasta Casserole, 41

Confetti Orzo with Ham and Vegetables, 376

Deep Chocolate Chiffon Cake, 101

Fettuccine with Chicken Sausage and Artichokes, 187

Pot Roast with Potatoes and Green Olives, 66

Slow-Cooker Lasagna, 67

11 SMARTPOINTS VALUE

Grilled Lamb Burgers in Pitas, 375

Linguine with Brussels Sprouts, Walnuts, and Parmesan, 140

Red Curry Beef with Pineapple and Snow Peas, 68

Rigatoni with Creamy Sausage Sauce, 152

Super-Easy Spaghetti and Meatballs, 183

12 SMARTPOINTS VALUE

Fresh Corn and Blueberry Pancakes, 84

Yogurt Pancakes with Fresh Raspberry Sauce, 82

INDEX